Orders:
  P.O. Box 660725
  Birmingham, AL 35266-0725

Editorial Address:
  306 Morningside Circle
  Birmingham, AL 35213

A Riffaterrean Reading of Patrick Modiano's

La place de l'étoile

A Riffaterrean Reading of Patrick Modiano's
La place de l'étoile:
Investigating the Family Crime

by

Charles O'Keefe

SUMMA PUBLICATIONS, INC.
Birmingham, Alabama
2005

Copyright 2005
Summa Publications, Inc.
ISBN 1-883479-48-7

Library of Congress Control Number 2005932236

Printed in the United States of America

To my students for inspiring me,
to Denison University for supporting me,
and to my wife for her inspiration and her support,
which are the least of it.

Contents

Introduction[1]

I. The Unlikely Success of Patrick Modiano's *La place de l'étoile*

The contemporary French novelist Patrick Modiano has known spectacular popular and critical success in France: his novels appear regularly on France's bestseller list, and they have won numerous significant French literary awards that are bestowed for fiction, most notably the highly prestigious Prix Goncourt in 1978 (Morris, *Patrick Modiano* [Rodopi] 7, note 6). The recognition of his literary achievements took on added luster with the especially impressive biennial Grand Prix de Littérature Paul Morand, awarded to him in 2000 for his oeuvre. As one might expect, recent surveys of contemporary French literature have declared him to be a writer of exceptional stature, perhaps one for the ages (Prince "Patrick Modiano," Roudiez, Taylor, W. Thompson, Wright).

Yet his work can be difficult, perplexing, and indeed outrageous, qualities not often associated with sweeping literary success. In none of his novels do those qualities appear more pronounced than in his first published novel, *La place de l'étoile* (1968). Those unfamiliar with *La place de l'étoile* will have to imagine an offensive book that not only savages such icons as "the heroes of the Resistance" of World War II (Cima 193-226), Jean-Paul Sartre, and Sigmund Freud, but that also is replete with nightmarish anti-Jewish buffoonery in which Adolph Hitler is portrayed as a perversely Disneyesque Captain Hook. At the same time they will have to imagine such grotesque racism appearing in a satiric book in which France's history of hostility to Jews is taunted with the most scathing irony, even while the state of Israel is compared to a neo-Nazi prison-state run by Jewish Gestapo agents. The task of imagining such a book will not be made easier by the fact that *La place de l'étoile* is also a fanciful historical novel that on page after page throws a hodge-podge of proper names at the reader, such that it takes the years-long independent travails of scholars to guide readers in sorting out which names refer to historical figures, which ones refer to imaginary characters, and which ones result from a saucy blend of the two.[2] For example, the following names appear in just the opening pages: Léon Rabatête, le docteur Bardamu, Charlie Chaplin, Marcel Proust, Alfred Dreyfus, Valery Larbaud, Scott Fitzgerald, Laversine, Cibao la Pampa, Silver Leys, Porfirio Rubirosa, Cléo de Mérode, Otéro, Émilienne d'Alençon, Liane de Pougy, Odette de Crécy, la comtesse de Ségur (*La place de l'étoile* 13-19). Into this confounding brew of historical and fictional names, Modiano tosses in a no less confounding brew of historical and imaginary book titles and textual passages (see Obajtek-Kirkwood 57, 73, and 82, for example). To get a better sense yet of this bewildering novel, those unfamiliar with the book will also have to imagine all of the above cast within a self-flaunting alternative to Marcel Proust's *A la recherche du temps perdu* in which the play of time, memory, and art, far from leading up to a Proustian aesthetic epiphany, frustrates any closure, reducing the text to a labyrinth of apparent dead-ends generated by insistent but contradictory memory.

For those who do in fact already know this novel, the above of course just begins to describe *La place de l'étoile*. In fact, so disturbing is this book that even its first preface-writer compared it to a scratching, clawing cat that pounces on the reader's face: "Ce livre, comme un chat fou de douleur, va te bondir au visage et te griffer jusqu'au sang. De cet assaut tu porteras les marques et l'on dira, en voyant ton visage labouré: 'Ce type-là a dû lire *La Place de l'étoile*. Il n'est que de voir ses cicatrices' " (Cau 3). And yet this baffling, unsettling book heralded the beginning of Modiano's extravagantly popular and critical success by garnishing two literary prizes in its year of publication, *le prix Roger-Nimier* and *le prix Fénéon*. Furthermore and no less astoundingly, baffling and unsettling though *La place de l'étoile* is, it was instrumental in changing the very way France views its recent history: Henry Rousso, expert on France's reappraisal in the seventies of "*le résistancialisme gaullien*" (the Gaullist triumphalist, salving myth of *la France résistante* in World War II), judges Modiano's publication of *La place de l'étoile*[3] to have made him a "lighthouse" to those seeking their way out of the fanciful fog of official French historical forgetfulness about France's official collaboration with the Nazis during the war (Rousso, 149, 152; see also Nettelbeck and Hueston, *Patrick Modiano* 8). But that point, made in the 1987 first edition of Rousso's authoritative *Le syndrôme de Vichy: de 1944 à nos jours*, was hardly unique or even new, although his book gave the issue its most resonance. As early as 1974, Michel Foucault, discussing Modiano's screenplay of the same year for Louis Malle's Occupation film *Lacombe Lucien*, was one of the many who saw how all of Modiano's work implied a reaction to Gaullist-era myths no less than to the wartime Collaboration whose shame virtually required those myths in order to shield itself from scrutiny. Subsequently, Odile Trioreau's research, for instance, highlighted the need for that point to be made. Her article, "La représentation de la seconde guerre mondiale dans les manuels d'école primaire de 1945 à nos jours," showed that state history books for elementary and middle-school classes *(les cours élémentaires et moyens)* did not even start to make merely timid, passing mention of the Collaboration until the early 1980s.

How can one explain the success of so unsettling a book as *La place de l'étoile?* Indeed, how can one explain the continued success of Modiano's many subsequent novels[4] (twenty-one as of 2003), given that the second and third ones (*La ronde de nuit* and *Les boulevards de ceinture*) aggressively even if a bit less belligerently continued to pursue troubling, unpleasant questions regarding the Collaboration; and given that the novels to follow, while sometimes letting the nettlesome Collaboration drift into a nagging background, developed a wistful, baffling style that some critics lamented served only to keep on producing the same story, a lament that Modiano himself has voiced (Ezine 25).[5] But the lament has done nothing to reduce both popular and sophisticated accolades that are regularly heaped on Modiano's novels. In fact, in France readers annually await the latest Modiano—in the words of one observer—with the same widespread excitement and enthusiasm as they do the year's *beaujolais nouveau* (Rachlin 121), lending the author "mini-cult status" (Guyot-Bender and VanderWolk, Introduction 7). Why?

Rousso maintains that, notwithstanding state amnesia about the Collaboration, the French came to experience considerable curiosity about the repressed past (Rousso 152-53). By Rousso's light, then, Modiano would owe his early success among the French to having been among the first to tap that latent curiosity on a national level. It should be noted that Modiano's invitation to collective anamnesis had nothing facile or market-oriented about it, since his reminder of the outrages went hand and hand with a developed sense of the moral complexities of the Collaboration. Natalie Rachlin has seconded Rousso's explanation of Modiano's early success and extended it even to Modiano's later works (which she views as an extensive rewriting of the same novel): "Modiano's enormous success and appeal are in large part due to the convergence of his private obsessions with what will become a national obsession with the memory of Vichy" (Rachlin 126). But Modiano has aroused interest far beyond the borders of France, having for example been translated into languages such as English, German, and Dutch (Gellings 9). That honor indicates an appeal based on more than national, historical considerations. How to explain the appeal? We can begin to answer that question by taking an overview of pertinent critical appraisal of Modiano.

II. Some Explanations of the Success of Modiano's Novels

Over the years several critics have used various but similar terms in expressing a rather broad explanation of Modiano's success. According to that opinion and in spite of the above off-putting characterizations, Modiano's books offer the pleasure of simply being very readable. In a much-cited 1977 article, Jacques Bersani established just that point:

> Si l'on veut prendre la mesure exacte de tout ce qui rapproche aujourd'hui, par-delà les disputes d'avant-garde ou d'arrière-garde, quelques-uns de nos romanciers les plus efficacement novateurs, point de meilleur exemple, sans doute, que celui de Patrick Modiano. Parce que point de plus retors. Simplicité de l'intrigue, rigueur de la composition, sobriété de l'écriture, et pour tout dire d'un seul et maître mot, lisibilité [. . .] . (Bersani, "Agent double" 78)

A 1986 article by Gerald Prince, for instance, concurred, finding Modiano's novels readable because of the "classic" quality both of his subjects ("the self, the quest, love and death, Oedipus and Theseus, Abraham and Isaac, time, memory") and of his style ("graceful, sober, and precise, [...] consistently pure"). As a result Prince viewed Modiano as having mastered narrative scale, purity, and effects with the aplomb of a virtuoso (Prince, "Re-Membering Modiano" 42). One year later and in the first book-length study of Modiano, *Patrick Modiano, pièces d'identité: écrire l'entretemps*, Colin W. Nettelbeck and Penelope A. Hueston reaffirmed that view, asserting that the young novelist was developing his art in the classical French tradition, *"accentuant les qualités de mesure, de simplicité et de continuité"* (*Patrick Modiano* 3). Six years later in 1993, Jules Bedner assumed a similar appreciation, compiling a collection of university essays primarily around the theme of ambiguity in Modiano's work, on the grounds that the oeuvre is *"un objet fascinant"* (Bedner, Présentation 1). In the same vein as Bedner, Thierry Laurent merely asserted the *"charme indéfinissable"* of Modiano's style (Laurent 9). He too offered indirect but substantial homage to Modiano's appeal by writing a book-length study, *L'œuvre de Patrick Modiano: une auto-fiction* (1997). Laurent explored the interplay between autobiographical details and fictional compulsions in Modiano's work. With great attention to biographical and fictional detail and with no less great prudence in respecting the unknowable border between a writer's memory and imagination, Laurent's study articulated the direction that Modiano criticism had—necessarily—been taking for some time. Given *"l'analogie flagrante et constante entre les premiers éléments biographiques en notre connaissance et les événements survenant dans les romans"* (Laurent 9), it is productive to recognize how Modiano's art uses his personal past as a trampoline into a fictional world that beckons him obsessively. What best characterizes that world for Laurent is a compulsive, painful wandering in the past on a search for answers to the questions posed by identity. That wandering in turn structures itself around the anguished themes arising from the author's boyhood memories of a family life scarred by parental abandonment and the early death of his only sibling, Rudy (Laurent 41, 181-83).

General readability as an explanation of Modiano's success continued to find partisans. In a 1998 collection of essays (*Paradigms of Memory: The Occupation and Other Hi/stories in the Novels of Patrick Modiano*) that too testified to growing scholarly interest in Modiano,

Martine Guyot-Bender and William VanderWolk would, like Bedner and Laurent, attribute Modiano's success to the fascination that his work exercises over readers (Guyot-Bender and VanderWolk 15). They go so far as to find his kaleidoscopic visions of France's recent past "addictive" (Guyot-Bender and VanderWolk 7). But like Prince, they root Modiano's reading appeal in specific terms, in universal interests such as his addressing the long-standing philosophical and literary interest in the relationship between recollection and representation, and in the role that memory plays in determining individuals' very existence (Guyot-Bender and VanderWolk 7). They even propose that Modiano's stories can be read as fables that tell us truths about the past that in turn enable us to advance into the future (Guyot-Bender and VanderWolk 15).

But even appropriate answers like Rousso's, and compelling homage to Modiano's readability like Prince's, Bedner's, Laurent's, and Guyot-Bender's and VanderWolk's, cannot restrain the terms of the debate over the success of a writer as richly complex as Modiano. For instance, Rousso's history-oriented observation that Modiano satisfied France's curiosity about its repressed memory of World War II does not address the question of why in France the appeal of Modiano's subsequent texts has endured well past that country's "*mode rétro*" of the early seventies, since starting with his fourth published narrative in 1975, *Villa triste,* Modiano broke with a subject matter focusing exclusively on the Collaboration.

Neither are paeans to Modiano's readable style universally sung, witness for example Robert Smadja's finding in Modiano's work: "un style qui s'élève rarement au-dessus de la plate relation journalistique" (Smadja 142). In fact neither are those paeans completely appropriate to the entire Modianesque oeuvre, since the latter has no strict uniformity of style. (Some would, however, categorically disagree: see Barrot 8-9.) For instance, the style of Modiano's first three published novels *La place de l'étoile* (1968), *La ronde de nuit* (1969), and *Les boulevards de ceinture* (1972) differs radically from that of the later ones, doubtless because of the change in focus that started with *Villa triste* (Avni 151-54). Or for other examples, one could point to Modiano's seventh published novel, *Une jeunesse,* in which for the first and so far only time, Modiano used an omniscient, third-person narrator; or one could point to the recent *Dora Bruder* (1997) and *Des inconnues* (1999, a compilation of three novellas), which, as Akane Kawakami indicates, show marked differences vis-à-vis Modiano's earlier works in for example the gender, voice, and verb usage of the narrators (Kawakami 121-31).

Understandably, then, other terms of debate and other answers to the question of Modiano's success have been proposed. Colin Nettelbeck and Penelope Hueston's *Patrick Modiano, pièces d'identité; écrire l'entretemps* expanded their affirmation of Modiano's general classical appeal by grounding it more specifically in aesthetic structures. Covering the novels published before the study's date of publication, 1986, that is, the first nine novels, Nettelbeck and Hueston argue with precision and persuasiveness that it is from musical and music-like structures (for example rondo, fugue, rhythm, measure) that Modiano's varied texts derive much of their emotional power, much of their transcendence, and much of their capacity to communicate Modiano's nuanced perception of time (Nettelbeck and Hueston, *Patrick Modiano* 23, 35, 37-39, 86-92, 124; see also Coenen-Mennemeier on the role of music in Modiano).

It is true that in 1996, ten years after Nettelbeck's and Hueston's ground-breaking study, part of the position taken by Prince and then Guyot-Bender and VanderWolk was reprised: Alan Morris proposed a strictly theme-oriented explanation of Modiano's success. Novel by novel (through the first fifteen), Morris shows how, in an increasingly reassuring attempt at self-definition, Modiano wrote an oeuvre that exorcises the demons of his troubled childhood. Identified as principal among those disturbances were the death of Patrick's brother Rudy, younger by two years, which occurred when Patrick was twelve, and a sense of abandonment brought on by the frequent absences of the touring-actress mother Luisa and the business-man father Albert who eventually left his family completely. Tracing the exorcism through the development of what he identifies as Modiano's key themes—remembrance, identity, time and the past, the relationship between life and art, indeed, between life and death—Morris turns to those universal themes in order to locate the appeal of this "king of ambiguity" (Morris, *Patrick Modiano* [Berg] 206, 207, 209).

A similar psycho-biographical approach was taken in 1999 by Baptiste Roux. The merit of the oeuvre, which for Roux too arises from Modiano's addressing his emotional demons, is to take its readers on an illuminating investigation of themes no less universal than those identified by Morris: human identity itself, the darkest corners of the human soul (Roux 88), and an understanding of the world and our place in it (Roux 263). Arguing forcefully and in detail against the claim (noted above) that Modiano writes the same book over and over, Roux scrupulously delineates the thematic, stylistic, and psycho-biographical evolution of the oeuvre from *La place de l'étoile* to *Dora Bruder*. Roux focuses on the role played by the Occupation as portrayed in Modiano's work. The critic finds the Occupation to be not a mere background on which the author putatively projects his neuroses, but rather a veritable actant in his narratives (see for instance p. 154). For his fundamental point, he maintains that there are two trilogies to be found in Modiano's oeuvre. The first, consisting of Modiano's first three published novels, *La place de l'étoile* (1968), *La ronde de nuit* (1969), and *Les boulevards de ceinture* (1972), are indeed a readily demonstrable trilogy. They stand tightly together because of their sequential publication, their nightmarish obsession with prenatal memories of the Occupation, and their shared characters (see for instance Roux 102), a sharing that generates an impression of circularity heightened, as Bruno Doucey notes, by the linking of locales from the end of one book to the beginning of the other, by their very titles as well as by their themes and concerns (Doucey 41-44). For Roux, a sense of void marks the writing of these three fantasy-driven books. For the second trilogy Roux proposes that nostalgia replaces the void with History, a maturation that allows Modiano to move beyond the traumas of Jewish martyrdom and the unsuccessful search for identity. This latter trilogy would consist of *Voyage de noces* (1990), *Fleurs de ruine* (1991), and *Dora Bruder* (1997), all three explicit and sustained revisitations of the Occupation. Roux considers the differences between the two proposed trilogies ultimately superficial, however, finding them united in what drives their production, namely Modiano's need to master his psychological demons.

Roux argues a good case for the two trilogies, and Modiano himself has indicated in *Dora Bruder* that Ingrid Teyrsen, the fictional character who haunts the memory of the narrator of *Voyage de noces,* was an initial, fictional incarnation of his thoughts about the historic Dora Bruder. Nonetheless, and the reprise of the theme of the Occupation notwithstanding, the latter three books do not have the striking number of links that weave together the former three. Furthermore, the ternary symmetry of Roux's argument requires his excluding the equally Occupation-haunted *Rue des boutiques obscures* (1978), postulating it as no more than a "bridge" between the two triads. But Roux justifies his extensive attention to the two triads with his claim that those six books are more interesting than the rest of the oeuvre. He sees them lending themselves more forcefully to Modiano's *"interrogations existentielles"* about identity arising from the Occupation (Roux 123). Roux observes in the latter trilogy Modiano's "natural universe," that is, the foundation of the identity quest undertaken by a writer in anguish over his uncertain relationship with an indifferent, sometimes hostile Jewish father-figure compromised by the Collaboration.

But in *Ontologie fantôme: essai sur l'œuvre de Patrick Modiano* (1996), there appear again in the critical debate over Modiano's success new terms and new answers. In his study Daniel Parrochia marks a different approach to Modiano by meditating philosophically on the latter's novels. Published in the same year as Morris's analysis but earlier than Roux's, Parrochia's book proposes a reading that, while less biographical than the latter two, is not unlike theirs: he finds in Modiano a captivating voice that communicates some of our more troubling contemporary preoccupations. Starting from the observation that in today's world our sense of materiality has been vaporized by the discoveries of nuclear physics, by the theory of relativity, and by the on-going "informationalization" of experience, Parrochia concludes that informed awareness today often makes us feel shadowy or ghost-like. He suggests that such awareness may have universal dimensions by wondering whether such ontological degradation of materiality does not resonate with neo-Platonism (24). He then proposes that the peculiarities of Modiano's characters combine to incarnate for the reader this sense of "desubstantialization." First of all, even the narrators occasionally assert their own nothingness (for example "JE N'EXISTE PAS," *La ronde de nuit* 11; "Je ne suis rien," "je n'étais rien," *Rue des boutiques obscures* 11, 124). And one could add that on occasion they and the characters comment on each other's "desubstantialization," comments made more telling through the use of suspension points, so frequent in Modiano: "—Non ... non... Je sais... Ça lui arrive de temps en temps... Il a des absences... Il fait le mort... Et puis il réapparaît..."; "Et Jansen semblait si absent, lui qui aurait dû être le lien entre tous ces gens..." (*Chien de printemps* 48, 70). Quite consistently with such assertions, the narrators and characters very often lack civil status because of their obsessive avoidance of any contact with the authorities. They invariably drift in that murky status because of a suspect but occulted past, and as a result of that drift they wrestle with conundrums created by the interplay of time and memory. For example, in conflating surges of memories and impressions, they view certain places like the Luxembourg Gardens or the Champs-Elysées as incarnating past and present events simultaneously and transparently (*Fleurs de ruine* 43, 103). Similarly, as narrators they constantly slip across the borders of past and present through a Henry James-like reliance on flash-backs and flash-forwards (Parrochia 81). But in a reprise of the general readability explanation of Modiano's success, Parrochia finds Modiano's special appeal in the pleasure brought on by the novelist's knack for bringing to life such wispy, evanescent characters (27), by the exhilarating sense of adventure arising from their perception of time's simultaneity and transparency (54), and by the delicate prose (*pace* Smadja) that makes the first two pleasures possible (28).

The next year (1997) saw yet another kind of explanation of Modiano's success. Taking a tack based much more on reader response, William VanderWolk offered *Rewriting the Past,* a comprehensive study of the interplay between memory, history, and narrative in Modiano's novels. In his book VanderWolk weaves various versions of the opinion that the key to the appeal of Modiano's work lies in the cooperation that it invites from, and enables in, its readers. For example, VanderWolk posits that, faced with the muddle of imperfect memory and lively imagination experienced by Modiano's narrators, we the readers become participants in the creative process, entering Modiano's unfamiliar realm, an activity that enables us to read both his narrators' worlds and our own (VanderWolk 2). Like the characters, the readers become detectives caught up in the search for meaning, a search all the more compelling because of the narrators' engaging human qualities (VanderWolk 35, 64). Furthermore, their dream-flecked searches open us up to our own dreams, charging them with the universality of literature and of myth (VanderWolk 45, 122). Modiano's characters, "even the most unrealistic, touch nerves in all of us and keep us constantly conscious of our past" (VanderWolk 104-5). Moreover, VanderWolk's approach to the novelist's oeuvre through memory derives considerable authority from his debt to Richard Terdiman, who has cogently argued that a study of memory gets to the heart of many of the vital questions in contemporary intellectual life.

The year 1999 marked the plowing of notably different critical terrain regarding Modiano. Taking an explicitly ethical approach to an explanation of Modiano's success, Martine Guyot-Bender's *Mémoire en dérive: poétique et politique de l'ambiguïté chez Patrick Modiano* suggests that Modiano's success lies in the value and appeal of his oeuvre's large ethical component. For her, his work shows how to maintain memory's vital encounter with the Holocaust, in opposition to dogmatic accounts that would settle the matter and so dispose of it.

> La voix des narrateurs de Modiano rappelle sans cesse que le chapitre du Génocide et des circonstances qui l'ont rendu possible ne peut être clos malgré la disparition des derniers témoins. Leurs investigations maladroites ne visent pas à combler mais à accepter le gouffre insondable de la tragédie. Si les mots et les sens se dérobent devant eux, c'est qu'ils ont pleine conscience de leur impuissance face à ce qui n'est plus. Mais cette reconnaissance ne les libère pour autant de leur désir de savoir. (Guyot-Bender 115)

We can corroborate this interpretation by an appeal to a larger context, noting that much the same point was made in 1999 in Myriam Ruszniewski-Dahan's *Les romanciers de la Shoa*. After a consideration of the work of Elie Wiesel, Anna Langfus, Romain Gary, Patrick Modiano, and Georges Perec, she concludes that they are: "cinq auteurs dont aucun ne peut dispenser de certitudes, mais cinq romanciers qui savent tous (et c'est sans doute ce qui les réunit dans ce même creuset du judaïsme) faire jaillir les questions, qui peuvent toutes se résumer en une seule et même: Auschwitz ne devra jamais cesser de nous interroger, et seule compte la question [. . .]" (Ruszniewski-Dahan 212).

The three chapters of Guyot-Bender's book methodically lay the groundwork for maintaining that Modiano's oeuvre authorizes this point of view regarding memory's dealing with the Holocaust. In her first chapter she looks at the oeuvre's author/narrators, all inextricably one for the reader. She highlights their unstable identity and the ways in which the instability is reinforced by their penchant for wandering and for writing place descriptions that project wrenching emptiness. She ends the chapter by connecting their identity to the Holocaust, finding that a sense of alienation, asserted to be frequent among post-Holocaust Jewish writers, underlies and explains their troubled identity. In her second chapter, Guyot-Bender first explores the abortive detective work characteristic of Modiano's work, finding in it an obsessive interrogation of how Modiano's/the narrators' (and France's) memory of the Occupation must dialogue with the present. She then argues that Modiano's language (the—only apparently—simple syntax and descriptions, along with his distinctive narrative breaks and slippages) works to "overdetermine the indeterminacy" of memory's workings (Guyot-Bender 90), all in a pronounced revolt against the triumphalist coherence advanced by the Gaullist myth of France's resistance to the Occupation. Her final chapter determines that Modiano's/the narrators' triple opaqueness (touching who they are, and what and how they write) and their detachment parallel our relationship with reality itself, as well as warn against the dogmatic inclinations of writers of history, especially of the Holocaust. Anticipating the charge that the effect is a relativism that would diminish the efforts of those who rightly try to understand and explain the Holocaust, Guyot-Bender argues for the uncertain oeuvre's positive impact, which for her results from the oeuvre's dogged insistence on several points. She sees it as insisting on truth as a difficult, imperfect process, thereby countering the corrosive simplicity of those who would make myths of the Holocaust; she sees it insisting on the merits of language in spite of the latter's unavoidable imperfections: "seul le langage peut perpétuer l'expérience et assurer la survie du souvenir" (Guyot-Bender 99); and she sees it insisting on ambiguity and so undermining the facile Gaullist myth of a unified France resistant to Nazism: "L'ambiguïté narrative et interprétative de son écriture ébranle les fondements du mythe gaullien [. . .]. Elle nous fait entrevoir [. . .] l'omniprésence d'un mal indéfini, indescriptible, insaisissable et inévitable, une composante à part entière de la dynamique nationale française [. . .]" (Guyot-Bender 104).

But subsequently, another critic returned to the earlier matter-of-fact inclination of Bedner and Laurent (see above) by assuming the obviousness of Modiano's success: Paul Gellings simply felt no need even to consider explaining it. In *Poésie et mythe dans l'œuvre de Patrick Modiano: le fardeau du nomade* (2000), he was content simply to observe Modiano's status as an established author of international stature (Gellings 9), being more interested instead in demonstrating that Modiano's novels are *"récits poétiques,"* poetic prose narratives as defined by Jean-Yves Tadié in *Le récit poétique* (Paris: Gallimard, 1994). As quoted by Gellings, Tadié proposes that poetic prose narrative borrows from poetry its means and its effects (Gellings 13), primarily through an exploitation of language as sound and image (Gellings 16-17). As a result, narrative structure becomes more formal (that is, circular, variational, nuclear, and repetitive) and thereby more communicative of the mythic, that is universal, structures behind human thought and activity (Gellings 13-17). Gellings argues that the universal structures at work in Modiano's oeuvre are to be found in its overlap on the one hand of the Freudian Foundling as explained in Marthe Robert's *Roman des origines et origines du roman*, and on the other hand of the Wandering Jew. Gellings maintains that for Modiano those myths come together because of the father figure, who comprises at once an Oedipal rival to be killed and a mysterious absence, knowledge of whom might fill in the anguishing vacancy of the author's identity. Gellings concludes that the father figure, more function than character, constitutes the driving force behind the poetics of Modiano's narratives (Gellings 200).

Two years later (2002), Annie Demeyère also wrote a careful, detailed study of Modiano's oeuvre on the unstated assumption that his impressive creative stature warrants such studies. Indeed, in an indirect sign of the oeuvre's substance, Demeyère managed quite easily to write close to three hundred pages focusing only on how the oeuvre portrayed the figure of the artist: *Portraits de l'artiste dans l'œuvre de Patrick Modiano*. Using a logic more associative than linear, and following a development more paradigmatic than syntagmatic, Demeyère's study responds to the oeuvre as the fruit of Modiano's compulsion. Driving the compulsion would be a need to create artistic figures fearful of failure and artistic powerlessness, who in their objectification allow the author to distance himself from his own identical fears (for example Demeyère 10). For her, Modiano's texts take their distinctiveness from the play among three key figures viewed as metaphors of novel writing (for example Demeyère 216 and following pages) and of each other (for example 259): 1) the author writing the narrator who narrates the artist, 2) the narrator narrating the artist, and 3) the tormented artist who offers a reflection of the author who is creating him/her and of the narrator who is narrating him/her. Let it be noted that Demeyère's scheme understands artists broadly: they often write, but can also engage in a gamut of other activities that extend from photography on through the entertainment fields of cinematography (an especially rich source of the oeuvre's themes, Demeyère 33 and following pages), sports, the circus, and the music hall, and the artist is sometimes represented even by the posturing dandy. So all-encompassing does she find this triadic play of author-narrator-artist—echoed, one might add, in the artist's triple exile from homeland, identity, and writing (121) and in the universal author-book-reader triad (235)—that she declares the artists, standing at the center of the triad for the reader (for example 182), to constitute "*les archétypes des personnages modianiens, leur métaphore absolue: évanescence, imposture, nihilisme et humour*" (Demeyère 9). The emptiness behind such a metaphor notwithstanding (or perhaps, as a result of such emptiness, 193), the artist for Demeyère incarnates an Orphic aesthetic that, by fudging the border between the real and the imaginary, still endeavors to resurrect fragmentary events and figures from the past. The paradoxical outcome of Modiano's long line of vacant artistic mediums to the past (Demeyère 192 and following pages), of course, is the very present existence of a distinctive, unified, accomplished oeuvre: "[Modiano] ne peut accomplir son œuvre propre qu'en intronisant des personnages incapables d'aboutir à une œuvre" (Demeyère 147, 148).

On the other hand, back in the same year as Gelling's book (2000), Akane Kawakami published a study that, although as impressive in its lexical, thematic, and structural mastery of Modiano's oeuvre, found it necessary to continue to address the issue of the novelist's success. But in a twist for Modiano scholarship, Kawakami defends *against* the "charge" of Modiano's readability, which she attributes to Modiano's skill in harnessing the strength of the popular novel. She maintains that Modiano's "readability seems to have the effect of banishing [him] from the realms of the academically interesting" (Kawakami 4). To counter the putative assumption of incompatibility between readability and academic interest, she takes a formal approach to the oeuvre, proposing that Modiano operates a self-conscious, sophisticated postmodern subversion of three of the very structures that make him apparently readable: first-person narration, chronological narration, and realist representation. Whereas readers expect first-person narrators to reveal authoritatively their own inner landscapes, Modiano's narrators strive to reveal as little of themselves as possible, drawing readers into a psychological, characterless void; whereas careful use of verb tenses like that shown by Modiano traditionally helps readers grasp the chronology of complicated narratives, in his novels verbal precision manages only to collapse past into present, undermining any sense of the temporal hierarchy of narrated events and thereby communicating the narrator's conflated affective stance toward those events; finally, whereas small and precise narrative details usually help create an impression of reality for readers, Modiano's use of such details, like his use of verb tenses, works in a way that helps to draw readers into the unreal atmosphere created by the narrator's inner void. She then goes on to argue that Modiano succeeds in being both readable and experimental by playing on the conventions of the detective story and by parodying autobiography. For Kawakami, Modiano has done this to such a consistent, accomplished degree that he has produced what she calls his own distinctive subgenre, which for her explains the steady popular demand for his books (Kawakami 109-10, 131).

To be sure, then, the list of attempts to explain the success of Modiano's oeuvre has grown in size and diversity. Let it be noted that indications of Modiano's impressive status as a writer have not been restricted to books, appearing as well in numerous articles. The fact that one of those articles was written by a critic of the stature of Michel Foucault suggests in itself that Modiano is more than just another important contemporary writer. Certainly that fact harmonizes well with the judgment expressed by a reviewer for *La Nouvelle Revue Française,* who declared as early as 1972: "Modiano s'affirme comme 'le' grand jeune auteur, comme le plus brillant de sa génération et peut-être aussi de celles des autres" (Amette 105). That lofty opinion has not gone without echo in other reviews (see Galey, Guillot, Pire, and Poirson, for example). Indeed, the assumption of Modiano's high literary achievements has reached the point where, as we have just seen, critics like Bedner, Laurent, and Gellings can feel free to offer analyses of the oeuvre without even bothering to explain its success.

III.   A New Explanation: *La place de l'étoile*'s Availability to Critical Variety

Nonetheless, like Kawakami and others doubtless to come, I find it useful to continue to make the effort to explain Modiano's success. Not surprisingly, given the survey above of historical, stylistic, thematic, aesthetic, ethical, and formal explanations of his success, I propose that Modiano's success is explainable precisely because the oeuvre lends itself fruitfully to a wide variety of approaches. To make that point through my own reading, I will first look primarily and closely at Modiano's first published novel, *La place de l'étoile,* and then I will apply the resulting critical template to key moments in the oeuvre.

But given the spirit of deliberate and outrageous provocation that permeates this novel, it seems more than acceptable to aim for critical provocation; indeed, it seems appropriate. Ora Avni offers an admirable example. In her *D'un passé l'autre: aux portes de l'histoire avec Patrick Modiano* (1997), she has used the multi-voiced, fractured, and discordant account by Raphaël Schlemilovitch, the narrator of *La place de l'étoile*, as a template to write a no less multi-voiced, fractured, and discordant analysis of France's anti-Jewish historiography, specifically its contradictory memory and forgetfulness regarding the Jewish French.

In the following pages, I will make my own attempt at provocation by viewing *La place de l'étoile* in the light of the controversial semiotic approach of Michael Riffaterre who, notwithstanding our critical era's widespread perception of the openness and undecidability of literary texts, posits a necessary way of reading them. The overriding implication of this study will be, then, that Modiano's oeuvre has experienced popular and critical success primarily because it is variously and richly readable in the way of all great literature.

It should be emphasized, however, that "variously and richly readable" does not necessarily mean readable only in the way practiced by the critics cited above and practiced in this study. Too often the assumption prevails that the critic's job is to find order, to find the "hidden" clue to order, the text's "deep structures," its "underlying structures." As read by Gary Saul Morson and Caryl Emerson, Mikhail Bakhtin for one resists the "semiotic totalitarianism" of decoding structuralist readings (Morson 28), such as the one that will immediately follow. Furthermore, Derrida-smart nowadays, we are sensitive to the meta-phoric—and so imperfect—fit of the concepts of what is "hidden" in texts, of what is "under" texts, and so forth, to the reality of texts. There is no compelling theoretical reason why Modiano's difficult, often hallucinatory texts should not be accepted as such, nor is there any compelling theoretic reason why we should not consider his verbal magic to be in the service of textual disorder as much as in the service of textual order. But for the following study, the choice has been made to imitate critically the detective story genre that will be seen to play such a large role in Modiano's oeuvre. So there will be a (critical) investigation hunting for the clues to a (literary) crime that is hidden beneath the "surface" of (textual) events, primarily because Modiano's texts can lend themselves to such an investigation, affording pleasure in the process.

Finally, a close study of *La place de l'étoile* has merit for other reasons as well. The results can help reinforce the arguments of Jacques Bersani,[6] Nettelbeck and Hueston,[7] Gerald Prince,[8] Pierre Daprini,[9] Jules Bedner,[10] and Annie Demeyère.[11] Those arguments propose that *La place de l'étoile*, while Modiano's most distinctive work,[12] is nonetheless a highly representative one, in that it offers a valuable base line for plotting the use and development of themes and images throughout the oeuvre.[13] So in the effort to strengthen those arguments, as well as to justify retro-spectively my extensive attention to *La place de l'étoile,* chapter 3 will show the usefulness of the conclusions drawn in the two chapters that precede it, by using those conclusions as a template for examining other Modiano novels. Furthermore, in the process of this analysis of *La place de l'étoile*, issues significant for contemporary literary scholarship will arise, such as the role of the referent in literature, and the tension in postmodern literature between aesthetic play on the one hand and the political and the moral on the other. To the degree that this study wor-thily raises (with no pretence to settling) those interesting, substantial issues, the reader will have one more sign of why Modiano's oeuvre has garnered so much success.

◆ ◆ ◆

Chapter 1[1]

A Riffaterrean Approach to
La place de l'étoile

Michael Riffaterre provokes: he "violates critical decorum" (Culler 91). Just on the basis of the spirit of provocation shared by both Modiano and Riffaterre, one should consider using the latter's approach in order to analyze the former's novel, on the grounds that the approach would suit rather well the far from decorous *La place de l'étoile*. But before considering applying Riffaterre's method to Modiano's novel, we should acknowledge that this important critic has been challenged for using technical terms from linguistics, rhetoric, and semiotics that are often difficult to follow, sometimes open to dispute, and on occasion not completely consistent.[2] Moreover, Riffaterre has made questionable assumptions. The most theoretically fundamental are that a critic's primary function in reading literature is to interpret it aesthetically, and that reading a literary text means dealing with a stable, purely objective entity constituted as text (and as text within a genre) independently of the act of reading. And of course that first assumption depends on the notoriously variable concept of "literature," which usually in turn has often entailed the concept of "serious literature," until very recently the only sort presumably deserving of aesthetic interpretation. So up through the middle of the twentieth century "literature" tended not to include texts like the one that this study focuses on, novels, because novels putatively served as mere amusement or escape (Wellek and Warren 219); as Boileau put it in Chant III of *L'art poétique* to enduring effect in French letters: "Dans un roman frivole aisément tout s'excuse." Or even worse, novels like *Les liaisons dangereuses*, *Madame Bovary*, *Ulysses*, and *Lady Chatterly's Lover* were regularly suspected of constituting a threat to moral order (May 8, 10, 257). (A good way to glimpse the sweep of variability in assumptions about what one is supposed to do with "literature" is to review approaches over the centuries to millennia-old texts like Homer's.) Nonetheless, the following pages will look past the shortcomings of Riffaterre's approach for three reasons, the weakest for so doing being that, as Antoine Compagnon has argued in his *Le démon de la théorie: littérature et sens commun*, no critical approach is free of substantial shortcomings; a stronger reason for looking past the Riffaterrean method's shortcomings is that his method produces excellent results[3] in explicating texts that are as difficult as *La place de l'étoile;* and a truly compelling reason is that, as the following paragraphs will maintain, Riffaterre's approach offers a uniquely excellent fit for *La place de l'étoile.*

I.   The Appropriateness of a Riffaterrean Approach to *La place de l'étoile*

As the opening paragraph of the Introduction above suggests, *La place de l'étoile* seeks to outrage, and Michael Riffaterre too does indeed violate decorum. And so *mutatis mutandis* and allowing especially for the shift from the world of publishing fiction to that of writing academic criticism, Riffaterre's work is driven by a spirit kindred to that of the Patrick Modiano of *La place de l'étoile.* The distinguished critic has spent his career offering ingenious explications of difficult texts, explications that tweak the noses of traditional explicators who tend to view textual conundrums as signs of artistic flights of fancy or as excuses for lofty expatiations (for example Riffaterre, *Semiotics* 61-62). His explications also tweak the noses of contemporary critics who view conundrums as signs of undecidability (for example Riffaterre, "Undecidability"). As we shall discuss below, Riffaterre insists that literary texts are exercises neither in freedom nor indeterminacy, but rather verbal constructs that dictate their own decoding. In brief, he violates contemporary critical decorum with insistence on textual necessity, much as Modiano violated artistic and political decorum with his flamboyant sortie into the Holocaust, the Collaboration, Israeli "tough guy" agents as Nazi-like, France's history of hostility toward Jews, and so forth.

Moreover, the critical tendency to peg Modiano as another "indeterminate postmodernist" has become too self-assured and deserves to be provoked, and Riffaterre's approach can help to do that. To be sure, the tendency has been more than justified by traits to be found in Modiano's work:

> In his grasp of his whole cultural heritage and his constant allusions to it; in his recourse to a considerable number of prose formats (autobiography, the war novel, the love story, the *polar*, and so forth) and to "borrowing" from what are often deemed to be less important genres (the cinema, popular music, or the comic-book); in his "skepticism about identity, causality and meaning" [Lodge 38]; in his use of the *mise en abyme* and blatant contradiction; in his antipathy for any form of closure; in his ever-present irony, ludism and pastiching; and in much, much more besides, he most clearly (if unwittingly) invites us to link him to the trend which is still on virtually all commentators' lips today: postmodernism. (Morris, *Patrick Modiano* [Berg] 208; see also Morris, *Patrick Modiano* [Rodopi] 113-17.)

So to question the growing facility with which Modiano's work is categorized as postmodern is not to say that it has not profited from being read as postmodern (see for instance Ewert, Scherman, or Kawakami). Such readings help highlight how Modiano's texts characteristically weave a wide range of contrary elements into an unrelenting self-conscious insistence on the epistemological difficulties created by narrative and memory. At the same time, however, should we not ponder the fact that many of the postmodern qualities mentioned by Morris and others apropos of Modiano would find significant equivalents in, say, *Don Quixote?*

But the provocative Michael Riffaterre points the way to a corrective and complementary reading of "the postmodern indeterminate Modiano." Over the years the critic's brilliant explications have willfully pitted textual necessity against the fashionable taste for conundrums, aporias, and so forth, because his staunchly rhetorical stance inclines him to view such textual difficulties as productive "ungrammaticalities" pointing to readings that embrace a text's distinctive, that is literary, features. In short, since for Riffaterre literariness in general is, even as the decorous Terence Cave has put it, "a disruption of the reader's normal linguistic habits" (Cave 278), textual incoherence on a mimetic level need not be limited to suggesting only a postmodern stance. When we read Modiano's texts in terms of Riffaterre's provocative semiotic necessity, those texts appear more in keeping with literariness and literary tradition, and less exclusively beholden to current ideology or "paradigm shifts." Nonetheless, the inclination that marks both the Riffaterrean and the postmodernist stance, while decidedly different in many respects, remains basically compatible, in that both stress how the signified is subordinated to the signifier, in spite of the reader's yearning for mimesis and reassuring referentiality.

A shared spirit of provocation between critic and novelist notwithstanding, the question arises whether Riffaterre's resolutely deterministic critical method will help explicate Modiano's no less resolutely phantasmagoric novel. But it is precisely because of the exceptional reading difficulties posed by *La place de l'étoile* that Riffaterre's approach should be considered. Riffaterre has a brilliant record in explicating puzzling texts that resist ready understanding, for example symbolist and surrealist poetry. Because he assumes that fiction "relies on codes" (Riffaterre, *Fictional Truth* xv), he has articulated a method demonstrably quite productive at the sort of literary structural decoding that the puzzling *La place de l'étoile* calls for. (For a sketch of the main features of Riffaterre's essentially identical approach to poetry, upon which he had tended to focus in his earlier work, see A. W. Lyle's "Practical Criticism à la Riffaterre.")

To crack fictional codes Riffaterre's reader starts with an initial "syntagmatic," "linguistic," heuristic reading dealing primarily with the fiction's meaning, that is, the relationship between its signs and their apparent referents. The heuristic reading tries to make sense. But Riffaterre emphasizes that the relationship between literary signs and their apparent referents is not only aleatory, subject to personal interpretation, it also invariably breaks down logically during the heuristic reading. After that first reading, which has identified where the "linguistic," "syntagmatic" sense breaks down, decoding of the text as an artistic whole requires repeated "paradigmatic," "literary," hermeneutic readings. The hermeneutic reading looks for significance beyond faulty signification. Riffaterre understands literary significance to be a global, unerring aesthetic understanding that semiotically incorporates and yet transcends the points of failure of linguistic sense. The reader is firmly guided to that significance in fiction by three textual feature, ungrammaticalities (elements that produce the break-down in meaning), subtexts, and a matrix.[4]

Riffaterre defines ungrammaticalities as "faults or rents in the fabric of verisimilitude" (Riffaterre, *Fictional Truth* 102), that is, they pose problems of understanding at the mimetic level of the text, not making mimetic *sense* because they work to make literary *significance*. Paradoxically, in posing problems they point to solutions for those problems, but they draw their indexing capacity not *from* the chain of events apparently surrounding the text or referenced in it, but rather *against* those events, making instead insistent reference to a primary hidden intertext (there may be several less decisive intertexts). But once identified, the intertext necessarily generates in the reader's awareness a sign of itself, specifically an interpretant, consistently with the theory of Charles Sanders Peirce (1839-1914), the American pragmatist philosopher who helped pioneer semiotics, that signs, already having an indirect relationship with their objects, generate no less indirect intermediate signs or interpretants of themselves. So in a Riffaterrean reading the intertext does not exist to the text in all the intertext's richness, complexity, and uniqueness (otherwise the intertext would be just its physical self within the text), but rather as an interpretant, a mediating concept between itself and the text in question (Riffaterre, "La trace" 9-10). The intertext, as interpretant, helps lead to semiosis, the integrative understanding of the entire text as symbolic, not referential, system (Riffaterre, *Fictional Truth* xvii-xviii). Or as Riffaterre had succinctly put it in *Semiotics of Poetry*, the ungrammaticalities where "linguistic" sense breaks down are "at one and the same time the locus of obscurity and the index to the solution" (161).

Next, he uses the term "subtext" to designate "a story or episode embedded in a narrative and mirroring the whole. The subtext enables the reader to grasp points and to be aware of the structure of that whole" (Riffaterre, "On Narrative Subtexts" 450). However, throughout the development of his theory Riffaterre repeatedly cautions that a subtext is *not* simply an episode, motif, theme, or even Barthesian *lexie* (see for example "The Mind's Eye" 37). Moreover, we should observe that in Riffaterre's opinion far more than mere enabling is involved, for he maintains that subtexts are "those narrative units of significance that account for readers' ability to find their way *unerringly* in fiction" (Riffaterre, *Fictional Truth* 54; my emphasis).

Finally, the matrix, unlike ungrammaticalities and subtexts, is for Riffaterre a hypothetical structure. A principle of conceptual unity, it is reflected in all the text's variants, that is, in its ungrammaticalities, its subtexts, its hidden intertext, whole segments of the text, and indeed in a general sense the textual whole itself. Readers can glimpse it in a word, a cliché, an expression, a sentence, or an image in the text (Riffaterre, *Semiotics of Poetry* 5-6, 13, 19). As the very term "matrix" should lead one to expect, it serves as a primary source from which springs the text along with the ungrammaticalities and subtexts. But for Riffaterre, of the three concepts, only a text's ungrammaticalities can typically be expected to reveal themselves on the first, heuristic reading that is spent getting over the hurdle of mimetic (mis)understanding.

So for Riffaterre it is as a result of successful hermeneutic (re)readings that one sees in semiosis how the ungrammaticalities, hidden intertext, and subtexts can be said to lead to the unerring perception of the matrix from which the whole text originates. Through the subtexts and ungrammaticalities, then, the text guides its own decoding, indeed, requires its own decoding on its own terms. The unerring decoding of fiction is of a piece with the necessary reading of poetry for which the early Riffaterre very quickly became notorious: "the system of inescapable ungrammaticalities makes *reading a restrictive process.* The only freedom left to the reader is the certainty that his reading is wrong, his task unfinished, so long as the ungrammaticalities are not removed" (Riffaterre, *Semiotics of Poetry* 150; emphasis in the original). As provocative as the language of "unerring," "necessary" reading sounds, however, it is only right to note that it arises from Riffaterre's attempt to encourage systematic, theoretically informed reading that, while inalterably grounded in the dynamic between reader and text, is not based on readers' personal whimsy:

> The text tends [. . .] not to be interpreted for what it is, but for what is selected from it by the reader's individual reactions. A segmentation of the text into units of significance thus occurs, and it is the task of the critic to verify the validity of this process. In pursuing this goal he must restrict himself to a seg-

mentation that can be proven as being dictated by textual features rather than by the reader's idiosyncrasies, by those elements the perception of which does not depend on the latter
and that resist erasure when they are in conflict with such individual quirks. (Riffaterre, "The Intertextual Unconscious"
372)

In addition to the shared spirit of provocation and the fit between
a decoding critical practice and a particularly baffling text in need of decoding, there are other reasons for viewing *La place de l'étoile* through
Riffaterre's semiotic prism: the critic's approach as a whole resonates
especially well with what is arguably the first-person text's very narrative instance, namely a psychoanalytic session that the narrator Raphaël
Schlemilovitch imagines spending with the Master himself, none other
than Sigmund Freud (*La place de l'étoile* 213 and following pages).[5]
Riffaterre has in fact articulated within the general context of literary
explication the overall fit between his semiotic concepts and Freud's ana-
lytical concepts. For instance: "The text functions something like a neu-
rosis: as the matrix is suppressed, the displacement produces variants all
through the text, just as suppressed symptoms break out somewhere else
in the body" (Riffaterre, *Semiotics of Poetry* 19). But in the specific context of a narrative conceived as an imaginary psychoanalytical session in
presumed search for the suppressed, the match between semiotic matrix
and the psychological impetus behind Raphaël's account becomes all the
more striking.

No less a fit is enjoyed between *La place de l'étoile*'s inferred
narrative instance and Riffaterre's ungrammaticalities specifically. Since
psychoanalysis aims to glimpse the workings of the subconscious, and
since it argues prominently that dreams provide a privileged path to the
subconscious, the reader may assume with confidence that what Modiano
himself calls the narrative "phantasmagoria" (*La place de l'étoile* 7) that
is offered up by Raphaël to his imagined Freud ferries or at least reflects
considerable dream-like material. No doubt because of fundamental
similarities between how dreams work and how symbolic systems work,
one of the three great functions that Freud ascribes to dream-work,
namely dream displacement,[6] works much like Riffaterre's ungrammaticalities, namely as an indication that an essential point has been sup-

pressed. Although vehicles of substantial information, dreams and symbolic systems both have elements that appear strange and incomprehensible at first glance, revealing precisely that they are hiding something (Riffaterre, *Production* 16), and those elements often occupy initially peripheral, secondary positions. Or as Derrida's language would have it, playing fully on the paradox at work here, those elements occupy supplementary positions:

> Car le concept de supplément [. . .] abrite en lui deux significations dont la cohabitation est aussi étrange que nécessaire. Le supplément s'ajoute, il est un surplus, une plénitude enrichissant une autre plénitude, le *comble* de la présence [. . .].
> Mais le supplément supplée. Il ne s'ajoute que pour remplacer. Il intervient ou s'insinue *à la place de;* s'il comble, c'est comme on comble un vide. (Derrida, *Grammatologie* 208)

Next, regarding the appropriateness of applying the concept of a repetitive "subtext" specifically to *La place de l'étoile,* one ought first to appreciate that the notion of a text's having embedded and similar reading units throughout is hardly unique to Riffaterre, nor is the present study the first to turn to such a notion in order to understand Modiano's work better. Indeed, we should recognize from the start that there is nothing startlingly new and revolutionary in the underlying thought here. Literary criticism has traditionally made profitable use of the simple notion of artistic repetition, and continues to do so regarding Modiano, as one sees in William VanderWolk's recent study of the interplay of memory, history, and narration in the latter's oeuvre (see the Introduction, above). For all his competence in the language and concepts of contemporary theory, VanderWolk does not hesitate to turn to tried and true traditional concepts, such as leitmotivs and repeated stylistic techniques, when they help explain how readers negotiate difficult texts such as Modiano's. In a borrowing from Milan Kundera, VanderWolk stresses how mere repetition in general can aid reading: "What Kundera calls '*le raffinement ludique de la répétition*' ([Kundera] 174) is evident everywhere in Modiano's work and serves as a signpost for the reader as we follow a trail of indistinct clues through his world of shadows" (VanderWolk, *Rewriting the Past* 52).

Nor is Riffaterre's concept unique among more contemporary-sounding critical moves. For instance, Junate Kaminskas makes use of Jean Ricardou's concept of *"germes d'agissements futurs"* when she reads one of Modiano's later novels, *Fleurs de ruine,* as an attempt on his part to reconcile feminine-masculine psychic poles:

> [Les femmes] constituent "un germe d'agissements futurs" (29) pour reprendre une expression de Ricardou [Ricardou, *Nouveaux problèmes*]. La description de ce procédé par Ricardou nous paraît pertinente: "le texte en disposant çà et là tels passages soumis à une certaine similitude, programme la verticalité des rapprochements qu'il revient à la lecture d'actualiser en passant de tel de ces passages à tel autre. Il s'agit d'un *texte court-circuité*" (Ricardou 124 [emphasis in the original]). (Kaminskas, "Les structures de l'échange" 242)

I prefer, however, Riffaterre's "subtexts" to other concepts, be they traditional or contemporary, first because the word itself better suits my comments above and below on textual suppression, that is, on the parallel role of a psychological and textual subconscious; second because Riffaterre, in distinguishing his reading unit from other concepts (for example themes or Barthes's *lexies)* articulates a more comprehensive, generative idea that better suits my attempt at describing semiosis in *La place de l'étoile.* A long quote from Riffaterre himself is now in order:

> A subtext must be derived from the same matrix as the whole narrative, or from a matrix structurally connected with that of the encircling text [. . .].
>
> The subtext manifests itself, and its limits—in particular the connection between closure and incipit—are identified when the reader becomes retroactively aware that one textual component is echoing another component, formerly read and now remembered. The component from out of the past, thus recollected or reread with the eye of memory, takes on features not noticed during the first or primary reading, for they

are noteworthy only because they are the first step or rung in a
repetitive series [. . .]. For the subtext to be identified, then,
there must be homologues within the narrative from which
flow recognizable, well-marked derivations constituting the
formal and semantic constants any literary text must be able to
show. (Riffaterre, "The Making of a Text" 61-62)

Another reason for my preferring Riffaterre's "subtext" formulation of the phenomenon lies in his repeated emphasis that the reader does
not become cognizant of the subtext's work (and so the latter does not
begin to function) until subsequent and similar textual components found
later in the text trigger a memory of an earlier subtext. Precisely through
its appeal to the workings of retroactive memory, Riffaterre's view of
textual components provides still another admirable fit with Modiano's
texts. Riffaterre affirms that "the principal mechanism of the written text
is memory" (Riffaterre, "The Mind's Eye" 30), a formulation that no less
admirably describes Modiano's oeuvre. As numerous critical studies
have convincingly argued (see for instance Guyot-Bender's and VanderWolk's collection of essays, *Paradigms of Memory: The Occupation
and Other Hi/stories in the Novels of Patrick Modiano*), Modiano's novels focus heavily on, indeed consist of, the imaginative play of memory.
Furthermore, Riffaterre's concept better adumbrates my position taken
below that the struggle between memory and its suppression motivates a
significant dimension of *La place de l'étoile* and indeed of Modiano's
oeuvre.

Even on an imagistic level Riffaterre's concept of the subtext has
special appropriateness for a reading of *La place de l'étoile*. The kaleidoscope figures prominently in Modiano's text as one of its controlling images, and just as a subtext offers "variants of a tautological paradigm"
(Riffaterre, "On Narrative Subtexts" 450) in a verbal context, so too a
kaleidoscope offers variants in a visual context. As Hilda Murzzuschlag,
one of Raphaël's girlfriends-whores, exclaims to him one day as she
looks into one of the kaleidoscopes manufactured by his father: "Re-
gardez dans celui-ci, Raphaël! Un visage humain composé de mille fa-
cettes lumineuses et qui change sans arrêt de forme..." (*La place de
l'étoile* 156). It has been apparent to critics that the rambunctious narrative tumbling from the hallucinatory narrator Raphaël can indeed be

profitably considered as a constantly evolving view of his own self-same character which, with each twist of the narrative barrel, takes on a striking kaleidoscopic visage made up of earlier, familiar elements that assume new alignments. Eschewing any traditional narrative linear thrust, the book spins itself out by means of a kaleidoscopic, more circular narrative principle. Colin Nettelbeck and Penelope Hueston have put the point nicely:

> Fils d'un fabricant de kaléidoscope [Raphaël] est lui-même un être kaléidoscopique dont la vie est faite de l'entrechoc d'expériences et d'images qui, aussitôt formées, éclatent, se transforment, portées et emportées dans un tournoiement perpétuel. Dans une série de travestissements grotesques et de burlesqueries sado-masochistes, il traverse le temps et l'espace dans tous les sens à un rythme délirant, à tel point que le roman lui-même finit par ressembler à un kaléidoscope [. . .].
> (Nettelbeck and Hueston, *Patrick Modiano* 13)

If we emphasize that the etymon of the word "aesthetic" of "aesthetic pleasure" means "perceive," we can appreciate how readers coping with Raphaël's demanding text could indeed experience pleasure in perceiving "kaleidoscopic" elements (among which principally the subtext) underlying and structuring the evolving text.

Finally, a narrative so studded on page after page with obtrusive references to its own intertexts calls to be viewed through Riffaterre's approach, because the latter stresses intertextuality as one of the keys to literary semiosis, emphasizing the literary text as a transform of an intertext (Riffaterre, *Semiotics of Poetry* 42). To be sure, like most good ideas, this one is hardly new: "Certains auteurs, parlant de leurs ouvrages, disent: 'Mon livre, mon commentaire, mon histoire, etc.' Ils sentent leurs bourgeois qui ont pignon sur rue, et toujours un 'chez moi' à la bouche. Ils feraient mieux de dire: 'Notre livre, notre commentaire, notre histoire, etc.,' vu que d'ordinaire il y a plus en cela du bien d'autrui que du leur" (Pascal, pensée 43). But Riffaterre's emphasis on the intertexts is distinctive, and the role of intertexts in *La place de l'étoile* is no less distinctive. In fact it becomes overwhelming, as can be readily surmised from the impressive list that Ora Avni has drawn up of merely the most obvious artistic and intellectual figures whose ideas and works are overtly brought into play in *La place de l'étoile* (Avni 35). The list includes Montaigne, Racine, Saint-Simon, Sartre, Charles d'Orléans, Rémy Belleau, Corneille, Scève, Colette, Giraudoux, Bazin, Proust, Céline, Nerval, Larbaud, Verlaine, Mauriac, Balzac, Benda, Maurois, Joinville, Zola, Halévy, Drumont, Joseph de Maistre, Barrès, Rebatet, Brasillach, Drieu La Rochelle, Maurice Sachs, Léon Daudet, Maurras, Marx, Kafka, and F. Scott Fitzgerald. Consequently, not to consider intertextuality as central in any analysis of the hyperliterary *La place de l'étoile* would be critically unrepresentative. In fact, it would ignore one of the explicit injunctions laid upon readers by the text itself. Quite simply, as Michel Nicolas has emphasized (Nicolas 344), Raphaël tells readers who want to understand him fully to go read some of his narrative's intertexts:

> Scott Fitzgerald a parlé mieux que je ne saurais le faire de ces "parties" où le crépuscule est trop tendre, trop vifs les éclats de rire et le scintillement des lumières pour présager rien de bon. Je vous recommande donc de lire cet écrivain et vous aurez une idée exacte des fêtes de mon adolescence. A la rigueur, lisez *Fermina Marquez* de Larbaud. (*La place de l'étoile* 20)
>
> [Raphaël] s'est rappelé les après-midi qu'il passait au Pré-Catalan et à la Grande Cascade sous la surveillance de Miss Evelyn mais il ne vous ennuiera pas avec ses souvenirs d'enfance. Lisez donc Proust, cela vaut mieux. (205)

Nonetheless, in tension with this overt intertextuality but in still another match with the psychoanalytic premise of *La place de l'étoile*, Riffaterre's vision of fictional narrative has it that the most important intertext, the one with comprehensive explanatory powers, "is hidden like the psychological unconscious and like that unconscious, it is hidden in such a way that we cannot help find it"; Riffaterre's vision postulates that narrative itself is "produced by repressing and displacing the intertext" (Riffaterre, *Fictional Truth* 86, 91). As we shall soon see, *La place de l'étoile* bears out that postulate.

II. Ungrammaticalities in *La place de l'étoile*

As we saw above, Riffaterre describes ungrammaticalities as "faults or rents in the fabric of verisimilitude" (*Fictional Truth* 102). The next few pages will address two kinds of "faults" to be found in *La place de l'étoile*, diegetic and lexical. ("Diegesis" will be taken to mean the "verbal representation of space and time referred to in the narrative," *Fictional Truth* 127). While diegetic ungrammaticalities index the hidden intertext whose interpretant helps explain them, the lexical "faults" will converge with the diegetic variety in illuminating the intertwining subjects that emerge from a reading of *La place de l'étoile* in the light of its hidden intertext. Those intertwining subjects are rootlessness, guilt, and art, which will intertwine in the novel's matrix.

For Modiano's text, the loss of narrativity characteristic of diegetic ungrammaticalities *à la Riffaterre* occurs in a variety of ways. For instance, even within the context of a hallucinating or mad narrator, the wildly incoherent physical displacements that mark the novel's fourth chapter give the reader pause, starting with its opening page: "Vienne. Les derniers tramways glissaient dans la nuit. Mariahilfer-Strasse [Vienne], nous sentions la peur nous gagner. Encore quelques pas et nous nous retrouverions place de la Concorde [Paris]" (*La place de l'étoile* 145). Raphaël will go on in the rest of the chapter to spin out a delirious account that lurches in an ever-accelerating rhythm back and forth among now Vienna, now Paris, now Tel Aviv. Since the reader can make little physical or psychological sense of the displacements on their face, the impression readily arises that their meaning lies on a site other than the immediate diegesis. According to Riffaterre, that textually generated impression of a failure of immediate meaning, the impression of meaning necessarily to be decoded elsewhere, characterizes ungrammaticalities.

To be sure, since the author himself in an opening paratextual[7] description has characterized Raphaël's account as hallucinatory and delirious (*La place de l'étoile* 7), readers could take that paratext as clear (and etymologically correct) authorization to try to locate the "elsewhere" that explains the text's various displacements in a murky psychological disturbance plaguing Raphaël, or even more accurately, in his imagination where he pursues his unbridled psychoanalytic session with his fantasized Freud. In that case, "the verbal representation of space and timc" would appear to be Raphaël's delirious fancy, out of which his narrative would arise. Riffaterre, however, would doubtless argue that attempts at a strictly psychological reading would result in a wide variety of idiosyncratic conclusions, depending upon what scientific judgments could be made about Raphaël's delirium, upon what school of psychology dictated the general approach, and so forth. Such psychological readings would of course each have varying difficulties in coming up with an integrative understanding of the gamut of the text's features. A Riffaterrean approach would insist that the reader should first determine how the text functions as text, before trying to import any extra-textually grounded explanations whatsoever, including the psychological (as, however, we will eventually do below).

Actually, the concluding pages of the text itself take a stand with Riffaterre when Raphaël finally rejects his imagined Freud, archetypal proponent of psychological explanations of literary texts, in favor of "Louis Ferdinand Bardamu," a cross between the novelist Céline (Louis-Ferdinand Destouches) and his creation Ferdinand Bardamu from *Voyage au bout de la nuit:*

> Je n'écoute plus le docteur Freud. Pourtant, il se met à genoux, m'exhorte les bras tendus, prend sa tête dans ses mains, se roule par terre en signe de découragement, marche à quatre pattes, aboie, m'adjure encore de renoncer aux "délires hallucinatoires," à la "névrose judaïque," à la "yiddish paranoïa." Je m'étonne de le voir dans un pareil état: sans doute ma présence l'indisposerait.
>
> —Arrêtez ces gesticulations! lui-dis-je. Je n'accepte pour médecin traitant que le docteur Bardamu. Bardamu Louis-Ferdinand... Juif comme moi... Bardamu. Louis-Ferdinand Bardamu... (*La place de l'étoile* 214)

In other words, for answers to his puzzling "case" or delirium, Raphaël himself calls for an analysis more grounded in fictional-historical textuality than in a personal unconscious. An antecedent for such a call enjoys considerable critical prestige: if one wisely accepts Lionel Trilling's observation in *The Liberal Imagination* that "all prose fiction is a variation on the theme of *Don Quixote*" (197), then the prose fiction of Raphaël's mad but compelling vision *à la Quichotte* ought for that reason as well to be viewed as fictional text before being viewed as psychological text. In fact, one may well wonder if the distinction between the two is not more apparent than real, when one reflects on the Lacanian view that language not only works like the unconscious, but is indeed constitutive of the unconscious (for example Lacan 267): the personal unconscious would be absorbed at least partially into fictional-historical textuality. A compatible conclusion derives from Richard Terdiman's efforts to study the interplay of language and memory:

> Words and concepts never stand alone and are never just synchronic. They carry the traces of their past, of the situations in which they have been made meaningful for their cultures, of the stresses under which they have come. Any specific signifier, any individual discourse, "remembers" the contents with which its culture has invested it. Its present always bears a past that the present is never free to ignore or to forget. This is the dialogic situation of all language, which Bakhtin sought to conceptualize through his notions of "heteroglossia" and "multiaccentuality" (see [Terdiman] *Discourse/Counter-Discourse* 35-41). Language is thus constituted by the adhesion of material it can neither speak nor forget. These spectral contents influence intention and expression [. . .]. (Terdiman, *Present Past* 192)

As Terdiman goes on to point out, even for Freud "the 'influence' of the unconscious upon the formations of the psyche may theoretically be indistinguishable from the spectral contents circulating in the cultural and linguistic realm and linked through their dialogism to every conscious signifier" (Terdiman, *Present Past* 193, note 10). But regardless of whether one views the unconscious in terms more personal or more textual, Raphaël and his text rejects a caricatured Freudian analysis, calling instead for a textual one.

Furthermore, *La place de l'étoile* makes no pretensions to being a "true document," like Prévost's *Manon Lescaut*, Constant's *Adolphe*, or Gide's *Isabelle* (to consider prominent examples of "true documents" from French literature spanning the last three centuries). So even if a devil's advocate were to claim that *La place de l'étoile* could arguably be viewed as a transcript of something resembling a psychoanalytic session and so something inviting the importing of a scientifically psychological framework for purposes of explanation, the claim would be undermined by the text's overt fictionality. That fictionality asserts itself in the novel's paratexts, for example in the dedication (*La place de l'étoile* 9; one would not likely dedicate a "found transcript"), and in the simple chapter divisions, as in the polished sentences and format of the body of the text. And it asserts itself most assuredly in the narrator's hilarious name that in and of itself points to story in full verbal play, and not to verisimilar document: "Raphaël Schlemilovitch."

Apropos of verbal play, fictional textuality asserts itself most poignantly in the introductory "*histoire juive*" that puns on the words *place de l'étoile*, punning that in opening the book intimates that in the pages that follow the play of textuality will prevail over referentiality: "Au mois de juin 1942, un officier allemand s'avance vers un jeune homme et lui dit: 'Pardon, monsieur, où se trouve la place de l'Étoile?' Le jeune homme désigne le côté gauche de sa poitrine" (*La place de l'étoile* 11). This ghastly pun assaults French pride in the iconic monument to much of France's historic glory, Paris's Arc de Triomphe at the "Place/Intersection of the Star," by conflating the name of its location with French shame over Vichy France's reprehensible imposition on its Jewish citizens and immigrants of the requirement to wear the yellow star on their clothes, the "place of the star (of David)." It was precisely in June 1942 that in Paris Jews over six years of age each received three yellow stars (Modiano, *Dora Bruder* 78), and that over twelve thousand foreign Jews—men, women, and children—were arrested in Paris and jammed together under abominable conditions into the Vélodrome d'Hiver for eventual deportation to the camps. Furthermore, in 1942 la place de l'Étoile represented France at its worst: "En 1942, la place de l'Étoile était le centre géographique des activités les plus folles de l'Occupation: dans les rues avoisinantes, on dansait, trafiquait, torturait, chantait, Allemands et Français, dans une étreinte obscène" (Nettelbeck and Hueston, *Patrick Modiano* 14). Just as there can be no doubt about the shame evoked, there can be no doubt about the pride evoked:

> In the French imagination, the Place de l'Étoile symbo-
> lizes not only the capital of France, but also the greatness of
> France's political and military past as enshrined in the Arc de
> Triomphe. As Maurice Agulhon notes, this monument, the re-
> sult of one of Napoleon Bonaparte's projects, was primarily
> intended "as a monument to the glory of the armies of the Re-
> public and the Empire" [Agulhon 4600]. This, at least, is how
> it is represented within the national memory. Maurice Barrès
> observes: "The Arc de Triomphe is the image of our righteous
> pride [. . .]" [Barrès 462]. (Khalifa 162)

In short, then, a reading of Modiano's first novel calls for an approach like that of Riffaterre, who insists that interpreting literature requires that considerations of textuality prevail over extra-textual considerations, such as psychology, in order to explain textual ungrammaticalities.

Therefore, regarding from a literary and not a psychological point of view the ungrammatical physical displacements related by the fourth section of the hallucinatory and delirious text, we note that in retrospect the reader can appreciate how the impetus behind those peculiar displacements had in fact been molding the text from the start, albeit less obviously. Early in his narrative, Raphaël describes how, even as a child and a youth, he drifted with casual ease between Deauville, Paris, Lausanne, and Geneva (*La place de l'étoile* 18-20), so casually that effecting the moves seems to have required no time or inconvenience at all. That sense of what could be called a radical lack of geographical fixity or radical rootlessness gets stronger when one recollects as well Raphaël's mentioning his dispersed, or perhaps more accurately, his ever dispersing family, for instance his grandfather from Odessa (36), his uncle from Venezuela (13, 46), his father from New York (55-56), and his mother often on tour in the French provinces (53).

Demonstrating their semiotic generativity, Raphaël's ungrammatical geographical displacements occur with a temporal counterpart in Raphaël's prenatal memories. For instance, his account opens with the implication that he had been a young man in the thirties and forties (*La place de l'étoile* 13-15): he recounts how the journalist Léon Rabatête (a mocking version of the name of the collaborator Lucien Rebatet (1903-

73) that plays on the words "rabattre" and "tête") and Céline had both vilified him in the full Jew-hating cry typical of their writings of that period, for instance Céline's pathologically hateful dithyramb *Bagatelles pour un massacre* of 1937. But ten pages later, ungrammaticality occurs when Raphaël blithely mentions the birth date of his friend and age-peer Des Essarts, "le 30 juillet 194..." (23). Lest uncertain readers attribute the difficulty to their own confusion about either the names or the dates, the text makes the difficulty explicit by having other characters point out the temporal problem: " 'Mais vous n'étiez pas né, Raphaël!' " (84); " 'Nous vivons actuellement dans un monde pacifié. Himmler est mort, comment se fait-il que vous vous rappeliez tout cela, vous n'étiez pas né, allons, soyez raisonnable [. . .].' " (214). This is narratologically logical, if unusual: Raphaël *is* nothing more than a textual entity for the reader, and so according to the dynamics of textuality, he must live outside of time, with a past no more prior than present. Raphaël's stepping outside of time, then, by having prenatal memories, along with his repeated affirmations of the intertextual—that is, literarily prenatal—nature of his experience, boldly and self-consciously emphasizes his literally essential literariness, a postmodern emphasis that will characterize Modiano's entire oeuvre. (For comments on the essential timeless of the intertextual, see Still and Worton 12.)

Finally, the geographical rootlessness also resonates with a no less arresting kind of rootlessness, one of an occupational, ultimately social nature. Raphaël airily shifts professions by becoming for example a journalist (*La place de l'étoile* 37), a member of the collaborationist militia (38), a student in the *khâgne* (the intensive course of study designed to prepare outstanding students of letters for the national admissions test to the most prestigious schools, 73), a white slaver (95 and following pages), a composer (162), and of course a writer. All these social metamorphoses doubtless erupt out of Raphaël's unstable sense of social identity, an instability that results in alternating impulses to reject French society and to be assimilated into it, see for example 50, 73. Although his career as a writer proves to be the most enduring and characteristic, rootlessness infuses it as well: he writes biographies, psychoanalytic studies, Latin and Greek translations, and even plays (15, 16, 20, 27, 49). In short, the diegetic ungrammaticalities of a geographical, temporal, and social nature all point back to the common sememe of rootlessness. ("Sememe" is understood to be *"Faisceau des sèmes correspondant à un lexème*, and *"sème"* is understood to be *"Unité minimale différentielle de signification"* [*Le petit robert*].) Albeit in less linguistic turns of phrase, the centrality of rootlessness for Modiano has been affirmed also by Pierre Daprini and Jules Bedner: "the basic topos underlying Modiano's novels [is] the expression of transcendental and existential homelessness" (Daprini, "The Existential Voyage" 198); Bedner sees the theme of the stranger running through the oeuvre (Bedner, "Patrick Modiano").

Faced, then, with these ungrammaticalities, and endeavoring to solve them first by viewing the text as a symbolic system that imposes the solution of its own difficulties, the Riffaterrean reader looks for the hidden explanatory intertext. To anticipate my discussion below of the impact of detective fiction on *La place de l'étoile*, it is hidden out in plain sight, much like Poe's famous purloined letter. Insofar as Raphaël is non-existent for readers apart from his narrative, in the simple terms of the reading process Raphaël *is* his narrative. The hyperliterary Raphaël/narrative tells us that he/it *is* "Schlemilovitch," the son/intertext of the canonic literary "Schlemihl." That Schlemihl, himself an offspring of the hapless fool of Jewish tradition, was introduced into the canon by Adelbert von Chamisso in his 1813 novella, *Peter Schlemihls wundersame Geschichte* (*The Wonderful History of Peter Schlemihl*) (Pinsker 7). Although other readers have noted the reference to Chamisso's character in Modiano's ("ce Charlot [Raphaël] se double de Peter Schlemihl, le héros de Chamisso..." (Kauffmann 141; see also Chasseguet-Smirgel 231, note 2), the Riffaterrean context would strongly emphasize the intertextual paternity.

The clue offered by Raphaël's surname is all the more obvious in this hyperliterary text because it too is hyperliterary, that is, it is emphatically overdetermined. The words "Raphaël Schlemihl" alone would have communicated that Raphaël is the son of Schlemihl. The addition of the Slavic patronymic in French therefore linguistically overdetermines the sememe "son of Schlemihl" by adding redundancy. That thrust toward overdetermination gains strength in that the attention-attracting "Schlemilovitch" not only is a neologism, but it is also very funny, for neologisms and humor overdetermine by emphasizing the arbitrariness of signifiers over their referentiality, of their relationship to the signified (see for example Riffaterre, *Production* 45-55).

Appropriately, the text by Chamisso itself arises from a matrix offered by the sememe of rootlessness. That derivation is in keeping with the frequent critical finding that the story owes much to the personal trauma experienced by the novella's aristocratic author. As Louis Charles Adélaïde Chamisso de Boncourt (1781-1838), he was forced to flee from Revolutionary France to Germany because of the risks posed by his noble lineage. It was only in Germany that he became Adelbert von Chamisso, who then struggled through much of his life as a political, social, cultural, and linguistic outcast (see Swales, Koepke). (By the way, that latter description would not be a bad description of Raphaël.) Critics have readily found textual support for their finding of Chamisso's auto-biographical inspiration, since it is patent that Chamisso was deliberately portraying himself in Peter. Through a paratextual "correspondence" between Chamisso and Peter that introduces the latter's story ("An meinen alten Freund Peter Schlemihl," Chamisso, *Peter Schlemihls wundersame Geschichte* 5), within the text Chamisso foists a narratological and ontological equivalence between himself and his creation, an equivalence that he firmly underscored: "Chamisso introduces Peter as his unmistakable double in looks and features, idiosyncrasy of costume, habits and disposition, including the gaucherie and lack of alertness that made him the butt of his friends' good-natured teasing" (Weigand 213; much the same doubling of traits, habits, and looks marks Modiano and his oeuvre's narrators; and as will be argued below, doubled identity lies at the center of a coherent reading of *La place de l'étoile*[8]). Finally, there are textual reasons for viewing Peter in terms of Chamisso's own traumatic displacements. Among the narrative's several winks and nods at the relationship, one can especially enjoy the mischievous twisting of a cliché that telescopes the two figures into one. Addressing his creator Chamisso, Peter exclaims, not that *he Peter* would not have believed something if *he Peter* had not seen it with *his* own eyes, but rather: "Wenn ich dir nicht beteuerte, es selbst mit eigenen Augen angesehen zu haben, würdest du es gewiß nicht glauben" ["if I did not assure you *I myself* had seen it with my own eyes, *you* would not believe it"] (Chamisso, *Peter Schlemihls wundersame Geschichte* 17; my emphasis and translation; see Weigand 212-14).

"The Wonderful History of Peter Schlemihl," the work for which Chamisso is most remembered, evolves from Peter's status as an outsider. It starts out as the story of a penurious youth from abroad among more privileged strangers, only to become the fantastic story of a shadowless man among the shadowed, and then the story of a rich man among the far less rich, having become rich because of a deal for a bottomless purse, unaware however of the identity of the dealer, the Devil, who exchanged the purse for Peter's shadow. Toward the end of the story (chap. 10), the sememe of non-belonging or rootlessness asserts itself most memorably when Peter acquires the seven-league boots that take him gliding prodigiously over and beyond all human communities, allowing him to repeat his original desocializing human-shadow-stripping bargain metaphorically while realizing more fully its consequences. Separating himself from society by distance instead of just by foreignness, penury, and shadowlessness, he transforms social and emotional isolation into the physical isolation toward which the former had been tending all along. He uses the magic boots to flee to uninhabited lands where, an intellectual monk, he produces scholarly works of geography and botany. He exchanges his life among people for a reclusive scholarly life.

In an only seemingly incidental detail, Peter is at one point classified as a Jew, principally because he had happened to let his beard grow (chapter 11). Notwithstanding the brief and "supplementary" quality of his Jewishness, the German narrative's final metaphor of rootless non-belonging, there is upon reflection nothing surprising about it. In fact, it has an air of semiotic necessity, since Chamisso obviously borrowed his character's surname from the Jewish tradition of the schlemihl, a figure itself already an outsider even within Jewish tradition, and a figure to which Chamisso had been exposed by his Jewish friends (Pinsker 7). So Peter becomes what his family name had been designating him to be all along: a doubled outsider, a Jew to the Gentiles, and a schlemihl to the Jews.

Furthermore, in the Bible-centered culture from which European literature largely springs, the threat of exile and wandering was widely seen to hang permanently over the Jews as punishment for not being faithful to their covenant with God (*Deuteronomy* 28: 36-45, 64-65). At decisive, determining moments in the Bible, the threat was of course realized: those Hebrews only just released from the Egyptian captivity were refused entrance into the promised land, enduring forty years of wandering and finally death in the desert, for having grumbled about their hardships (*Numbers* 14:26-35); and their distant descendants had to suffer humiliation and captivity in Babylon for in time turning to the worship of false gods (*Jeremiah* 1:11-17). In addition, many Europeans viewed the Diaspora as the result of the Jews' rejection of Christ as messiah. Finally, through the seven-league boots, Peter gets readily linked to the legend of the Wandering Jew, Ahasvérus, doomed to wander until the return of Christ for having refused to help the Calvary-bound Messiah.

Because, then, of Peter's surname "Schlemihl" that posits his origins in Jewish culture, when viewed semiotically this schlemihl's entire story of rootless non-belonging becomes an extended development of precisely that surname. He is another example of the hapless Jew of so much literature, doomed like many other prominent Jews of traditional literature to wander in one way or another, in one form or another. An important consequence flows from this view of Chamisso's novella as an "indexing" intertext or interpretant of *La place de l'étoile*. In their bafflement, readers of the geographically delirious *La place de l'étoile* will typically turn away from the world of the textuality to look for verisimilar extrapolations that are either external (the indeterminacy of Patrick Modiano's postmodernism) or internal (the narrator occasionally seems to be hallucinating). But a Riffaterrean explanation would have it that Raphaël's various "ungrammatical" displacements remain so powerfully jarring that any verisimilar truth is still less literarily satisfying than the intertextual truth: Raphaël's text—a text that is hyperliterary—is harking back to a fabulous intertext where a magic purse and magic boots comfortably explain all shifts in social status and location of a Jew-like wanderer. And just as the geographical action of the boots is of a piece with Peter's social wandering, so too Raphaël's geographical rootlessness is of a piece with his temporal and social lack of fixity.

But before leaving the argument that diegetic ungrammaticalities in *La place de l'étoile* point to *Peter Schlemihl* as the indexing intertext of Modiano's novel, one should reckon with a peculiarity attached to the German figure's rootlessness, namely the feeling of guilt. Even at the very beginning of the story, before Peter has struck his deal exchanging his shadow for a satanic bottomless purse, he submits to the condescension of an inn-worker and of a porter, a submission due in large measure to what even he recognizes as his anxiety and introversion (chap. 1). In brief, he shows extreme deference to others. In and of itself, such deference might not be seen to hint at the defensiveness of guilt, were it not for two details. First, Peter never explains why he left whatever place he came from, and why he was prepared to endure social and emotional hardships to stay away from that place once his subsequent troubles started. Second, all the other characters are completely unaware of any bargain on his part with the Devil, an inherently innocent bargain at that, since he was ignorant of the fact that he was dealing with the Devil, and he bargained only over his shadow and not over his soul. Nonetheless and strikingly, the other characters very quickly and vocally reproach Peter for the loss of his shadow. Indeed, on occasion Peter is reproached by means of physical abuse. The "givenness" of the inexplicable, irrational, and virtually universal reproaches—even Peter finds fault with himself for having lost his shadow (chap. 2)—suggests that it is a marker of unexplained guilt. It is symptomatic that just before he had made his bargain with the unrecognized Devil, he feels apprehensive that some one will reproach him for walking across some grass. In fact, one has to wonder if Peter's "incidental" name, "Number 12," when he is categorized as a Jew, does not spring from a notorious marker of guilt in the West, evoking as it can for many Christians the most guilty Jew, the twelfth disciple, the traitor Judas, the only disciple of Christ whose very name defines him as a Jew (Steiner xiii). Whatever the implications of "Number 12," the most striking feature of Peter's guilt is the fact that, for all its power and pervasiveness, it goes unexplained and unexplored. As we shall see in subsequent sections of this chapter, the very absence of explanation and exploration regarding guilt will carry over to *La place de l'étoile*.

In keeping with the guilt, the end of the tale finds that Peter— isolated to the point of penitent monkishness—has become himself most fully. Even though now a beneficent scholar, he achieves explicitly and with acceptance the status that he had been resisting all along, that of an individual unable and unwelcome to establish roots in society. That his final, enduring need to flee people parallels his initial need presumably to flee his home, closes the circle on his status as someone permanently convinced and convicted of reproach and rejection, that is, as someone convinced and convicted of permanent but unexplained guilt. I maintain, then, that *La place de l'étoile,* in carrying over its hidden-in-plain-sight intertextual interpretant, carries over also the guilt woven throughout the hidden intertext, such that, like Peter's, Raphaël's geographic rootless-ness exists too under a cloud of permanent but unexplained guilt. So one finds through intertextuality a contributory explanation of still another odd detail of *La place de l'étoile,* namely why Raphaël feels compelled to act as a *juif collabo,* that is, to act guiltily: son of Peter the schlemihl, he has no choice but to carry on the mysterious guilt of his textual father.

But there exists as well in both texts the coincidence of guilt with artistic activity itself. In this regard, we have to note one of the opinions of Heinrich Heine, who on the one hand was to become a notable figure of the German literary world in which Chamisso had participated, and who on the other hand appears in German on the pages of *La place de l'étoile* (159). Like Chamisso, Heine knew material and social anguish, in his case not because he was a political refugee, but because he was Jewish, and, like both Chamisso and the latter's creation Peter, Heine was obliged to leave his home for a new land, even though for Heine the direction was opposite to Chamisso's, from Germany to France. To Heine, the hapless schlemihl was "a metaphor of the artistic quest itself" (Pinsker 7), a view apparent in "Jehuda ben Halevy," the second of Heine's three "Hebräische Melodien" ("Hebrew Melodies"). Toward the end, the German poet recuperates into "schlemihldom" even the Greek god of poetic inspiration himself, along with the latter's poet "sons":

> Dichterschicksal! böser Unstern,
> Der die Söhne des Apollo
> Tödlich nergelt, und sogar
> Ihren Vater nicht verschont hat,
>
> Als er, hinter Daphnen laufend,
> Statt des weißen Nymphenleibes
> Nur den Lorbeerbaum erfaßte,
> Er, der göttliche Schlemihl!
>
> Ja, der hohe Delphier ist
> Ein Schlemihl, und gard der Lorbeer,
> Der so stolz die Stirne krönet,
> Ist ein Zeichen des Schlemihltums.

Was das Wort Schlemihl bedeutet,
Wissen wir. Hat doch Chamisso
Ihm das Bürgerrecht in Deutschland
Längst verschafft, dem Worte nämlich.
(Heine, Werke 221-22)

[What a fate's reserved for poets!
Star of evil, deadly gadfly
Of Apollo's sons, and one that
Did not even spare their father.

On that day when, chasing Daphne,
He reached out for her white body
And instead embraced a laurel—
What a big divine Schlemihl!

Yes, the highborn Delphic god is
A Schlemihl; indeed, the laurel
That enwreathes his brow so proudly
Is a sign of Schlemihldom.

What the word Schlemihl denotes is
Known to us. Long since, Chamisso
Saw to it that it got German
Civic rights—I mean the word did.
(Heine, *Jewish Stories* 125-26)]

The preceding verses show that Chamisso and his novella sub-stantially inspired Heine's vision of a bond between schlemihldom and the artistic quest, at least in its poetic formulation. Furthermore, torn as Chamisso was by mixed feelings and divided loyalties as he shuttled back and forth between the warring French and Germans in the early nineteenth century (Koepke v-ix), he had quite possibly found in his own artistic quest a source of guilt: in turning to the German language that offered him the only realistic chance of artistic life, he did it a disservice, in that he never mastered it and needed the help of his German friends to use it well (Koepke vi-vii); by the same token, practicality obliged him to abandon his mother tongue, French. So the irrational guilt of the verbal creature Peter Schlemihl doubtless reflects the guilt at work in his crea-tor's own verbal, and so artistic, life. But in mentioning Heine, Raphaël's own narrative links him to that nineteenth-century Jewish writer, who also was influenced by Chamisso and who viewed the schlemihl in terms of the artistic quest. Quite consistently, then, Raphaël too knows the yearnings of the artistic quest: in the midst of the account of all his geographical and occupational displacements, he repeatedly mentions books and plays that he writes, and he even mentions a requiem that he is composing. Consequently, Modiano's schlemihl can be viewed as carrying over from Chamisso's hidden intertext the guilt of the latter's schlemihl, and from Chamisso and/or Heine schlemihldom as artistic questing itself. Guilt and the artistic quest combine, then, in schlemihldom.

This conjunction or matrix of rootlessness, guilt, and artistic questing in schlemihldom, in the open secret of Raphaël's being Schlemilovitch, anticipates the decoding of a particularly difficult lexical ungrammaticality found in *La place de l'étoile*. Generally in a Riffaterrean argument, the more singular the obscurity with which the suppressing textual unconscious charges an ungrammaticality, the more singular is the attention that the ungrammaticality draws, and the more singular the promise of revelation that its decoding holds. In the case of *La place de l'étoile*, however, we can expect the decipherment to be far more difficult (and therefore more revealing) than most, because this text's forces of suppression are multiple. In addition to the typical covert suppression brought on in *La place de l'étoile* by the textual unconscious, there exists another covert, even more elusive, force for suppression, this one brought on by a devastating trauma inflicted on the author in his childhood. In the section below on the subtext of *La place de l'étoile*, that trauma will be shown to have produced deeply rooted guilt feelings on Modiano's part, and guilt of course is a notable source of psychological suppression. Furthermore, on an overt level, trauma, guilt, and suppression grip *La place de l'étoile*, because it rages about French contributions to the Holocaust, that massive effort to suppress Europe's entire Jewish population, and it rages about official France's attempt after World War II to suppress the very memory of French contributions to the Holocaust. In explaining the following particularly difficult lexical ungrammaticality, we should then anticipate a heightened need for careful linguistic and psychological detective work. In turn, that need for detective work will be seen to be especially appropriate when it comes to dealing with the semiotic coherence of *La place de l'étoile*, because its subtext is an interrogation scene dealing with a crime.

The ungrammaticality in question first appears when Raphaël, concerned about his new, suicidal acquaintance, a concentration-camp refugee named Tania Arcisewska, acknowledges a dizzying, overpowering suicidal desire of his own, that of wanting to swallow razor blades: "je cache avec soin mes lames de rasoir. J'éprouve en effet un curieux vertige quand mon regard rencontre ces petits objets métalliques: j'ai envie de les avaler" (*La place de l'étoile* 45). At first blush, the expression "swallowing razor blades" is not only grotesque and disturbing, made all the more so by its suicidal context, it is barely if at all conceivable, even if one assumes *La place de l'étoile* to be a hallucinatory work. So its ungrammaticality prompts us to search for a suppressed meaning, a meaning that has been driven through cryptic association into the initially inconceivable, instead of being allowed to expose itself directly.

Upon reflection, however, a speaker of French might suspect that, literally, *avaler des lames de rasoir* should be only slightly more grotesque, disturbing, and inconceivable than the common-place expression *avaler des couleuvres*, "to swallow (serpents) insults." But over the centuries the latter expression has had time to slip into usage without first incurring substantial semantic resistance. It evolved from an initial medieval sense of *couleuvre* alone as an insulting description applied to the perfidious. Arguably, the description of the object of the insult, a metaphoric snake, eventually metamorphosed metonymically into the effect itself of the description, namely an insult. Whatever the precise history of the expression, we can be confident that by the eighteenth century (and perhaps as early as the seventeenth), *avaler des couleuvres/insultes* had become a comfortable part of the French lexicon (Rey 918). *Avaler des lames de rasoir* had no such period of gentle lexical transition, being grotesque, disturbing, and inconceivable from its apparent birth at Modiano's idiosyncratic hand. But a French speaker who is casting about trying to make sense of this resistant expression will be working with a verb, *avaler*, that has a long history of being especially open to distinctly nonsensical metaphors, for example *avaler une canne, son parapluie* "to be stilted, stiff," *avaler son bulletin de naissance*, "to die," *avoir avalé un chat*, "to be hoarse." But *avaler* has also taken within its metaphoric reach a number of less inconceivable, less nonsensical expressions, for instance *avaler sa langue*, "to keep silent, to refuse to speak," and *avaler la pilule*, "swallow the [bitter] pill." Apropos of the latter expression so similar to its English equivalent, the verb can similarly be used with *affront* to mean "swallow an affront," and finally *avaler* often means simply "to put up with it," a meaning that dominates in the classical French of the seventeenth century (Rey 1064-65). In light of that lexical terminus, a French speaker could rightly wonder whether the cutting *lames de rasoir* in *avaler des lames de rasoir* are not an unexplained subterfuge for simply "insults" like those figured by the biting snakes of *avaler des couleuvres*.

That interpretation recommends itself for a text like *La place de l'étoile*, characterized as it is by its fixation on Jewishness. Consider that too often when Jews appear in French texts, the representations can be insulting or "cutting." Among only the most prominent literary examples one finds Hugo's Manassé in *Cromwell*, Balzac's Gobseck, Maupassant's Walter in *Bel ami*, Zola's Busch in *L'argent*, Bourget's Hafner in *Cosmopolis*, and the Jewish cinematic milieu in *France la doulce* by Paul Morand (of L'Académie Française, to which he was elected in 1968, the year in which *La place de l'étoile* was published).[9] Lest it be assumed that such representations were socially marginal, a bit of bibliographic history deserves mention: "[Edouard] Drumont, in *La France juive* (1886), wrote a thousand pages intent on promoting left-wing anti-capitalist anti-Semitism as *the* political philosophy of modern times. It was one of the two best-selling works in France in the latter half of the nineteenth century" (Mehlman 3, emphasis in the original). Such representations of Jews diminish, that is, "slash" the human worth of Jews, even to the point of threatening the emasculation of a Jew like Modiano's narrator. The very image of emasculation happens to set both the emotional tone and the metaphoric field for the novel, since Raphaël's opening paragraph explodes with one of Bardamu's/Céline's anti-Jewish diatribes, which expressly pleads: "qu'on l'étripe... le châtre. [. . .]. que les Aryennes ses esclaves lui arrachent le gland!" (*La place de l'étoile* 14). So the text's introductory stream of stereotypically demeaning expressions about Jews opens with a powerful example that conflates cutting images with hatred of Jews. The emasculating metaphor reaches far and deep in *La place de l'étoile*, in that the suppression of Jewish reproductivity serves as the focus of the book, because the annihilating Holocaust stands out as its fundamental preoccupation. Furthermore, a metonymic glide is at work here, linking Holocaust and razors, in that the razors that suicidally haunt Raphaël have in Jewish tradition been viewed as a threat to Jewishness (see *Vayikra/Leviticus* 19:27), since Jewishness is frequently symbolized for Jews and Gentiles alike in Jewish men's unshorn beards (like Peter Schlemihl's) and sideburns.

But if we listen to the homonymy of the word *avaler,* it whispers that *qui avale (donne son) aval*, "who swallows gives approval," perhaps a whispered memory of the time in French when *avaler* meant both "to swallow," and "to give approval" (see *avaliser* in Rey 1066). This painful issue of French that demeans Jews becomes even more painful when Jewish French writers, often cast by others as rootless outsiders, themselves willy-nilly becomes purveyors of the very insulting anti-Jewish texts that hurt and alienate them: Jewish writers' and narrators' voices in French both cut and get cut because the very language they use—the only practical literary vehicle available to those putative "rootless outsiders," to those, in Modiano's terms for himself, *Français de hasard* (Ezine 22) who are acculturated as both Jewish and French—gives continued life and so indirect approval to the anti-Jewish stereotypes too often conveyed by the sociolect incarnated in the French language itself. (For a general psychoanalytic explanation of how "to swallow" signifies "to identify with," see Chasseguet-Smirgel 223; for the latter's interpretation of *avaler* specifically within *La place de l'étoile*, see her pages 250-51.) As Richard Terdiman, drawing upon Foucault, articulates the theoretical argument: "a culture's tropes and commonplaces, its figures and its characteristic locutions, [are] essential reservoirs and enforcers of its habitus" (Terdiman 51). Or as the resulting anxiety will be more simply put by a later Modianesque avatar of Raphaël: "tâcher de parler et d'écrire une langue le mieux possible afin d'être bien sûr de ma nationalité" (*Chien de printemps* 117).

To observe the wounding power of the sociolect on even innocent looking French, one need only consider the apparently harmless words "*place de l'étoile.*" As explained above those words communicate not only the iconic Parisian intersection, but also "*la place de l'étoile,*" the place where Jews in Vichy France were obliged to wear the star of David. French history wills it of course that even the very word "*Juif*" too often continues to convey stereotypic potential such as "*avare*" (or of course vice versa), as enshrined in no less a text than Molière's *L'avare*. Cléante, reacting to the usurious lending terms proposed by Harpagon through La Flèche, sputters: "Comment diable! Quel juif, quel arabe est-ce là? C'est plus qu'au denier quatre" (*L'avare*, II, 1). Indeed, early in the twentieth century, in order to avoid that and other connotations, many assimilated French Jews felt pushed to reserve the disparaging "*Juifs*" for recent Jewish immigrants, and the less charged "*Israélites*" for themselves (Lazarus 3, see also Berl 13). In order to advance the argument for what is starting to appear as a possible semantic bridge ("texts insulting Jews") between *avaler des lames de rasoir* and *avaler des couleuvres*, we do well to observe that we are dealing not just with a literary French context such as that created by any French novel, but rather with the overtly hyperliterary context of Raphaël's literature-obsessed narrative. It is literature-obsessed because, of course, the narrator is literature-obsessed, making on page after page explicit and often-repeated allusions to, and occasionally pastiches of, no fewer than thirty different writers, the vast majority of whom are novelists (as we saw above in Ora Avni's list). In French, to express how avid a reader of novels Raphaël must be, one would commonly say: Raphaël avale roman après roman, "he swallows novel after novel." So within the hyperliterary context of *La place de l'étoile*, the reader attempting to make sense of the resistant expression *avaler des lames de rasoir* moves on from *avaler des couleuvres* to the no less available and far less repulsive *avaler roman après roman*. The odd semantic conflation of *lames de rasoirs* and *romans* gets ever so subtle reinforcement in the fourth and final section, where a more explicit and so more revealing use of the first expression occurs four times. The simple *lame de rasoir* becomes *lame de rasoir Gillette extra-bleue* (137, 149, 153, 186). In a context unfailingly fixated by literary texts, the word *extra-bleue* teases with the recollection of the expression *conte bleu*, that is, a "wild" story, wild like Raphaël's own extravagant *roman*.

One rightly suspects,[10] then, that for Modiano/Raphaël, a Jewish/French (that is, "rootless") reader/writer obliged to read/write in French, a language and literature too often expressing and in fact incarnating anti-Jewish sentiments, swallowing/producing offensive novels equates with swallowing/producing insults that bite like snakes and slash the throat's voice like razors. That suspicion finds corroborating if less imagistic resonance in an observation by Charlotte Wardi: "Modiano vit le drame de l'écrivain qui s'exprime dans une langue qui véhicule des valeurs, des symboles et des mythes étrangers à son être" (Wardi, "Mémoire et identité" 95; see also her "Mémoires romanesques" 122). Nonetheless, so subtle and obscure is the mutual echoing of the expressions *avaler des lames de rasoir*, *avaler des couleuvres*, and *avaler des romans*, that they hint at a unified literary meaning that is strongly resisted indeed.

The problem of Jewish writers' contributing to their own insulting, moreover, is hardly unique to Raphaël/Modiano in French. Franz Kafka, a haunting presence on page after page of *La place de l'étoile*, had articulated early in the century a similar problem regarding German, a problem with what he called "a self-tormenting usurpation of an alien property":

> In a letter to Max Brod about German-Jewish writers he [Kafka] said that the Jewish question or "the despair over it was their inspiration—an inspiration as respectable as any other but fraught, upon closer examination, with distressing peculiarities. For one thing, what their despair discharged itself in could not be German literature which on the surface it appeared to be," because the problem was not really a German one. Thus they lived "among three impossibilities...: the impossibility of not writing" as they could get rid of their inspiration only by writing; "the impossibility of writing in German"—Kafka considered their use of the German language as the "overt or covert, or possibly self-tormenting usurpation of an alien property, which has not been acquired but stolen, (relatively) quickly picked up, and which remains someone else's possession even if not a single linguistic mistake can be pointed out" and finally, "the impossibility of writing differently," since no other language was available. (Kafka, *Briefe* 336-38, in Arendt 31)

When Jewish writers of a non-Jewish nationality are confronted with the extent to which anti-Jewish representations, destructive of their own worth and voice, inhere in the "alien" language, images such as Raphaël's *avaler des lames de rasoir* become possible.

But it must be emphasized that for Jewish writers who happen to be French or vice versa, the image becomes all the more possible: Revolutionary France, the first country to offer Jews complete acceptance as equal citizens, had conditioned its offer on Jewish assimilation into the state, a status that acquired a distinctive linguistic dimension. "Assimilation" first came to mean of course abandoning Jewish education for the state's centralized schools and turning away from a defining Jewish enculturation for the state's centralized enculturation (see Lazarus 1-3). And the foundation of state enculturation was nothing less than the French language itself. But after the Dreyfus affair, the Holocaust's "opening act" in modern France, and after France's collaboration in the Holocaust itself, Jewish/French writers like Raphaël/Modiano were affirmed as rootless again. Again they had good reason to be sensitive to the wounds being inflicted by this language-culture that as writers they had in large measure become.

Riffaterre insists that a reading resulting in semiosis occurs in retrospection, after an initial heuristic reading of initial (de)familiarization has been performed (Riffaterre, *Semiotics* 4 and following pages). Indeed, retrospection makes taking the proposed semantic conflation *avaler lames de rasoir/couleuvres/romans* seem not just possible but advisable for those attempting to view French as Raphaël's narrative views it. The two opening pages of the text not only help establish the subject of emotional/verbal emasculation as we have already seen, they also explicitly make use of the potential enjoyed by literate French going back at least as far as Rabelais to situate vigorous language within the oral-digestive frame of reference created by verbs like *avaler*. That frame of reference became all the more assertive in French when novels—Raphaël's passion—made the historic turn to pot-boilers, in French "*de la littérature alimentaire.*" On its very first page, Modiano's text activates this potential by viewing le docteur Bardamu's disapproval of Raphaël as so many verbal belches: "le docteur Bardamu éructait sur mon compte [. . .]" (13). Lest we restrict to Célinesque pastiches this view of French in Raphaël's narrative, rereading observes that Raphaël himself describes the language used in his play as *borborygmes*, "rumblings from the gut" (51). Moreover, on the last pages Freud's imagined pleas being described by Raphaël as so much barking does nothing to weaken the link between oral-digestive events and language. Finally, we should note that since so much of writing is the searching for, the creating of, voice, it is hardly surprising that the problem of a voice "cut" by cultures at odds with each other is not restricted to European Jews such as Modiano and Kafka who use languages with a history of hostility to Jews. It appears for instance in Maxine Hong Kingston's *The Woman Warrior*, in which the narrator's voice is imperiled by her having to speak across a Chinese and American divide. This tale of silences triumphant and silences vanquished incorporates not only the image of a throat torn by words (200-201), but also of a snipped frenum (for example 163-64).

An analysis of the lexical ungrammaticality *avaler des lames de rasoir* alerts us, then, to the fact that Jewish writers in French might easily persuade themselves that they cannot be creative without guiltily contributing to the life of all the elements that comprise that language and its sociolect, including anti-Jewish insults. Indeed, in this light, Raphaël/ Modiano the writer in French in the sixties has every reason to view himself as a "*juif collabo*" of the forties, because by assuming the act of writing in French, he assumes the language of Céline, Morand, and others that facilitated and encouraged French collaboration in the Holocaust. This, then, helps explain the narrative's need for guilt-driven suppression of a painful truth. Incapable of consciously addressing the implicit anxieties for him—as an "alien," "rootless" outsider, how can a Jewish/French novelist read/write without the very French that threatens and harms Jewishness?—Modiano/Raphaël finds himself in psychic displacement, fixating instead on suicidally swallowing razor blades. The ungrammatical *avaler des lames de rasoir* lets Raphaël's/Modiano's account veer away from recognizing and addressing its necessary and painful dilemma: a text by a French Jew must guiltily slash much of its own Jewishness, its very self, because it accepts the necessity of taking an alienated voice that inevitably echoes with denials of the author's existence and worth as a Jew.

It is an issue whose racist foundation has been often—and painfully for Jews—dismissed: "LE JUIF N'EXISTE PAS, comme dit très pertinemment Schweitzer de la Sarthe [aka, Sartre]" (*La place de l'étoile* 213). But there is a problem: Raphaël's/Modiano's narrative highlights that racist foundation with the intensity of a concentration camp spot-light: it articulates in frantic forthrightness one anti-Jewish stereotype after another (for a comprehensive list, see Khalifa 163-64), and it repre-sents with telling reminders one famous French enemy of Jews or Collaborator after another (Saint Louis, Céline, Drieu La Rochelle, Bra-sillach, and others). Moreover, critics have been quick and numerous in observing that one of the major issues raised by *La place de l'étoile* is: "comment un Juif peut-il être français ? et comment peut-il être écri-vain ?" (Nettelbeck and Hueston, *Patrick Modiano* 14; see also Chasse-guet-Schmirgel, Wardi "Mémoire et écriture," and Khalifa 162). In fact, Raphaël's very name originates in the *Book of Tobit,* the precise subject of which is the Jew living as an outsider (O'Keefe, "Patrick Modiano" 68-69). However, if Raphaël/Modiano is forthright about anti-Jewish stereotypes and if the novel poses in an obvious way the problem of be-ing a French/Jewish writer, why is suppression at work regarding that problem? The answer to that question, we may be sure, will have some-thing to do with the unexplained and unexplored guilt carried over from that other schlemihl, Raphaël's forebear Peter Schlemihl. To reach an answer, we need first to do more decoding, more detective work. In the meantime, we can conclude this section on ungrammaticalities by ob-serving that both diegetic and lexical ungrammaticalities in *La place de l'étoile,* along with its hidden intertext *Peter Schlemihl,* converge on the subjects of rootlessness, art, and guilt.

III. Riffaterrean Subtext in *La place de l'étoile:* The Interrogation Scene

As we have seen at the beginning of this chapter, Riffaterre uses the term "subtext" to designate "a story or episode embedded in the text and mirroring the whole. The subtext enables the reader to grasp points and to be aware of the structure of that whole, because the subtext is brief and thus makes its point obvious, either by itself or through cognate subtexts" (Riffaterre, "On Narrative Subtexts" 450). The following pas-sage from *La place de l'étoile* will be considered a Riffaterrean subtext, that is, a passage that prepares us to perceive at a later point elements at work organizing the narrative kaleidoscope:

J'achevai bientôt ma pièce. Tragi-comédie. Tissu d'invectives contre les goyes. J'étais persuadé qu'elle indisposerait le public parisien; on ne me pardonnerait pas d'avoir mis en scène mes névroses et mon racisme d'une manière aussi provocante. Je comptais beaucoup sur le morceau de bravoure final: dans une chambre aux murs blancs, le père et le fils s'affrontent: le fils porte un uniforme rapiécé de S.S. et un vieil imperméable de la Gestapo, le père une calotte, des guiches et une barbe de rabbin. Ils parodient un interrogatoire, le fils jouant le rôle du bourreau, le père le rôle de la victime. La mère fait irruption et se dirige vers eux les bras tendus, les yeux hallucinés. Elle hurle la ballade de la putain juive Marie Sanders. Le fils serre son père à la gorge en entonnant le *Horst-Wessel Lied*, mais il ne parvient pas à couvrir la voix de sa mère. Le père, à moitié étouffé, gémit le *Kol Nidre*, la prière du Grand Pardon. La porte du fond s'ouvre brusquement: quatre infirmiers encerclent les protagonistes et les maîtrisent à grand-peine. Le rideau tombe. (*La place de l'étoile* 51)

As one readily sees, the passage—as grating as the complete text itself— comprises elements of a preternaturally clear Oedipal triangle: in one corner, the rabbi-like Father who incarnates the Law in his recitation of an ages-old Jewish prayer that evokes the submission of countless generations; in the second, the Son who wears Nazi (that is, eminently Lawless) clothes that screech opposition to the values of the Father and who endeavors to replace the Law by eliminating the Father; and in the third corner of the triangle, the Mother who, in singing Bertolt Brecht's "Ballade von der 'Judenhure' Marie Sanders," announces herself to be a whore, as Oedipal rage against parental sexuality would have her.[11] The raw clarity of the triangle is matched by the archetypal appropriateness of the context, that of *un interrogatoire*, an interrogation. Oedipus of course stands as the question-answer master of Greek mythology, for having successfully answered the Sphinx's deadly question on human identity, and for having relentlessly and ruthlessly, in spite of his mother-wife's opposition, led the interrogation on the criminal identity of the defiler of Thebes. As we will see, in Modiano's Oedipal instance as in others, the Son turns out to be the criminal that he himself is seeking.

The perpetrator's identity, moreover, also fuses with that of the victim in a way that, in keeping with much contemporary art, undoes any essentially singular identity of the unified subject, an essential consideration for much of what follows.

Several other features of the subtext draw attention and too will figure below in the analysis of the work of the subtext. There is the fact that, like the entire novel itself, the *morceau de bravoure* is determinedly intertextual, in fact reaching not just beyond itself but well beyond the confines of French literature, incorporating as it does overt references to the Kol Nidre, the Horst-Wessel Lied, and Brecht's ballad. That the latter two are German resonates with what has just been shown above to be the primary intertext of *La place de l'étoile,* Chamisso's German novella. There is as well the degree to which the Oedipal struggle and the question of identity is fused with Jewishness. The prayer recited by the Father is after all not just any Jewish prayer but the sacred Kol Nidre that prepares Yom Kippur, the Day of Atonement, a prayer far more tied to the ritualistic memory and assertion of Jewish identity than most; the Son's clothes are not just any clothes but a hybrid SS-Gestapo uniform, and so one doubled in its intense hostility to Jews, one doubled in its incarnation of the Nazi aspiration to the absolute annihilation of Jewish identity, that is, annihilation not just of being, but even memory. In addition, if the Mother and Father figures are marked by Jewishness, the reader has to wonder what crisis of identity has led the son to become a doubled anti-Jewish thug of the worst possible stripe. What is no less attention-grabbing, the scene plays out its luridly neurotic elements in a more than appropriate setting, an asylum.

It should be noted as well that rootlessness, art, and guilt—the three semantic features found above suppressed in the diegetic and lexical ungrammaticalities—penetrate the subtext. Guilt most starkly infuses it, as one would expect in any interrogation scene, and the scene's theatricality represents of course art. Less immediately obvious but nonetheless present is rootlessness. It insinuates itself chronologically in the unstable lurching among the mythical time of the Oedipal struggle, the millennia-spanning Kol Nidre, the more modern Nazi-era mixed uniform worn by the son, and the contemporary voice of the narrator describing the scene. It insinuates itself geographically in the dispersing implications of the German *"Nazi,"* the Hebrew borrowing from Aramaic *"Kol Nidre,"* and the Flemish *"Sanders."*

But all of the subtext's principal elements—the Oedipal triangle, the interrogation, the echo of hostility to Jews and of the Holocaust, the theatricality, the questions of identity, of psychological pathologies, and of porous place- and time-frames—are indeed constitutive, and indeed the most significant constitutive elements of *La place de l'étoile,* as the text later prompts us to see in recollection.

One of the places where this occurs is in a sentence toward the end of the third of the book's four sections. In the sentence, Raphaël momentarily describes himself, and he does so in an arresting use of a past-tense third-person that, like his frequent prenatal memories, defies chronological distinctions and verisimilitude. His description sums up for bewildered, needy readers his transformations to date: "après avoir été un juif collabo, un juif normalien, un juif aux champs, il risquait de devenir [. . .] un juif snob" (128). Those are indeed the transforming roles played by the troubled Raphaël in the course of his imagined wanderings in what most often seems to be Nazi-Occupied France. During each trans-formation, Raphaël copes with prenatal, time-warping memories of anti-Jewish history, as he repeatedly and variously raises questions about his identity, and as he gravitates toward a variety of shifting father-figures, for example Maurice Sachs, Schlemilovitch père, Adrien Debigorre, "mon père le vicomte Lévy-Vendôme"[12] [*La place de l'étoile* 121], le colonel Aravis, l'abbé (that is, "mon père") Perache, and in the fourth section le commandant Bloch among others. He gravitates no less toward uneasy relationships with women who, in keeping with the subtext, range from maternal to whorish, such as Maman, Miss Evelyn, Loïtia, Véro-nique de Fougeire-Jusquiames, and in the fourth section Hilda Murz-zuschlag, Yasmine, and Rebecca. Some of these figures—most notably Maman—combine both qualities: "Maman me délaisse pour des joueurs de polo" (*La place de l'étoile* 18). Readers are cued to appreciate the work of these constitutive elements because immediately after Raphaël's summary of his transformations and just before fully taking up his sec-ond role of *juif normalien* in his on-going search for a secure sense of identity, his mother abandons him to go on still another theatrical tour to the presumed delight of other men, and he fantasizes about going on vaudevillesque tour himself with Schlemilovitch père in terms strictly reminiscent of the above *morceau de bravoure:* "Schlemilovitch père et Schlemilovitch fils ne se ressemblent pas: le premier traîne un physique de poussah abyssin, au second le costume de S.S. sied à ravir. Il le porte souvent, tandis que Schlemilovitch père se déguise en rabbin. Les deux clowns parodient alors un interrogatoire" (*La place de l'étoile* 75). The family circumstance, the costumes, and the interrogation clearly hark back to the *morceau* that had appeared about twenty-five pages earlier. As a result, this second passage serves as did the first occasion when, as per Riffaterre's concept as quoted above: "The subtext manifests itself, and its limits—in particular the connection between closure and incipit— are identified when the reader becomes retroactively aware that one textual component is echoing another component, formerly read and now remembered" (Riffaterre, "The Making of a Text" 62).

But the subtext of *La place de l'étoile* undergoes its most dramatic transformations in the fourth section. Shortly after the third section's helpful list of Raphaël's transformations to date, the fourth section opens with a truly arresting metamorphosis in the form of a remembered nightmare. In the nightmare the father-figure and the son-figure reverse positions within the subtext triad. The father-figure moves into the violent, dominant Nazi role by becoming none other than Adolph Hitler himself (the nature of this substitution will be discussed in the next chapter), while Raphaël the displaced son-figure becomes the passive, victimized Jew trying to get back to his waiting mother (*La place de l'étoile* 145). The power of this father-son switch is such that, shortly after Raphaël breaks free of the memory of the dream, it inevitably takes him and his narrative back under its sway. His present becomes the remembered past (and another expression of the subtext), as the bulk of the rest of the chapter takes the form of an extended, vicious interrogation scene during which various father-figures assault the narrator (for example 174 and following pages) and various whorish women appear (for example 151). Consistent with subtextual dynamics, the description of the interrogation proper opens with language borrowed from the initial theatrical interrogation scene ("La porte s'ouvrit brusquement"; "La porte du fond s'ouvre brusquement" 175, 51). Various Israeli/Nazi authority-figures then question, torture, and execute Raphaël the callow son who now insists that: "je suis JUIF français, JUIF français" (175). The final incarnation of the mother-figure, the uniformed Rebecca, is executed shortly before the son.

Finally, so generative is the subtext in *La place de l'étoile* that it may be seen as being implicated in the book's very narrative instance as inferred above, a psychoanalytic interrogation. Even the functioning of the proposed narrative instance derives from subtextual dynamics, because the closing of Raphaël's text would create a helicoidal narrative structure, that is, one the ending of which requires the reader to go back to reread the whole text on a new narrative plane:[13] one may argue that it is only on the final pages that the reader learns that the entire narrative appears to have been an imagined psychoanalysis session, that Raphaël has all along been imagining relating his account to none other than Herr Freud himself. By this reading, only at the end, then, do readers discover that they do not hear a direct account of events, but rather merely overhear Raphaël's imagined account to an imagined Freud. This origin would clearly require another, different reading of what went before, because intentions about audience have considerable significance for an understanding of rhetorical strategies, and Freud is not just another audience. So it would be no exaggeration to observe that in order merely to begin to read *La place de l'étoile* with appropriate understanding, one can only reread, a necessity that is the product of—or at the very least in thorough harmony with—the repetitiveness driving the subtext itself.

This observation permits—in retrospect, of course—further recognition of the denseness and self-referentiality of the subtext, because the Mother, we recall, had been singing a ballad in the *morceau de bravoure*. In its choice of a ballad, then, the subtext can be seen to be pointing to its own dynamics: a ballad achieves its peculiar effects through repetition of usually three stanzas, often of three rimes, and characteristically of the same refrain in the last line of each stanza. That line, of course, has its own helicoidal thrust, in that, while its identical repetition is circular, its meaning rises to a new plane upon repetition because of its progressively evolving, enlarging context from stanza to stanza. The ballad mentioned in the *morceau de bravoure* occurs, moreover, in a theatrical play, that is, in a literary piece intended for numerous repetitions, one in which the audience does not hear, but strictly speaking only overhears, the characters' exchanges that are addressed directly to each other.

Raphaël's intentions regarding his distinguished primary audience would mark the second, more obvious way in which the subtext implicates itself in the narrative instance. Freud clearly stands as one of the most famous and greatest readers of the Oedipal tale. Like the helicoidal narrative structure, Raphaël's laying out his Oedipal tale to Freud, fellow Jew and the Oedipal Master himself, would contribute to the organizing semiosis by calling back to mind the interrogation scene, this time in terms of its psychological pathology. Furthermore, for modern observers Freud's identity is not only inseparable from Oedipal considerations, but—not coincidentally for Raphaël and for how he pitches his story—he was also a Jew who knew a thing or two about the Nazis and persecution of the Jews. Still another flash of readerly recall organizes the narrative under the rubric of the interrogation subtext, when it occurs to the reader that Freudian psychoanalysis is in effect a self-interrogation, under guidance. Thus at the end of the novel, at the moment of retrospecting narrative instantiation, we would also find ourselves harking back to the subtext's principal points of reference, namely the Oedipal struggle, anti-Semitism, Nazis, and interrogation.

Given the ability of the subtext to generate cognates, there is no surprise in noticing that some of the expository details of the inferred narrative instance at the end facilitate evocation of the *morceau de bravoure* by paralleling some of the latter's own expository details. The closing setting takes us back to an asylum-like room ("ma clinique de Potzleindorf," *La place de l'étoile* 213), and the final recollection that Raphaël recounts to Freud has the Father (Bloch), Son (Raphaël), and Mother-Whore (Rebecca) locked in ever murderous relationships, with the Son still garbed in an SS uniform. In only the second but the last reference to nurses, moreover, we learn how the Son was taken into the control of nurses (as in the *morceau de bravoure*) who took him to Freud's clinic ("mes infirmiers vous ont ramassé cette nuit," 213). Finally, in an echo of the hysterical singing by the subtext's original trio, the Mother-Whore Rebecca—after being used sexually like a whore and as she was being executed—had burst into laughter that filled the entire Bois de Boulogne, reaching "*une hauteur vertigineuse*" (206), and the Son Raphaël himself had been overcome by body-shaking laughter, as the Father-executioner Bloch howled at him while shooting him in the head (212).

The all-absorbing power of the subtext makes itself felt even on indirect, highly subtle levels, for example in the very French used to situate the subtext in *La place de l'étoile*. As is only fit in a novel whose very title is a pun, word play that underscores the absence of single stable meaning in language declares itself in our subtext too. It turns the elusive presence of the whole play into even more of a phantom, with *pièce* "a play" sliding lexically into *pièce* "a part of something larger" and indeed "a patch," a device covering up a hole, as we are reminded through the contextually iterative adjective used to describe the son's uniform, *rapiécé*.[14] Or let us consider the actors. Having already taken on the names of their roles *le fils, le père, la mère,* they compound the theme of role-playing by having their roles assume roles in the play within the play, the roles of *bourreau, victime,* and *putain juive*. This furnishes an organic reflection of Raphaël's plethora of role- and name-changes within *La place de l'étoile*.[15] In a similar if more recondite vein, we note that this feeling of absence of identity is not without parallel in the feeling of semantic absence that too characterizes *La place de l'étoile*. Here, the theatrical passage is presented as a *morceau*, that is, as already truncated, plucked from the wholeness of a complete text only alluded to, teasing the reader into speculation about a (non-existent) missing whole. But the wholeness of the complete text of *La place de l'étoile* itself is also only apparent (and the subtext's sense of absence thereby organic), because of for example *La place de l'étoile*'s ceaseless intimations and indeed occasionally explicit affirmations of a fuller sense to be found only elsewhere, in its bewildering number of intertexts mentioned above. In short, then, the theme of absence arises in identity (actors hiding behind family roles that hide behind action roles) and in meaning (the play/*pièce* is only a part/*pièce* of a whole, which part serves as a patch/*pièce* covering a semantic hole).

However, we need to keep in mind that the current chapter is proposing a semiotic reading, that is, one based on the assumption that literature ought to be viewed exclusively as a linguistic construct exclusively explainable in terms of linguistic concepts. But language deals essentially in absence not presence, or as Richard Terdiman, citing Maurice Blanchot, has put it, a word is not an expression of a thing, but of its absence (Terdiman, *Past Present* 137). Consequently we can be sure that absence will paradoxically figure prominently in a proper understanding of the subtext, in spite of/in keeping with the indirect and subtle way in which we have just seen the subject of absence arise for the subtext. Furthermore, at first blush, the subtext's indirectness and subtlety seem to be consistent with the unexplained, unexplored questions about guilt raised by the diegetic ungrammaticalities, as well as with the question left suspended at the end of the above section on lexical ungrammaticality, namely why *La place de l'étoile* suppresses direct and clear treatment of the anxiety produced by a French Jewish narrator's use of French in an otherwise stunningly outspoken text. The detective decoding has yet to be concluded.

But in the meantime, thus alerted to the interrogation subtext's insistent and highly varied echoing effects, readers can appreciate how it helps to structure *La place de l'étoile,* and they can take pleasure in the perception of its repeated patterns. This would complement on the semiotic level Nettelbeck's and Hueston's early finding mentioned in the Introduction above that the perception of musical structures explains much of Modiano's appeal.

The functioning of a subtext does not restrict itself merely to serving as a perceptual guide to content. As Riffaterre conceptualizes it, a subtext can also act as a commentary on modes of representation itself: "The subtext, its repetitions and its generating cognates, all concur to form a conspicuous and consistent commentary on the methods used [by the novel] to represent reality and to convey its significance" (Riffaterre, "On Narrative Subtexts" 463). If then in our decoding we turn back to Modiano's interrogation subtext in order to interrogate it in turn about ways in which it might comment on this novel's representation of reality, we do well to linger over its being precisely an interrogation. Taking pause, we observe that the interrogation in *La place de l'étoile* is never concluded. Its object—an answer to its question—remains forever absent. So in paradoxical retrospect the subtext can be seen to anticipate and prepare the delayed narrative instance inferred above (an aborted session of psychoanalysis that must start all over again), in that they both consist only in the start of an inquiry, the answer to which is never found. That situation reflects *La place de l'étoile* as a whole, for throughout the hallucinatory novel itself reality

and its significance remain forever elusive, as will be the case throughout the oeuvre.

In fact each and every one of Modiano's novels comes quite
close to being, in one guise or another and with varying degrees of explicitness, an extended interrogation scene. And in all of his novels, as
in this subtext, the inquiry never offers answers, as one would expect
from an oeuvre frequently characterized as postmodern. In fact, so
penetrating is *La place de l'étoile*'s interrogation scene that Modiano's
novels have been described as texts that approach and often meet sub-
stantially the content-structure criteria of hard-boiled detective novels,
but postmodern versions that systematically raise questions and expec-
tations only to frustrate them no less systematically (see Kawakami 93
and following pages). The stance vis-à-vis reality proposed by Modiano's oeuvre is then, as in the subtext, that of an interrogation that is
doomed to interference and interruption, an interrogation that, although
compelling and haunting, will go nowhere before the curtain is brought
down on it.

But this interrogation of the interrogation requires us to take account of still another problem. Not only do we not learn the answers to
the questions of this *morceau de bravoure*, we never learn even the ques-
tion(s). Several critical doors are opened by this observation about what
begins to assume the lineaments of a repetitive absence regarding the
representation of reality. Such absence will be found to permeate the subtext, an absence not unlike that at work in Poe's "Purloined Letter," the
one that famously for Lacan symbolized the nature of signifiers.

The first door opens onto a consideration of the relationship between Modiano's novel and the very nature of the detective story from
which it borrows its subtext. Tzvetan Todorov has drawn an insightful
corollary from the observation made by the writer George Burton, a
character in Michel Butor's novel *L'emploi du temps,* that every detective story consists in fact of two stories, that of the crime and that of the
inquiry into the crime: in detective fiction the first story, that of the
criminal act (which by the way almost invariably deals with a violently
"absented" character, the victim) has one defining, necessary quality,
namely initial absence. That is because its presence at the beginning
of the story would "kill" the second, longer story, a situation that Uri
Eisenzweig's book *Le récit impossible* subsequently explored at length

and splendidly. Paradoxically, the bulk of the most present text, the detective story proper stands—in one functional sense—in inverse proportion to its diegetic significance, because all it does is to get between the reader and the desired first story. But it remains insignificant in only that one, limited diegetic sense, because its indispensable narrative function is to spin out the text by delaying the revelation of the first story while highlighting precisely its absence (see Todorov 57-59). But paradoxically the detective story's presence is a function of absence, being both the product and purveyor of an absence. In that sense, it lays bare the dynamics of all narrative desire. Or as Geoffrey Hartman has pithily put it: "Instead of a whodunit we get a whodonut, a story with a hole in it" (Hartman 214).

To better understand the absence that will be found paradoxically to possess Modiano's subtext, we should continue this detour into the detective-story genre whose interrogation scene appears to have so profoundly impacted Modiano's novel. At first glance, the narrational paradox just mentioned may appear more slick and fashionable than appropriate for the traditional detective story with its satisfying logic that in the end *affirms* what putatively is, that is, a traditional sense of morality, truth, and identity. Critical reflection has revealed, however, that the traditional detective stories have always been riven by paradox, and that the paradoxes made manifest in more modern detective stories merely demonstrate the traditional detective story becoming more patently itself. Even Edgar Allan Poe's stories of ratiocination, "The Murders in the Rue Morgue," "The Mystery of Marie Rogêt," and "The Purloined Letter," texts canonically said to be at the origin of the contemporary detective story genre,[16] and the Sherlock Holmes series by Conan Doyle become less than reassuring when interrogated themselves. Without even taking into account Lacan's and Derrida's arguments that Poe's "The Purloined Letter" relates the less than traditional, less than reassuring, story of the absences worked by, respectively, the signifier and *différance,* the ratiocinations of a Dupin or a Holmes always sprang from a core of irrationality:

> What saves Poe and Conan Doyle from sterility is not that,
> like [Wilkie] Collins, they came first, but that the relentlessly
> logical process of ratiocination is thrown into question by a

deeper irrationality. Dupin seeks the dominance of pure intel-
lect, but, as with Holmes, there is always the presence of some
profound personal disturbance which impinges on the apparently objective vision of the detective; Dupin, "enamored of
the Night for her own sake," loathe to interact with others except at a distance and through a distancing mind, anticipates
Holmes and his need for seclusion, his addictions and depres-
sions. (Hutter 232)

Moreover, the irrationality can, and at its revealing best often
does, reach the status of a condition of dual personality.[17] A more pal-
atable and less ominous sign of this in detective fiction occurs when, as
is often the case, the solution to the puzzle of the crime is found by the
detective's managing to "get into the shoes" of the criminal. Usually,
this means no more than the simple efforts of detectives to imagine the
thoughts and feelings of criminals, simple efforts that do not, however,
preclude moral or philosophical sophistication, as in the case of G. K.
Chesterton's Father Brown: "[Father Brown] solves his cases, not by
approaching them objectively like a scientist or a policeman, but by
subjectively imagining himself to be the murderer, a process which is
good not only for the murderer but for Father Brown himself because,
as he says, 'it gives a man his remorse beforehand' " (Auden 156).
Sometimes, as with Doyle's Holmes, the substitution becomes as literal
as the sleuth's disguising himself as a character from no less a psychologically suggestive site than the hidden, mysterious, and menacing
underworld. Most illustrative for my purposes, and as Colin Davis has
pointed out, in Modiano's sixth novel *Rue des boutiques obscures*, the
most detective-like of his many detective-like novels, Modiano himself
creates a "narrator-detective, who is [. . .] both the investigator and the
person under investigation" (Davis, "Disenchanted Places" 667).[18]

Furthermore, in some instances appearing as early as 1891 (see
Eisenzweig 310, note 12), this dual impulse expressed itself in some
most striking examples. Whereas detective fiction narrators-characters,
for example Dr. Watson, usually act as instruments of narrative revelation and sometimes even of detection, these narrators occasionally turn
out to have been from the beginning the guilty party, that is, the agents
of concealment, as in Agatha Christie's *The Murder of Roger Ackroyd*

or James Cain's *The Postman Always Rings Twice, Double Indemnity,* and *The Butterfly* (see Bradbury). In this light, the detective in Alain Robbe-Grillet's *Les gommes,* who in the course of the novel actually turns into the murderer whom he has been seeking, appears to spring less from literary revolution and more from literary evolution. Even this striking development had arguably been adumbrated by a socio-logical understanding of the traditional detective:

> Loaded with the criminal burden of society, isolated and even
> exiled from the social system by inclination, design, and the
> curious combination of awe and hatred with which police are
> always regarded, the detective is both above and outside the
> law, an individual both despite and because of himself. He has
> always been seen as the mirror-image of the criminal both by
> sociologists and the mystery writers, symbolized occasionally
> by pairings—Batman and the Joker, Sherlock Holmes and
> Moriarty [and of course Dupin and D____ of "The Purloined
> Letter"]—and often by the action and description itself. But
> the link between detective and murderer is more than the mur-
> derer as "negative representative" of the detective as Kenneth
> Burke would have it. Rather the two are the same person
> whose opposite roles are merely accidental, like those children
> of the slums who become either cops, priests, or gangsters. It
> is this identity of the seeming opposite which makes the detec-
> tive uniquely suited to his job. (Van Meter 18)

Paradox permeates, then, even the detective-versus-murderer distinction most fundamental to the mystery novel. At the core of representation in the detective story, and arguably in all of literature, absence of fixed identity has always already presided.

Even if one prefers to consider more hackneyed representatives of the genre, unease about the clarity of traditional identity distinctions starts stirring when one questions how the genre works even at its most plodding. First of all, readers of all traditional detective stories learn quickly enough that appearances—especially and principally human ap-pearances—are not at all what they seem. It follows, here as in the better examples of the genre, that identity is never a given, never fully present, as the text goes along teaching readers that assuming otherwise invites both error and danger, even death. And if the detective/murderer confusion appears less apparent in undistinguished examples of the genre, more often than not—and hardly less threatening in its implications—the murderer in traditional detective fiction is in fact "one of us," a member of the community, a member of the literal or figurative family that would reassure us. Not only that, but multiple suspects being de rigueur, *any* member of the family is a potential murderer. Finally, the moral reaffirmation thought to be offered by the scapegoating of the guilty party crumbles too under interrogation:

> It is traditional to argue that detective fictions posit the temporary disordering of the moral universe only to reestablish that moral order more forcefully in the identification and ostracization of the criminal. This process of recentering, however, depends on the resistance of moral precepts to the tales' mode of analysis. Detection reduces evil to a simple model of stimulus/response, accepting efficient causes as sufficient explanations of crime. The very notion of "motive" is both psychologically and morally impoverished. It asks us to believe that one murders simply for money or for revenge. The motive's motive—the sources of (and cultural encouragement for) jealousy, greed, or anger—remains unexamined, as is the paradox of why people, who should be moral, are in fact not. In this respect, the relative amorality of Dupin's detections implicitly acknowledges the deficiency of their moral vocabulary. (Van Leer 77-78)

Therefore, far from being a slick, extraneous proposition, the detective story's constitutive narrative paradox of absence, whereby the narrative consists of a present text spun out of an absent text, harmonizes well—indeed, most appropriately and perhaps necessarily—with all the other paradoxes that expose themselves when even traditional exemplars of the genre are interrogated.

The case becomes more convincing still when one considers "hard-boiled" detective fiction, something readers of Modiano should in fact do, because several of his novels are cut from that mold, for instance, *La ronde de nuit, Rue des Boutiques Obscures, Une jeunesse, Quartier perdu, Dimanches d'août, Fleurs de ruine, Un cirque passe,* and *Du plus loin de l'oubli.* Moreover, many of his narrators and characters refer to detective novels or to their authors, and they often claim to read and sometimes to write them, for example in *Villa triste, Rue des boutiques obscures, De si braves garçons, Dimanches d'août, Voyage de noces, Un cirque passe, Du plus loin de l'oubli, La petite bijou,* and *Accident nocturne.*[19] In "hard-boiled" fiction, the traditional but ultimately untenably sharp distinction between victim, criminal, and detective not only implicitly but also explicitly and manifestly evanesces: victims run the gamut from underworld types to robber barons; corruption eviscerates the moral authority of "the good guys," the political and community leaders, the judges, and the policemen; and on occasion investigators become "dicks" themselves who are not averse to breaking either bones or the law. On the other hand (dare we say, paradoxically?), the "dick" often has a rigorous code of conduct almost existential in its individuality, as for instance in the unshakeable commitment of Chandler's Marlowe to the (not always savory) interests of his clients, as suggested by the following exchange from Chandler's *The Big Sleep* between Marlowe and a district attorney incredulous at the former's commitment to his clients:

> "And for that amount of money [$50, the fee Marlowe bills his client for two days' work] you're willing to get yourself in Dutch with half the law enforcement of this county?"
>
> "I don't like it," I said. "But what the hell am I to do? I'm on a case. I'm selling what I have to sell to make a living. What little guts and intelligence the Lord gave me and a willingness to get pushed around in order to protect a client. It's against my principles to tell as much as I've told tonight, without consulting the General [his client]. As for the coverup [of criminal events that concern the General], I've been in police business myself, as you know. They come a dime a dozen in any big city. Cops get very large and emphatic when an outsider tries to hide anything, but they do the same things themselves every other day, to oblige their friends or anybody

with a little pull. And I'm not through. I'm still on the case. I'd do the same thing again, if I had to." (Chandler 137)

So unswerving if arbitrary is his moral compass that the "dick" deserves inclusion among the knight-errant heroes of literary romance, as is intimated by Marlowe's reflections from the very opening scene from *The Big Sleep,* one of the foundational texts of "hard-boiled" detective fiction:

> The main hallway of the Sternwood place was two stories high. Over the entrance doors, which would have let in a troop of Indian elephants, there was a broad stained-glass panel showing a knight in dark armor rescuing a lady who was tied to a tree and didn't have any clothes on but some very long and convenient hair. The knight had pushed the vizor of his helmet back to be sociable, and he was fiddling with the knots on the ropes that tied the lady to the tree and not getting any-where. I stood there and thought that if I lived in the house, I would sooner or later have to climb up there and help him. (Chandler 589)

But literary romance—a form "of intensified reality, overheated imagina-tion, where the irrational (the dense, nightmarish, fantastic) plays an im-portant role" (Tani 25)—only reinforces the already noted intimations of an assault on rationality.

Recognition of the pervasiveness of irrationality inevitably en-tails of course the collapse of epistemological certitude. When that hap-pens, the detective genre more clearly becomes itself, finally dismissing "the" truth that logic had sought repeatedly but unsuccessfully to produce on its own as the solution to the mysteries confronting it. Most "logical" solutions to traditional detective stories have been shown to be unsatis-factory (Aydelotte 76-77), perhaps even necessarily so (Eisenzweig 50-62). Poe himself, the widely acknowledged originator of the genre, had "cheated" in "Murders in the Rue Morgue" by allowing Dupin and Dupin alone and at a late date to stumble onto the final but obvious key to the puzzle posed by murdered corpses in a room apparently sealed from within, the key that makes Dupin's ratiocination superfluous: the observation of orangutan hairs and of non-human nail-marks on the victims (Eisenzweig 67). Actually, in Dashiel Hammett's *The Dain Curse,* the Op, like Marlowe another "hard-boiled" foundational figure, blithely dismisses "the" truth of detective logic, when his more or less traditional mid-narrative up-date of "discoveries" is interrupted by the question coming from the character Fitzstephan about the identity of a victim:

> "His wife?" Fitzstephan asked.
>
> "Yeah, but what difference does that make? It might as well have been anybody else for all the sense it makes. I hope you're not trying to keep this nonsense straight in your mind. You know damned well all this didn't happen."
>
> "Then what," he asked, looking puzzled, "did happen?"
>
> "I don't know. I don't think anybody knows. I'm telling you what I saw plus the part of what Aaronia Haldorn told me which fits in with what I saw. To fit in with what I saw, most of it must have happened very nearly as I've told you. If you want to believe that it did, all right. I don't. I'd rather believe I saw things that weren't there."
>
> "Not now," he pleaded. "Later, after you've finished the story, you can attach your ifs and buts to it, distorting and twisting it, making it as cloudy and confusing and generally hopeless as you like. But first please finish it, so I'll see it at least once in its original state before you start improving it."
>
> "You actually believe what I've told you so far?" I asked.
>
> He nodded, grinning, and said that he not only believed it but liked it.
>
> "What a childish mind you've got," I said. "Let me tell you the story about the wolf that went to the little girl's grandmother's house and—"
>
> "I always liked that one, too; but finish this one now."
> (Hammett 284-85)

The Op's skepticism is of course well founded, as one eventually realizes in the third section when it is revealed that Fitzstephan was in fact the author of the mayhem and murder. Cleverly and deviously manipulating one dupe after another only to kill them after they had helped him kill each other, he nefariously advanced his incestuous plan to possess his niece. But this concluding chapter of the middle, second section *does* offer an explanation for the confused and confusing goings-on that had preceded it. To assault this sound-seeming explanation is to cast into at least momentary question the convention of the tidy, comprehensive explanations that the genre calls for. The assault, however, takes on permanent effect some hundred pages later, when the Op proposes in "hard boiled" language an epistemological stance on what he calls "beliefs and opinions" (an echo of Plato's *δόξα?*) that makes possible his and Hammett's contempt for what literary critics have come to call totalizing explanations:

> "Nobody thinks clearly, no matter what they pretend. Thinking's a dizzy business, a matter of catching as many of those foggy glimpses as you can and fitting them together the best you can. That's why people hang on so tight to their beliefs and opinions; because, compared to the haphazard way in which they're arrived at, even the goofiest opinion seems wonderfully clear, sane, and self-evident. And if you let it get away from you, then you've got to dive back into that foggy muddle to wangle yourself out another to take its place."
> (Hammett 342)

Lyotard himself would have approved the Op's dismissal of controlling narratives: "En simplifiant à l'extrême, on tient pour 'postmoderne' l'incrédulité à l'égard des métarécits" (Lyotard 7)

Not surprisingly, when the second and "real" explanation of the crimes is offered in the third and last section of *The Dain Curse,* that explanation is unsatisfying and vaguely unconvincing. It is long winded, flat, and shot through with off-putting improbabilities; for example only after the arrests have been made do stray witnesses come forth with information that would have easily done away with the "mystery." Hammett's *The Dain Curse* has the genre question itself, and it has the genre find itself wanting: the genre's logic and truth are always and already turned up absent. Knowing that, one is in a position to realize that, much as the libidinous Fitzstephan says, wanting—suffering an absence—is what the subject of this book and of the genre itself has been all along.

Fitzstephan the killer should have known better than most characters, since his profession was that of writer.

Of course the wanting, the lack or absence, which has always possessed the paradox-permeated detective story, ultimately invites readers to deal with the absence always already at the heart of the signifiers-representations of reality that make up the languages that make up literature. Working from that final recognition of the absence generative of all representational and literary absences, we can leave the detour into the quintessentially "absent" nature of detective fiction, to return to the subtext drawn from it. Now we can note for instance that the subtext's interrogation is not a "real" interrogation, but rather only a parody of an interrogation. But then again, it is not a "real" parody of an interrogation, but rather a theatrical representation of a parody of an interrogation. But then again, it is not a "real" theatrical representation of a parody of an interrogation, but rather a narrative recollection of a theatrical representation of a parody of . . . Well, in short and as we know, in the detective story, in the subtext, and indeed in all texts, there is no fixity along language's slippery, ever receding chain of signifiers.

We may conclude, then, that *La place de l'étoile*'s subtext owes a heavy debt to the detective story, not only in the interrogation form that the latter lent to the molding subtext, but also in the detective story's derivation from absence. No wonder, then, that the above examination of diegetic and lexical ungrammaticalities closed on unanswered questions, that is, absent answers, about guilt and language.

Possible answers to those questions will finally suggest themselves after a consideration of one more absence. Since the subtext portrays an interrogation, that is, the most characteristic common place of the detective story, may we not approach it with an interrogatory mindset and look for clues in an attempt to identify, if not the question(s) asked, then at least the crime that leads to the interrogation? Indeed, if we read Modiano as William VanderWolk would have us do (see the Introduction above), on this and on many other subjects his texts inevitably lead us to read him precisely as detectives.

The subtext's appearances suggest that Jewishness or perhaps Oedipal strife is somehow criminalized here. But the detective-story genre teaches us not to trust appearances; rather, we should look for clues, and it is a common place of detective fiction that clues involve nothing other than absences, or gaps. To quote from Marty Roth's book, *Foul and Fair Play: Reading Genre in Classic Detective Fiction:* "Poirot calls the clue a 'little curious fact,' because it suggests no associations into which it can enter; it does not want to fit anything, and yet its great virtue is that it fits whatever gap there is. As we know from the legend of Sherlock Holmes and the dog that didn't bark, the clue may also be the gap itself [. . .] " (Roth 180).

First of all, on the level of this subtext we may note the "little curious fact" that *four* nurses rush into the room to control only *three* characters. What need is there for the explicit number "four"? On the imaginary stage, what would the extra nurse do? What is prompting the text to bring to awareness a seemingly gratuitous detail that creates an incoherence, another ungrammaticality? One effect of the discordant numbers is to raise the possibility that a member of this bizarre family is somehow missing, that is, somehow there yet not there. For the patient reader the legitimate suspicion that we may be dealing with no more than a nugatory detail weakens considerably some fifty pages later when there occurs still another "little curious fact," again a numerical discrepancy. In his *juif aux champs* incarnation, Raphaël describes himself in Savoy reading a regional newspaper: "J'apprends qu'un film des Marx Brothers passe au cinéma de T. Nous sommes donc *six frères,* six juifs exilés en Savoie" (*La place de l'étoile* 103; my emphasis). But are the Marx Brothers five or four? Although offstage the famous brothers were actually five in number (Chico, Groucho, Harpo, Zeppo, and Gummo), only the first four at most appeared in their films. Given that the explicit context here is a Marx Brothers film, we should assume that Chico, Groucho, Harpo, Zeppo, and Raphaël make only five. We have the strong probability then that someone is missing again. If we work from that probability, the explicit "*six frères*" indicates that the missing family member is a brother.

An even more curious "slip" occurs many pages later, in a passage where the narrator says of himself and apparently of a heretofore occluded brother: "Nous étions *né* à Boulogne-sur-Seine, Ile-de-France" (*La place de l'étoile* 145-46; my emphasis). What is the reader to make of the grammatical error, whereby the *né* of "*nous étions né*" is in what appears to be an incorrect singular instead of the correct plural? Another merely incidental detail? That is not likely, if we take our cue from a second example that occurs hard on its heels and that insists on the curious construction: the passage in question concludes: "Après *nous* avoir *tué,* notre ennemi parcourrait ces rues désertes comme un fantôme, jusqu'à la fin des temps" (*La place de l'étoile* 147; my emphasis), the singular *tué* being used instead of the usually required plural *tués.* There exist more than one possible interpretation, to be sure. The most glib would have it that Raphaël has momentarily slipped into the *"nous" de modestie ou de royauté.* That hypothesis collapses instantly, as in the very next sentence one encounters an instance of *nous* modified by a perfectly normal plural: "Il *nous* sembla que *nous* étions *les seuls habitants* de la ville" (*La place de l'étoile* 147; emphasis mine). We may assume then that two close but distinct appearances of the usually plural *nous* in a singular sense, in immediate proximity to a *nous* that is properly plural in both form and sense, raise the former above the status of mere grammatical lapses or of preciosity, making them instead part of a very clear polar pull between singularity and plurality in Raphaël's view of himself.

For help in understanding this, we can turn back to the subtext, specifically to its muddle regarding the son's clothes: an S.S. uniform that is both "patched together" and topped off by the incoherent Gestapo raincoat, in other words, a uniform that is not whole, that is more multiform than uniform, and that consists of clothing for two individuals not one. In the retrospective light of the grammatical sliding of singular/plural brother/s, the vestimentary confusion appears to be a preliminary symptom of a fragile, patched-over single but vaguely doubled identity, ready in its tightly familial context to burst into a fraternal plurality that would require the inclusion of the fourth nurse. Recalling that the subtext's topos is an interrogation, the essence of the detective-story genre, we see that this identity split/doubling is completely consistent with the doubled psychological state and identity often characteristic of fictional detectives and with the paradox of presence/absence generative of the detective story.

As we shall see in Chapter 3 below, the issue of the double will bubble up progressively closer to surface awareness throughout the rest of the oeuvre. It reaches its most explicit textual awareness in Modiano's later (1993) *Chien de printemps:* "un frère, un double est mort *à notre place* à une date et dans un lieu inconnus et son ombre finit par *se confondre avec nous*" (*Chien de printemps* 121; my emphases). In keeping for instance with the words "*à notre place*," Annie Demeyère will find in the oeuvre's double a substitution that she connects with the typically Modianesque theme of superimposed time (Demeyère 44). Although doubling as substitution clearly manifests itself in the preceding quotation's expression *à notre place* and throughout the oeuvre, the words *se confondre avec nous* and the notion of *la surimpression du temps* suggest in addition an even more striking phenomenon. That phenomenon, shrouded over by the power of psychological repression, is more conflation than substitution. So it will be the contention of these pages that a brother's ghost does not substitute, and is not substituted, for the narrator and/or author, but is rather a conflated part of their porous identity.

Similarly in retrospect, the recognition of the pattern of split/doubled identity in Raphaël and in the subtext's Son raises a question about the identity of the subtext's Father. In a work like *La place de l'étoile* whose very title becomes a play on words, can homonymic play on *père/pair[e]* "father/peer[pair]" be appropriately heard, whereby the Son's Father also becomes split/doubled by the Son's *frère/pair[e]* "brother/peer[pair]"? If it is in fact appropriately heard, it would help explain the poignantly fraternal and curiously reversed youth/elder qualities of Raphaël's relationship with his father that Raphaël suggests when he notes his father's silly clothes, when he stands the youth/elder relationship on its head by leaving his father an inheritance (*La place de l'étoile* 55), and when he links him with kaleidoscopes, that is, toys. That curious relationship is hinted at in Modiano's next two novels as well, *La ronde de nuit* and *Les boulevards de ceinture*, where the narrators often assume the protective role of an older brother toward the father figure. Furthermore, in *Les boulevards de ceinture* the narrator underscores the reversal of his position vis-à-vis his father, after the latter switches the typical parricidal flow of Oedipal hostility by trying to kill his son by attempting to push him under a moving subway (*Les boulevards de ceinture* 104). This curious relationship would also intimate that in a family consisting of a mother, two sons, and a largely absent father, the older son may have in his own mind assumed the role of father in Oedipal competition with the sibling for the affection of the mother often abandoned by the father, a role that would help illuminate exacerbated sibling antagonism.

The possibility of a porous identity shared by the Son, Brother, and Father offers another opportunity to emphasize in passing the multi-leveled coherence of *La place de l'étoile*. These shifting boundaries in character identity offer an analogue to the shifting in textual identity, that is, to the intertextuality of this book, whereby the lines between it and for instance *The Great Gatsby* and *A la recherche du temps perdu* are, as we saw, explicitly eroded, and whereby the weaving into itself of quotes from Rebatet, Céline, Verlaine, and others further dissolves textual boundaries. In short, the grammatical "slips" involving *nous* and the sliding of character identity revealed by the subtext parallel the text's explicitly emphasized intertextual sliding. Those parallels provide still another indication of the extent to which the passage identified in these pages as the subtext is imbricated in the very forces that generate the entire text. The fact that the sliding among both character and textual identity calls to mind the workings of basic linguistic tropes such as metaphor, metonymy, and synecdoche suggests as well the extent to which Modiano's text—like so many rich contemporary texts—leads its readers back to pondering the workings of language itself.

Let us summarize our "investigation" into the identity of the crime leading to the subtext's interrogation. When we approach the subtext in a search for clues that will help articulate the putative crime, the number of nurses and the Son's clothes intimate a gap evocative of an absent family member, probably the Brother, a gap that in its peculiar use of *nous* in the singular repeats itself grammatically at later points and in ways that heighten the probability that the absent one is indeed the Brother. But the absent one in detective fiction being of course the murdered victim, the subtext's crime—the knowledge of which has too been absented, that is, suppressed—appears then to have been nothing less than the murder of a brother.

This conclusion allows us to view the Oedipal character of the interrogation subtext, on the one hand and in a traditional light, as appropriate: once again, it appears that the interrogator will turn out to be the assassin that he is seeking, doubtless out of rivalry over the mother (but a sibling rivalry). On the other hand, however, this conclusion also allows us to view the Oedipal character of the interrogation subtext in a slightly new light. Given the overt hostility between the narrator and his parents and the erotic charge given off by the maternal figures, there is little that is latent in *La place de l'étoile*'s Oedipal display or for that matter in the entire oeuvre's Oedipal situations. But if one assumes with the myth, with Sophocles's play, and with the Freudian hypothesis that "the truest memories are the one that we cannot recall" (Terdiman, *Present Past* 212), one has then to ask precisely which "truest memory" is being occulted in this seemingly overt Oedipal situation. As we have just seen, the answer may well be the "murder" of the absented brother. So, whether one views the subtext's Oedipal interrogation in a traditional or a new light, the result comes out the same: parricidal tendencies seem to be occulting fratricidal tendencies. Similarly, if one assumes with the myth, with Sophocles's play, and with the Freudian hypothesis that the Oedipal drive hides itself necessarily, in order that the Law may manifest itself as that which opposes the latent, one has then to ask to where the latency has retreated, on what it is operating. The answer for *La place de l'étoile* is the rivalry with the Sibling not the Father, a "murderous" rivalry which then becomes the source of the prohibition that becomes the occasion for the revelation of the Law. For Modiano the novelist the compelling Law is the revelation of the Text that refuses to remember the unforgettable crime of fratricide.

The suppressed will out in subterfuges, however, and in its subterfuges within this novel the suppressed memory of the brother does indeed bear the mark of fratricide. Its first subterfuge would be the text's generally murderous instincts that, while never far from the surface, burst out most dramatically on four occasions. The very opening pages of *La place de l'étoile* consist of two violent pastiches of tracts from Lucien Rebatet and Céline (see Obajtek-Kirkwood) pleading for homicidal rage to be directed against the Jew Raphaël. In typically breathless Célinesque style, the second pastiche reaches a crescendo with pleas for Raphaël's mutilation (*La place de l'étoile* 14). That thirst for murder and savage mutilation later grips Raphaël himself. In his *juif normalien* incarnation he beats his classmates (his intellectual brothers, we should observe) with casual sadism (81), one of the details of which—crushed vertebrae—repeats itself in a later, particularly grizzly scene (137). In that scene, Raphaël first murders Gérard, the Marquise de Fougeire-Jusquiames's chauffeur, and then mutilates the corpse's ears, eyes, and mouth (thereby reinstituting the murk of identity), while making eventually unrealized plans to stuff the disemboweled corpse, much as the

Célinesque Dr. Bardamu wanted Raphaël's body to be disemboweled. Finally, approximately forty pages of the penultimate section of the novel relate Raphaël's vicious fantasies of himself being tortured and executed, fantasies that had been prepared by earlier fantasies of his own and others' suicide (for example 43-46) or death (for example 106). In short, Raphaël's narrative fairly bursts with images of others mutilating and killing him, of him mutilating and killing others, and of him mutilating and killing himself. Given the looseness of the oft transforming Raphaël's sense of identity, given the splitting/doubling psychology haunting the controlling interrogation trope, and given textual details pulling the son's single identity into a fraternal splitting/doubling, those permutations of murder and mutilation that center in turn around Raphaël, center also around an unstable self/brother identity.

It should be recalled that the issue of doubled identity is hardly a subtle, unfamiliar one for Jews:

> Mais qu'est-ce qu'un Juif, sinon toujours un autre, sinon une image qui ne lui appartient pas, qui ne lui ressemble pas, sinon cette fiction que l'on insulte, torture et massacre sous le nom de Juif? Se contenter d'être Juif, c'est accepter de ne pas être. Si je veux à la fois être et être Juif, si je veux enfin coller à ma condition et à ma peau de Juif, il me faudra donc, par tous les moyens, m'identifier à cette image qui m'est étrangère, à ce reflet où je ne me reconnais pas. (Bersani, "Patrick Modiano: *La place de l'étoile*" 334-35)

We should observe as well that W. E. B. Dubois had similar comments about the "double-consciousness" inflicted on African-American victims of racism (Meisel). But the subject of unstable doubled identity, while certainly brought easily to the fore in victims' reflections on racist identity, also comes to influential explicitness in literary texts such as Edgar Allan Poe's "William Wilson." We will return to Poe in the next chapter.

The suppressed murderous urges against the self/brother come closest to clear eruption when Raphaël's addresses his relationship with Jean-François des Essarts, the character who will in fact become Raphaël's brother. Intimate friend and companion, Des Essarts gets a false passport from Raphaël in the name of "Jean-François Lévy," making him in his own terms the narrator's *"frère de race"* (*La place de l'étoile* 23). We should note as well that, like Raphaël, Des Essarts is both a journalist and a writer of books (24-25, 27), making the doubling self/brother identification even more insistent. The fraternal glow takes on a murderous cast a few pages later, however, in the conclusion of one of Raphaël's extended fantasies: "En décembre, lors de l'offensive von Rundstedt, je me fais abattre par un G. I. nommé Lévy, qui me ressemble comme un frère" (38). The deadly favor is quickly returned, when Raphaël recounts Des Essarts-Lévy's suspicious death in an automobile accident (50), an accident that Raphaël later admits was in fact the murder of his brother: "Quant à Des Essarts, mon frère, mon seul ami, n'était-ce pas moi qui avais déréglé le frein de l'automobile pour qu'il puisse se fracasser le crâne en toute sécurité?" (149). In keeping, however, with the suppression-serving tendency seen frequently thus far to conflate rather than distinguish antagonistic identities, after Des Essarts's death Raphaël quite simply usurps the identity of *"mon frère, mon seul ami"*: "j'ai décidé d'usurper l'identité bien française de mon ami Des Essarts" (100; see also 127). Raphaël thereby once again smudges any sense of identity boundaries, and thereby obscures a fratricidal urge neither explained nor denied. The same process takes hold of the end of the narrative when Raphaël is led to torture and ultimately death by an admiral significantly named "Lévy" and when in his escape attempt he uses the papers of still another Lévy and wears the latter's uniform (196, 198): Lévy repeatedly kills Lévy.

The postulation of a splitting/doubling self/brother at homicidal odds with himself offers a way of interpreting one of the more inflammatory aspects of *La place de l'étoile*, its equating Nazis and Jews. In the subtext, for instance, the Nazi Son questioning his Jewish Father suggests that for *La place de l'étoile* Nazism has its origin in Jewishness. The suggestion would be repulsive on its face and so undeserving of consideration, except that Raphaël is quite clear on the matter: *"Tous juifs, [. . .] les nazis sont des juifs de choc!"* (*La place de l'étoile* 158). Moreover, he repeatedly insists on a parallel proposition, that the most virulent anti-Semites are in reality Jews. For instance, he pronounces at the start that: "le docteur Bardamu [that is, Céline, one of the most notorious, overt, and literary haters of Jews in French history] est l'un des nôtres, c'est le plus grand écrivain juif de tous les temps" (15). A few pages later, Raphaël performs much the same act of assimilation. First he effects the metamorphosis into a Jew of another notorious, overt, and literary enemy of Jews, Drieu La Rochelle: "Drieu avait une vocation d'odalisque. Il fut la courtisane juive, l'Esther Gobseck de la Collaboration" (32). Then he invites André Maurois to resume his birth identity, that of Emile Herzog: "Maurois m'enviait mes amitiés fascistes. Je lui donnai la recette: abandonner définitivement son exquise pudeur de juif honteux. Reprendre son véritable nom" (36). Furthermore, Raphaël's assimilation of Jewishness and Nazism/hatred of Jews doubtless helps generate his fantasy of having become an intimate of the epicenter incarnate of Nazism, Adolph Hitler himself. The assimilation turns more aggressive still when Raphaël substitutes for Hitler by becoming Eva Braun's lover (152-53), and of course in its Oedipal evocation, brings the father-figure into the Nazi-Jew conflation. Finally, in a section that must have caused considerable pain in Israel, Raphaël fantasizes a Tel Aviv-Paris in which Israelis assume Nazi roles (177 and following pages). This forcing of intense cultural and moral polarity into a single identity would, therefore, be a cognate of the personal self/brother antagonism, that is, another expansion of the unstable psychological rootlessness that grips Raphaël.

The final task in this interrogation of the interrogation is, then, to explore a bit more the apparently Oedipal source of this urge to kill the self/brother. To do that, we will start drifting away from a theoretically pure version of Riffaterrean semiotic analysis, that is, one that eschews extratextual—in this case, psycho-biographical—criticism. This study's drift away from strict intratextual criticism of our primary text *La place de l'étoile* actually started in remarks seven paragraphs above. It was there that notice was taken of two Modiano texts other than *La place de l'étoile,* specifically *La ronde de nuit* and *Les boulevards de ceinture,* both of which have elements of the shifting Oedipal identity *père/pair(e)* that operates in *La place de l'étoile* and that includes the Self/Brother pair/peers. The preparation for a break into psycho-biographical explanation of the triangular *père/pair(e)* occurs when we take note that—true to the dynamics of suppression—a clue has been pushed out to the final margin of *La place de l'étoile,* its last paratext, where another "curious little fact" comes into play. In the autobiographical summary on the back cover of the early Folio editions of the book, Modiano listed the year of his birth as 1947, although the public subsequently learned that he was actually born in 1945. Annie Demeyère finds in the discrepancy no more than a hallmark of the author's autofictional work, a tampering with reality in the cause of fiction that she calls "*les fondations de tout travail romanesque de déplacement et de réinvention*" (Demeyère 206, 207). But the suspicion arises that far more is involved here than just autofictional tampering: the later date was in fact the birth year of Rudy, who died of apparent anemia when he was ten and Patrick was twelve. Is this a trace of a psychological tectonic that could yield a personal explanation of the conflation of dates, that is, the suppression of one of the dates? Why the deception about an event so traumatically personal, deception that is the detective story's second standard sign of the guilty party, the first being murder? Can the author's relationship with his sibling indeed cast light on the fratricidal urges identified through a strictly textual analysis of *La place de l'étoile?*[20]

We can start formulating an answer in the affirmative if we temporarily make a move back to strict textuality, to a close consideration of the novel's fourth section, in which the narrative's hallucinatory pace accelerates:

> Vienne. Les derniers tramways glissaient dans la nuit. Mariahilfer-Strasse, nous sentions la peur nous gagner. Encore quelques pas et nous nous retrouverions place de la Concorde. Prendre le métro, égrener ce chapelet rassurant: Tuileries, Palais-Royal, Louvre, Châtelet. Notre mère nous attendait, *quai Conti.* Nous boirions un tilleul menthe en regardant les ombres que projetait aux murs de notre chambre le bateau-mouche. (*La place de l'étoile* 145; my emphasis)

Unquestionably and quite literally the scene is nightmarish (taking place at night, charged with fear, and allowing dream-like confusion and displacements) and thus more open to the unconscious, the suppressed, that is, that which is absented from consciousness. The nightmare has, moreover, the cast of a childhood memory or perception, since when Hitler eventually appears in it, he does so as a Disneyesque Captain Hook in an especially disturbing passage in which he will repeatedly scream the enduringly chilling figure, "*Sechs Millionen Juden!*" (*La place de l'étoile* 147).

Significantly (but in a move again away from a properly intratextual explanation), those familiar with the autofictional dimensions of Modiano's oeuvre (see the discussion of Thierry Laurent in the Introduction above) know the scene to resonate with a passage from *Livret de famille*, in which the narrator "Patrick Modiano" describes presumed incidents from the author's and his brother's own childhood. Patrick and Rudy had lived on the quai Conti (Nettelbeck and Hueston, *Patrick Modiano* 4-6; see also Modiano's autobiographical *Un pedigree* [2005] but with caution: he designates some of his texts now autobiography now fiction, Introduction, note 4). The passage in question recounts how the narrator and his brother Rudy used to watch at night the shadows cast on their bedroom walls by the bateaux-mouches passing by on the Seine (*Livret de famille* 209). So in viewing *La place de l'étoile* as part of the autofictional oeuvre, it would be difficult not to understand an allusion to Rudy carried in the possessive adjective of *notre mère* (and a few lines later of *notre cousin* and *notre père*) and in the pronoun *Nous* when it occurs in the sentence (discussed above): "Nous étions né à Boulogne-sur-Seine, Ile-de-France" (*La place de l'étoile* 145-46). Moreover, the *Boulogne-sur-Seine* merges the biographically accurate Boulogne-Billancourt with the Hauts-de-Seine *département* of which Boulogne-Billancourt is the *chef-lieu*, where Patrick was in fact born. So it is a biographical detail, the author's relationship with his brother, that seems to be implicated in the narrator's self/brother identity.

No less significantly, we learn from a very personal and provocative interview given to Pierre Assouline by Modiano and by his wife Dominique in 1987 that our author declares the death of his brother as the single most troubling event of his childhood, and indeed of his life, and—most importantly for our purposes—as the most identifiable reason why he writes. Even if one maintains—properly, as we will see below—a guarded acceptance of those comments, they are consistent with much else in the oeuvre. In his book on the interplay between fiction and autobiography in Modiano's oeuvre Thierry Laurent considers the impact of Rudy's death on Modiano so decisive that he devotes an entire chapter to sorting out the role of that death in Modiano's work. Echoing a point made about the oeuvre earlier by Nettelbeck and Hueston (*Patrick Modiano* 5), Laurent observes for instance that:

> De 1968 à 1982, les huit premiers romans sont dédiés à Rudy; le premier l'étant même à lui seul, alors que les suivants associeront son nom à ceux d'intimes de l'écrivain (parents, épouse, enfants, amis très proches). C'est dire l'importance de l'hommage et la place privilégiée du disparu dans le cœur de l'écrivain. Même si les récits ne concernent absolument pas le frère cadet, son image plane quelque part. (Laurent 125)

While he correctly cautions against simplistic conclusions about Patrick's guilt in this regard, he does deal with it as a legitimate subject that has to be taken into consideration. Marja Warehime shares that approach: "While it is essential to distinguish between Modiano the author and his narrators, it is not irrelevant to raise the issue of the death of Modiano's own brother Rudy in conjunction with the theme of guilt that emerges in the narrative" (Warehime 52-53, note 10).

Apropos—in perplexing contradistinction and most suggestively in terms of the author's psychological suppression—another not so little "little curious fact" is that on the explicit, overt level the brother, putatively the reason behind the writing of the oeuvre, is appreciably absent from the family-obsessed oeuvre, his name appearing in only three works, *Livret de famille, Remise de peine,* and *Fleurs de ruine.* And on one of the occasions when the beloved figure Rudy does appear, he accompanies his brother the narrator past a pair of statues in the garden of the Louvre, statues that tellingly appear in the guise of the less than loving Abel and Cain (*Fleurs de ruine* 90).

So in summary, the pages of the *La place de l'étoile* itself lead to the two strictly text-based suspicions that the crime at the root of the subtext's interrogation is that of fratricide, and that the interrogation is interrupted and frustrated because of psychological suppression of the unacceptable memories/drives that make up this fratricide; the paratextual clue involving the author's year of birth and the extratextual clue involving Abel and Cain, when viewed within the decidedly autofictional nature of the oeuvre, allow the suspicion that at an unconscious, irrational biographical level for the author the "crime" may be a sense of responsibility for the death of his brother. That suspicion grows only stronger because of still another "little curious fact," another extratextual one: Modiano's eleventh published novel *Remise de peine* (1988)—but only the second novel in which the brother explicitly appears and the one in which he appears extensively for the first time—had actually started out to be Modiano's first novel. But true to the dynamics of suppression asserted by these pages, the author had found himself incapable of finishing it in a timely fashion, for reasons unclear to him: "Bizarrement, ce livre [*Remise de peine*], j'avais commencé à l'écrire il y a longtemps, avant mon premier roman. Mais je n'y suis pas arrivé. Alors j'ai écrit tous mes bouquins. En fait, c'est un peu le livre que j'aurais voulu comme mon premier livre. Mais je n'avais pas le courage, enfin, de remuer tous ces..." (Joselin 59). The suspension points so characteristic of Modiano serve as well as anything to evoke the suppressed trauma of the death of the brother to whom Modiano was so attached, and with whom, as his paratextual conflation of their years of birth suggests, Modiano had a relationship of self/brother. As Nettlebeck and Hueston put it, Rudy was: "*son ami inséparable, son 'jumeau' presque, dont l'identité se confond avec la sienne* [. . .] "(Nettlebeck and Hueston, *Patrick Modiano* 5).

So all these textual, paratextual and extratextual "curious little facts," these additional absences or gaps, make it possible to argue that the semiotic absence/suppression marking the constitutive elements of *La place de l'étoile* (which is indebted to the absence-centered detective story) is compounded by a psychically searing family absence, one probably irrationally and subconsciously feared by the author to be the result of the detective story's classic pretext, a murder. This means that semiotic absence bleeds into a psychological absence in Modiano's novel, tingeing the abstract, purely aesthetic with the deeply personal. Such a compounded absence would surely help explain the unusually strong suppressive strains of the otherwise flamboyantly overt *La place de l'étoile*. In fact, the semiotic/psychological gap or absence inaugurates what Annie Demeyère considers a paradoxical source of the oeuvre's writing: "Autour d'un manque, d'un vide l'obsession d'écrire se construit" (Demeyère 92). But for her, the oeuvre's sense of void and remorse result from the Modianesque artist's capacity to assume imaginatively the lives and sufferings of others (119).

The text itself, however, poses a major caveat for too facile a psycho-biographical reading. As we have seen, it concludes with a decisive rejection of Freud, father of many such readings. Der Herr Doktor becomes a figure of ridicule as he is made to perform like a trained dog eager for approval, rolling on the floor, walking on all fours, and even barking, in order to get Raphaël to take him seriously, but all to no avail. This suggests strongly that Raphaël and his text find fault with the figure at the root of so much psycho-biographical criticism. In other words, it suggests that there may be fault to be found precisely with the sort of conclusion just reached. As well it should. Even painstaking, lengthy psychoanalysis between individuals in actual contact has obviously more than a few pitfalls as a path to certain knowledge, especially if in a Freudian context one accepts that "certain knowledge" can just as easily be based on retrospective fantasizing (*Nachträglichkeit*) that is true to one's psychic needs, as it can be on actual experiences. A fortiori, psychoanalysis—or more accurately, sketchy use of psychoanalysis-derived notions, even the more accessible Oedipal notions—by a reader like myself untrained in the practice, applied to an enigmatic writer through the latter's no less enigmatic texts, holds out little to no hope of even approaching secure findings. (For a reading of *La place de l'étoile* by a prolific psychoanalyst, see Chasseguet-Smirgel 217-55.)

The abjection of Freud is very pertinent to this chapter, then, in that it serves to warn against taking the psycho-biographical link between Modiano and his first published novel for more than it is here intended to be. The intention is *not* to explain the psyche of Patrick Modiano the man, but rather to offer an arguable, coherent reading that, faced with the especially resistant *La place de l'étoile,* tries to take into speculative account the threads of that other *textus* that consists of the interrelated stories that Modiano writes and that he tells the public about himself. Those stories about himself and his own work can be contradictory, and in the view of two authoritative Modiano scholars are most assuredly not to be taken at face value:

> Quand Modiano parle de sa vie, il fabule avec une effronterie presque célinienne. "Effronterie" n'est d'ailleurs peut-être pas le mot juste; comme Céline, Modiano semble avoir compris que pour se dérober à une attention potentiellement stérilisante

de la part des médias, il fallait créer un personnage public, un rôle plus vrai que nature, qui le protégerait. (Nettelbeck and Hueston, *Patrick Modiano* 4)

So here and throughout this study, "Modiano," his family members, and incidents in his life are understood to represent elements of another auto-fictional story, one that the author relays to readers and observers through the media, but one that while more "auto" than most of his fictions, is more fictional than most autobiographical public comments of many artists. (See Dickstein 146-47 for a nuanced but different acknowledgement of the problem.) With all due caution, then, we can safely say that Modiano's public statements about his brother comprise at the very least another imaginative text quite compatible with the oeuvre.

To bring this chapter to a close, let us turn back one last time to exclusively textual details, in order to identify another and more than adequate source of the urge in *La place de l'étoile* to kill the self/brother. Looking under a certain light at the earlier discussion of textual ungrammaticalities, we can spot a source of the murderous urge in nothing less than Raphaël's use of the French language. To bring that light to bear, let us first recall that the diegetic ungrammaticalities of *La place de l'étoile* pointed to the hidden intertext *Peter Schlemihl* in a way that made the ungrammaticalities and intertext converge on the subjects of rootlessness, guilt, and the artistic quest. Let us also recall that those same subjects erupted in the notably indirect and obscure lexical ungrammaticality *avaler des lames de rasoir* that pointed to what—for a post-Holocaust Jew who would write in French—must be the "cutting" character of French and its sociolect. Compared with the clarity of the hidden intertext and the diegetic ungrammaticalities once both are revealed, the lexical ungrammaticality in its heightened obscurity betrays heightened suppression, so much so that it stands linked to the only other subject of highly resistant suppression, the source of the destructive urges aimed at the self/brother. Viewed semiotically, that source then would be Raphaël's situation as a writer. Rootless or uncertain in his identity (a French Jew or a Jewish Frenchman?), Raphaël in his frequently evidenced compulsions to write has no choice but guiltily to use French favorable to his creativity and its concomitant elements hurtful to Jews; being a post-Holocaust writer in French, true to both his Jewish self and

his French self, he attacks and affirms alternate parts of himself (a situation aptly captured by Raphaël's oddly moving description of himself as
a boxer in a match against himself [*La place de l'étoile* 76]). On the one
hand, what better setting for the portrayal of such a dilemma than the
Holocaust years, when collaborating France itself lived out its own
self/brother destruction, a setting in which the writer Raphaël, trying to
portray his inner artistic life, could fantasize himself a "*juif collabo*"? On
the other hand, what worse setting for that portrayal than the Holocaust
years, if the writing then becomes a personal reenactment in subconscious fratricide of the genocidal-suicidal Collaboration? The psychological need to keep that reenactment from clear awareness would go far
in explaining the powerful forces of suppression at work in this outrageous novel that draws much of its power from the outrage of having to
deal with being a post-Holocaust Jewish writer in French.

It becomes clear, then, that Raphaël the artistic schlemihl suffers
from guilt-ridden rootlessness linguistically, textually, and psychologically, like the hybrid that he is of archetypal Abel-Cain and of shadowless Peter Schlemihl ("he who killed his brotherly shadow"). This
indicates finally that the semiotic matrix out of which *La place de
l'étoile,* its ungrammaticalities, its hidden intertext, and its subtext issue
is the notion of an artist's guilt-ridden rootlessness.

There is great appropriateness, of course, that it is largely on the
subject of writing and language that this chapter should close. First of all,
it has dealt with a text frenetic in its intertextuality, that is, in its awareness of how its subjects and origins are to be found in other writing and
language. Secondly, the pages above kept leading back to reflections on
the nature of language, for example how signifiers perpetually recede,
how words deal in absence, and how language confounds tight distinctions by gliding on the play of tropes. Nonetheless, recognition of the
ultimate obviousness of the basic conclusion arising out of all the preceding pages—the subject/source of this self-conscious use of language
called *La place de l'étoile* is the literary use of language, that is, the self-
conscious use of language—should neither surprise nor disappoint us:

> Altered by the mimetic anomalies, [Riffaterre's reader] sets
> out on his quest for the hidden hypogram [or subtext and inter-
> text, *mutatis mutandis*] and is, up to a point, rewarded with its

discovery—with the important proviso that, in this case, getting there is definitely much more than half the fun. What is finally revealed can, as in dreams interpreted by Freud, seem very little compared to the intricacy of the work that was needed to disguise it. In can, in fact, be nothing at all. Yet its existence, actual or potential, is indispensable for the entire process to take place. (de Man 26)

Nor should self-conscious use of language in *La place de l'étoile* blind us to its poignancy. When a text implicates the Holocaust, an event that cries out for language to work at its referential best, how could it not reflect the torment of confronting language's difficulty in breaking away from mere linguistic and textual self-referentiality? As we have already seen, this text's textuality asserts itself in exceptionally prominent ways, for instance, in the punning of the very title and of the paratextual introduction, in the comical neologism that is the narrator himself "Schlemilovitch," and in the self-referentiality that constitutes the nature of the variously reincarnating interrogation subtext. But a referent as powerful as the Holocaust resists mere textual play, and therein lies an especially difficult problem for a semiotic approach to *La place de l'étoile*. To what extent if any does this self-conscious novel in fact use the Holocaust of history as an extratextual referent? It is a problem that the next chapter will address.

◆ ◆ ◆

Chapter 2

Referentiality in *La place de l'étoile:*
Challenging Riffaterre and Aestheticization

I. Objections to a Riffaterrean Approach

As mentioned at the beginning of the preceding chapter, there are a number features of Riffaterre's theory to which objections can be raised. Of the more noteworthy objections most pertinent to making a retrospective critique of the Riffaterrean approach as used above, not the least is the objection against the most striking feature of Riffaterre's work, namely the insistence that a text dictates its own necessary decoding, that literature is *"une machine à contrôler l'attention et l'imagination"* (Riffaterre, *Production* 21). But if, as post-Derrida opinion accepts, one cannot pin down once and for all the precise referent of just a single linguistic sign, and if Riffaterre is correct in observing that a literary text is a system of linguistic signs, it is hard to accept theoretically that *the* referent (*the* Riffaterrean intertext, for example Chamisso's *Peter Schlemihl*) of an extensive literary text can be consistently, and a fortiori conclusively, determined, such that it would work with the mechanical determinism argued for in a Riffaterrean reading. Moreover, there is no reason even to assume a shared and accurate meaning of "referent": identifying the referent of a verbal expression is in turn largely a function of the logical analysis that one makes of the entire expression, an operation open to wide divergence. For instance, is the referent of "Caesar crossed the Rubicon" Caesar, or the Rubicon, or the crossing of the Rubicon, and so forth (Descombes 770-71)? Answers to such a question depend upon contexts of course, and as Stanley Fish argues, in language a context is not a single external given independent of sign interpreters but rather multiple internalized structures of assumptions shared by members of various interpretive communities, which of course are always in flux. More generally and simply expressed, if a text dictates its own necessary decoding, why do readers come up with so many different decodings and readings (Dragoş 104; Culler 93 and following pages; Ginsburg 452), and why do readers intuit that they read freely and idiosyncratically? To be sure, the accuracy of the intuition is an open, very interesting question. Moreover, the fact of the intuition's virtual universality is an incontestable, no less interesting, matter, but one based ultimately upon the frequently challenged "notion of an autonomous unconstituted subject." The pioneering semiotician Charles Peirce "suggests that our minds are accessible to us in *exactly the same way* that everything else is. The self, like the world, is a text. Hence the notion of an autonomous unconstituted subject is just as problematic (and for the same reasons) as the autonomous and unconstituted world" (Michaels 199; emphasis in the original). If that is so, then the intuition of free and idiosyncratic readings is wrong in an absolute sense, and needs rectification in a relative sense. All three points however—the intuition of freedom in reading, the universality of the intuition, and the justification of the intuition in a certain view of the subject—should be taken into account for a comprehensive explanation of the role of necessity in semiosis.

Of course, Riffaterre has answered the general point that diverse, sensible readings argue against his position that a literary text dictates its own necessary decoding. For instance, in a 1981 interview given to *Diacritics* he posited semiotic necessity more in process than in product. He was asked whether "accomplished readers *have* to agree on what constitutes the matrix and the hypogram" (Riffaterre, "Interview" 14; emphasis in the original), the hypogram playing in poetry a semioticizing role similar to that of the intertext and subtext in fiction. He replied that in the reading process the text's "troublesomeness," its ungrammaticalities, keep pointing to a need to resolve the "troublesomeness" with an intertextual hypogram ("already a system of signs comprising at least a predication, and it may be as large as a text," Riffaterre, *Semiotics* 23), or with an intertext (the term that he will subsequently use instead more and more, see for instance "La Trace de l'intertexte"). Equally involved in the resolution of the ungrammaticalities is a matrix that "most economically accounts for the greatest number of formal and semantic features in the text" (Riffaterre, "Interview" 14). "Normal readers" will track the intertexts down "imperfectly or vaguely," whereas "analysts" will use special knowledge and training to prove the necessity, with more or less success, trying to "locate more accurately what texts, or to pinpoint more precisely what textual references a native sense of language and human memory have *already* tracked down" (Riffaterre, "Interview" 14, emphasis in the original). In expanding on the emphasis that he would give to process over product, Riffaterre finds logical room to allow himself the equivocation that even the most informed of readers will articulate the necessity only "more accurately," only "more precisely," and not with the definitive accuracy or precision of a deterministic reading. As we shall soon see, this is not the first time that Riffaterre the superb reader and observer of the reading process will, to his credit, let the realities of practice trump the absolutes of theory, and thereby avoid what Stanley Fish has called Riffaterre's lack of connection between description and interpretation, which Fish takes to lead to a confusion of message with meaning (Fish 86-87).

Another, more obvious problem here is the use of truly tendentious adjectives (in such expressions as "native sense of language," "natural reader-perception," "normal readers," "natural awareness," and "natural reader," Riffaterre, "Interview" 24), all of which go undefined. Another problem is that a text's occasional "troublesomeness" is considered only in the context of a search for semiosis, and not in other contexts. The most fundamental of those contexts would be the workings, not just of literature or literariness, but also of language itself, and so the presumption of Riffaterrean "non-troublesome" or "grammatical" language too becomes problematic.

Along those lines, in a penetrating article Paul de Man addresses that problem in terms of the unavoidability of figuration. Toward the end of the article's third part, he argues that Riffaterre's article, "La trace de l'intertexte" betrays a misreading of Hegel, in that Riffaterre understands the German philosopher to have shown precisely what Riffaterre tries to show, the loss of referentiality, whereas de Man's Hegel has instead and more consequentially shown the loss of determination itself (de Man 29). De Man then goes on to observe that, whereas Riffaterre proposes that his techniques and concepts do away with the mimesis-wrought arbitrary

reading of literary texts and result in an agrammaticality-enforced necessary reading, ultimately Riffaterre's putative certainty-inducing concepts—like all concepts—are rhetorical figures. The difficulty then is
that rhetorical figures cannot be anchored in determination because they
necessarily arise from epistemological tension (de Man 33). The confident determinants of Riffaterrean readings have an ultimately indeterminate ground themselves.

On other philosophical grounds, ones more related to the reader-
response emphasis of Riffaterre's approach, the question arises whether
the text exists as an empirical object to be observed, or rather as a sub-
jective object in the experience of readers enculturated to such socially
determined phenomena as genre (Freadman 32). In a related but less philosophical way, the question arises whether for any literary work, especially for canonical texts showing up in different editions, there even
exists such a thing as "the" physical text about which to argue, and on
which the necessary semiosis will be performed. For just one of several
examples of the ways in which the issue arises we need only reread
Gérard Genette's list of paratexts (see p. 177, n. 7 for the list) that complicate the question of where a text begins and ends. In light of the assault on textual boundaries represented by that extensive list, and since
Riffaterre's is a reader-response approach, we can wonder to what extent
the reader of *La place de l'étoile* does/should respond to, for example the
editor's?/author's? preface to "the text proper"; to what extent does/
should the reader respond to the cover of the early Folio editions of the
novel that show a raincoated man whose head is a Star of David embla-
zoned with "Juif," or to the fact that subsequently to initial publication
Modiano issued a version of *La place de l'étoile* less offensive to Israel.
Jacques Derrida certainly would concur that textual boundaries are more
supposed than real, having said apropos of Edgar Allan Poe's "The Purloined Letter": "no totalization of the border is even possible" (Derrida,
"The Purveyor" 99). (See below page 120 for a fuller quotation, at which
point the special pertinence of Poe to Riffaterre's position on referentiality will be under discussion.) For all that, I suspect that Riffaterre would
pragmatically and rightly have readers attempt semiosis on whatever text
has been reasonably if not absolutely determined to be "the text proper"
or even "*a* proper text." But the high likelihood of heated arguments
about what constitutes "the text proper" or "a proper text" suggests that

contingency will further compromise the necessary character of any proposed Riffaterrean reading.

Entailed in the necessary decoding, in the necessary transformation of mimesis into semiosis argued for by Riffaterre, is a position not explored in the previous chapter, a position concerning the object of mimesis, representation itself. But a position on representation has important implications for a reading of *La place de l'étoile* that aims to be faithful and thorough, since Modiano's novel deals prominently with the referentially charged subject of the Holocaust. Riffaterrean decoding, however, ultimately requires breaking away from the referent, breaking away from the representations of mimesis.

The general philosophical issue of representation is as old as Plato, of course, who maintained that what most people experience as reality consists actually of mere shadows of imperfect representations of what truly is, of the ἰδέαι or transcendent forms (*The Republic* 7.541 and following pages). As ancient as the issue is, however, if we are to judge, for example, from Hans Bertens's comprehensive study of postmodernism, *The Idea of the Postmodern,* even our own postmodern time finds itself in a veritable "crisis of representation" (Bertens 11). Regarding contemporary theoretical discussions of that issue, it almost seems prescient on Plato's part that his metaphor to help explain representation postulated a cave that was dark, presumably claustrophobic, and not easily accessible. But there is a little niche off the less than inviting main cave, a niche that teachers/scholars of literature have been visiting more and more frequently, namely the niche where the talk deals with representation that is more specifically literary. Riffaterre has for some forty years now been holding forth in that niche with provocative brilliance, but also with inconsistency on the question of whether what is represented in literature, the referent, is pertinent to literary analysis. The point of this chapter will be less to joust with Riffaterre on this or other inconsistencies to be imputed to his approach (for the names of critics finding Riffaterre inconsistent, see note 2 of chapter 1). Rather, his inconsistency itself regarding representation will serve to argue that, Riffaterre's frequent declarations to the contrary notwithstanding, the referent does indeed remain pertinent to literary analysis. Furthermore, it does so in a way suggesting that Riffaterre's inconsistencies reflect a tension inherent in literary representation itself. Awareness of this tension in literature is, however, hardly new (see for example Paul de Man's "Lyric and Modernity" in his *Blindness and Insight*), but observing it at work in an application of a Riffaterrean approach to *La place de l'étoile* underscores that the issue has continued deservedly and necessarily to attract the attention of the best critical minds (see for example Barthes, *Littérature et réalité*), all the more so in a culture still dealing with the problem of generally representing the Holocaust (see for example Friedlander, *Probing the Limits of Representation: Nazism and the "Final Solution"*). In addition, the fact that Patrick Modiano's first novel raises the issue of literary representation in terms of the problem of representing the Holocaust suggests that his work achieves a blend of timelessness and urgent topicality, a blend that in his case suggests another reason why he is both a popular and critical success.

Let us first briefly review some of the Riffaterrean reading principles addressed in the previous chapter, but with more of a view to bringing out some of the logical tension. Grounded from the start of his career in what he called "*la stylistique structurale*" that combines stylistics with a focus on reader-response, he has maintained as a sensible first linguistic-critical principle that, although everyday language does in fact manage to work referentially, in literature of imagination the referent tends to become purely verbal as the text's aesthetic autonomy prevails (Riffaterre, *Essais* 154-55). Elaborating upon that first principle, he has—at some points—acknowledged "the actual literary experience" to be what he calls "the double reading" or "double meaning" as the reader goes from a mimetic or referential reading to a semiotic or aesthetic reading. To be clear on key terms, we should observe that by "mimesis," Riffaterre understands "the literary representation of reality" (*Semiotics of Poetry* 2); "What is shown or enacted [in a narrative structure] is mimetic" (*Fictional Truth* 127). Regarding "semiosis," we read: "Semiosis: the three-way relationship between a sign, its object, and its *interpretant* (C. S. Peirce, *Collected Papers* 5:484). It is therefore opposed to referentiality, the assumed relationship between a sign and nonverbal objects taken to be reality" (Riffaterre, *Fictional Truth* 130; his emphasis). Apropos of "doubled reading" between mimesis to semiosis, he explained:

> [One phase of Riffaterrean analysis] is based upon my concept
> of a double reading that only literary texts require—a primary

reading [elsewhere called "heuristic" or "linguistic" by Riffaterre] which deciphers the text at the level of mimesis [and which unfolds syntagmatically]; and a retroactive [or "hermeneutic" or "literary"] reading, which effects the semiotic transformation [that is, which arises in a moment of paradigmatic discovery when one suddenly sees how a text's various elements are expansions or conversions of the abstract "matrix"]. The matrix structure sets everything going, triggering as it does the back-and-forth scanning of the textual space. But this *double meaning* is the actual literary experience: my analysis explains and preserves its complexity and its richness. For I ascribe two facets to each component, mimetic and semiotic; I place the literary phenomenon at the moment of transformation. Third, I have pointed out that every reader's effort to make sure of the semiosis makes him go through a new reading at the mimetic level. This accounts for the continuous rereading, the inexhaustibility of the experience that is peculiarly literary. (Riffaterre, "Interview" 15; emphasis in the original. For "heuristic" and "hermeneutic," and the Freudian "expansion" and "conversion" of a "matrix," see *Semiotics of Poetry* 4-6, 13, 47-80.)

On the other hand and at other points, however, Riffaterre has made notorious apodictic statements about the inconsequentiality of mimesis's referent in the presence of semiosis, statements that are so provocative that one is entitled to wonder how compatible they are with his locating the actual literary experience in a text's double meaning between semiosis and the representations of mimesis. For instance, in his 1979 book *La production du texte* he states with emphatic underlining in the original:

Il me reste à considérer le problème de la littérature comme *représentation*. Dans ma description des caractères propres à la communication littéraire, je notais que la réalité y est un succédané du texte. Cette propriété demande un changement radical du point de vue traditionnel dans l'explication. Il s'ensuit en effet que *le référent n'est pas pertinent à*

> *l'analyse*, et qu'il n'y a aucun avantage pour le critique à comparer l'expression littéraire à la réalité et à évaluer l'œuvre en fonction de cette comparaison. (Riffaterre, *Production* 19; emphasis in the original)

Similarly, in his 1990 book *Fictional Truth* one reads apropos of literary verisimilitude:

> [Criticism based on the traditional interpretation of verisimilitude] privileges the mimesis, a sign system seemingly based on the referentiality of its components, that is, on the assumption that words carry meaning by referring to things or to non-verbal entities. [Criticism such as Riffaterre's based on a semiotic interpretation of verisimilitude, however,] privileges the narrative sequentiality that is entirely within the text's boundaries.
>
> This opposition, however, is more apparent than real. In fact, *exterior referentiality is but an illusion*, for signs or sign systems refer to other sign systems: verbal representations in the text refer to verbal givens borrowed from the sociolect, but such verbal givens are actually present in the text, explicitly or implicitly, as presuppositions. (Riffaterre, *Fictional Truth* 3; my emphasis)

Paul de Man has pointed out the same problem in Riffaterre's 1984 *Semiotics of Poetry*, but de Man calls it just a "shift in tone":

> Riffaterre seems to have reacted to pressures such as these [tensions between descriptive observation and hermeneutic conclusions], for the concluding chapter of *Semiotics of Poetry* reveals shifts in tone that cannot be ignored. The ghost of referentiality, which has theoretically been exorcized in the model of the hypogram, does not seem to have been entirely laid to rest. We hear that reading is "at once restrictive and unstable," which is surprising, since the main reason for one's willingness to accept the restrictions was they had such stabilizing power. We hear that the "revelation" of correct read-

ing "is always chancy, must always begin anew," that "the reader's manufacture of meaning is thus not so much a progress through the poem ... as it is a seesaw scanning of the text, compelled by the very duality of the signs," that reading "is a continual recommencing, an indecisiveness resolved one moment and lost the next" (*Semiotics* 165-6). This language surprises [. . .] . (de Man, "Hypogram and Inscription" 29-30)

Terrence Cave, in his review of Riffaterre's *Text Production*, noted retrospectively the same problem in the earlier *Semiotics of Poetry* (Cave 278). But we should respect the fact that the turn of phrase by de Man, one of our time's most penetrating readers of literature, seems to inflect accuracy with a generosity cognizant of Riffaterre's outstanding contribution to critical understanding and his many superlative explications. But be it "shift" or "inconsistency," this example is not the only one about which Riffaterre has been taken to task for definitional problems, see for instance Freadman 35-36 concerning "interpretant."

Regardless of what I term "inconsistency," for practical-minded teachers/scholars of literature trying to decide which critical approach to take toward especially difficult texts, Riffaterre's productive, stimulating approach has much to recommend itself. Certainly de Man has credited Riffaterre with developing "the most reliable didactic model for the teaching of literature, regardless of period or language, available at the present [1981]," and he has called Riffaterre's essays "masterful, witty, learned and altogether enlightened," as well as a source of "considerable pleasure [. . .] " (de Man 18). This encomium, one of the most glowing about Riffaterre's work and one with which many would agree, might however be viewed as self-serving: it comes of course from a critical theorist not only instrumental in drawing deconstructive attention to the problem of the referent-text relationship dear to Riffaterre, but also notorious for the convenience with which that chasm served him and his adherents to argue away the historical referents of his own shameful past.[1] This possibility of self-serving praise on de Man's part highlights as well as anything the specter haunting approaches like his and Riffaterre's: their approaches eschew a text's extratextual referents at the price of being challenged as occultations of the most serious political issues.[2] That specter will hover over the argument to follow, which contends that

Patrick Modiano's *La place de l'étoile* illustrates a tension that binds together what Riffaterre would—at least on apodictic occasion—keep at essential odds with each other, namely a text's mimetic referent and its semiotic transformation into an exclusively symbolic system. As incarnated in Modiano's novel, that transformation will be shown to be unsuccessful in avoiding traces of the referent.

But to begin with, Riffaterrean semiosis cannot avoid the trace of the referent even in its own very conception. That trace can be identified at work behind the logical circularity mentioned in Antoine Compagnon's recent examination of the limits of literary theory, *Le démon de la théorie: littérature et sens commun*, at one point in which he faults Riffaterre's conceptions of referentiality and literary significance:

> L'aporie [. . .] est celle de la littérarité elle-même: comment distinguer en effet le langage poétique, doté de signifiance, du langage ordinaire, pour sa part référentiel? On touche tout de suite à la pétition du principe, car il n'y a pas d'autre critère de l'opposition entre langage ordinaire et langage poétique que, précisément, le postulat de la non-référentialité de la littérature. Le langage poétique est signifiant parce que la littérature n'est pas référentielle, et vice versa. D'où la conclusion quelque peu dogmatique et circulaire à laquelle Riffaterre aboutit: "La référentialité effective n'est jamais pertinente à la signifiance poétique" ([Riffaterre, "L'illusion référentielle"] 118). Circulaire, parce que la signifiance poétique a été elle-même définie par son antagonisme avec la référentialité. (Compagnon 127-28)[3]

The circularity centers on the trace.

However an important, necessary distinction can be made that at first glance might promise to redeem Riffaterre's distinction between the two kinds of language. For example the philosopher Joseph Margolis points out that: "criticism and interpretation require referentially successful discourse [for their own expression]; but providing for that says absolutely nothing about, and sets no significant constraints on (though it does require constraints on), the intrinsic nature of artworks and other cultural entities" (Margolis 241). And the intrinsic nature of literature is based on intentionality, that is, the reader's agreement to "make believe," to suspend practical reference, to read a text as literature. In Margolis's words:

> texts and artworks do not form natural kinds and cannot be identified merely physically or as physical bodies. They differ essentially from natural objects in possessing Intentional [sic] properties. It is, in fact, just in virtue of that, paradigmatically, that texts *are subject to* [adequational and constructive] *inter-pretation* [. . .] . (Margolis 247; emphasis in original)

Similarly, from within a strictly literary context Murray Krieger defines "intentional object" as follows: "an illusion of a single entity created through the complicity of the reader who, sharing the author's habit of seeking closure, allows the work—even as he does his share in creating it—to lead him toward the act of sealing it off within the aesthetic or fictional frame that his perceptual training leads him to impose" (Krieger 89). Of course a variety of other terms could be used to describe the intentional or literary nature of a literary text. Consider for example "literature" as a "functional term" as opposed to an "ontological term" (Eagleton 8).

Up to a point, this view works harmoniously with the crux of Riffaterre's approach to fiction: after one has set one's critical terms and concepts using referential language, and although one discusses the pragmatics of literature (for example identity of an edition, other examples of an author's writing, and so forth) using referential language, within the literature itself analyzed *qua* literature the choice entailed thereby to consider the literary functioning of the language literally forecloses logically simple extratextual referentiality. In more pedestrian terms, if we want to understand systematically what happens when we "make believe" with a literary text, that is, intend the text to be literary, a consistent analysis should focus on the literary "make-believing-ness" of the experience. A study of literary "make-believe," however, even on those terms is not perforce pedestrian. For an introduction to the expression "literary text as prop in a game of make-believe," the latter an expression used in fictional world semantics, one could read Uri Margolin's article, according to which, if we want to argue systematically, we should not consider what happens when in reading literature we uns-ystematically yield to signs that disrupt the "make-believe," that is, the literary intention (Margolin). However, a problem would still arise, were in fact the justification of a Riffaterrean non-referential reading to take refuge in intentional, functional, make-believe properties: Margolis, Krieger, Eagleton, and Margolin say nothing about whether literary lan-guage excludes traces of non-literary uses, and there is no reason to be-lieve that in fact they would argue for exclusion. So in spite of this clarification about the nature of a literary text, Compagnon's objection holds: Riffaterrean semiosis cannot avoid referential traces on at least this count, that it arises from and exists in its resistance to referentiality.

II.   Incorporating Referentiality into Semiosis

But if one can cannot eliminate the trace of the referential under ordinary non-referential reading of fiction, referentially charged circum-stances would a fortiori underscore the phenomenon: *La place de l'étoile*'s numerous historical references include some so powerful that, even after the initial heuristic reading, they offer special resistance to purely aesthetic integration into semiosis. For instance, and as seen in the previous chapter, the novel regularly introduces especially resonant his-torical figures ranging from Captain Dreyfus (*La place de l'étoile* 16 for example) to Maurice Sachs (page 28 for example, the Jewish French writer who, after collaborating with the Germans, was in all likelihood executed by them toward the end of the war [Cima 322]), and it intro-duces historical events ranging from anti-Jewish tendencies in the reign of Saint Louis (page 125 for example) to the Holocaust itself. Regarding the last example, and certainly an especially arresting one, we ask (as Theodor Adorno did regarding poetry) to what extent if any the Holo-caust can be aestheticized by *La place de l'étoile*. To get a sense of how the Holocaust "figures" in Modiano's novel, one can consider the open-ing segment of the last of *La place de l'étoile*'s four chapters, where indi-rect reference is made to Adolph Hitler himself:

> Nous entendîmes tout à coup le bruit d'une jambe de bois qui
> frappait le sol. Un homme s'avançait vers nous, un infirme

monstrueux… Ses yeux étaient phosphorescents, sa mèche et
sa petite moustache luisaient dans l'obscurité. Le rictus de sa
bouche nous fit battre le cœur. Son bras gauche, qu'il tendait,
se terminait par un crochet. Nous nous doutions bien que nous
allions le rencontrer à Vienne. Fatalement. Il portait un uniforme de caporal autrichien pour nous effrayer encore plus. Il
nous menaçait, il hurlait: *"Sechs Millionen Juden! Sechs Millionen Juden!"* (*La place de l'étoile* 146-47)

Since the scene belongs to nightmarish fancy working within a childhood
context (for example *"notre mère nous attendait"* 145), and since the
novel abounds in explicit intertextual references (see Avni 35), the peg
leg and the hook at the end of the left arm combine with the traits of
Adolph Hitler to suggest a "Hitler as Captain Hook." And because of the
childhood preference for movies over books, of such cinematic features
as phosphorescent eyes, and of the novel's references to for instance
Charlie Chaplain and the Marx brothers, the figure harks back more
likely to the Disney movie than to the original Peter Barrie book. But the
aestheticizing impact of a kiddy-movie intertext notwithstanding, surely
this figure screeching *"Sechs Millionen Juden!"* is as referentially
charged as any figure in literature.

However, arguing against Riffaterre from this powerful—some
may say unfairly unrepresentative—example is quite useful because,
evoking starkly the mimetic pole of the mimesis-semiosis tension, even it
can be decoded à la Riffaterre within an exclusively semiotic context for
La place de l'étoile. That is, even "Hitler as Captain Hook" can indeed
readily generate what would appear to be a sign internally adequate to *La
place de l'étoile,* one not requiring an appeal to external reference for
comprehension and aesthetic appreciation. The background necessary to
defend this proposition is situated in the novel's first chapter, where we
had found the interrogation scene exemplifying the novel's considerable
Oedipal charge, a charge that will help to impart a semiotic orientation to
"Hitler as Captain Hook." It will be recalled that in that scene (quoted
above on page 53), Raphaël describes a musical scene from a play that he
had written, in which a strong Nazi son-figure strangles his weak Jewish
father-figure, while the whorish Jewish mother-figure tries to intervene,
with all three figures singing their way through the struggle. The scene's

Oedipal hostility leaps from the text, as argued in the preceding chapter. In light of that passage, the "Hitler as Captain Hook" of the later passage from the fourth chapter could indeed be decoded within the exclusively semiotic context of *La place de l'étoile*. In keeping with this novel's kaleidoscopic reconfiguring of key scenes—and we recall that the kaleidoscope is widely considered this novel's chief metaphor (Nettelbeck and Hueston, *Patrick Modiano* 13)—"Hitler as Captain Hook" can be read as representing a reversal of the power terms suggested by the scene from the play. So "the father-figure, now the Nazi and supremely strong," turns the tables by threatening "the son-figure, now the Jew and supremely weak." Moreover, the evocation of Disney's Captain Hook resonates with the text's Oedipal elements in other, more symbolic, intertextual ways, for instance when we notice that like Oedipus (etymologically "Pierced Foot") this Captain Hook has been wounded in the foot (that is why he has a peg leg), and then when we recall that the plot of the Disney film opens with the question of whether the story-telling mother-figure Wendy will sleep with the children or in the father's section of the house (*Peter Pan*), an Oedipal question consistent with Peter Barrie's original novel.[4] The young man Peter resists the father not only by refusing to grow up and by trying to steal Wendy away, but also by his having cut off the hand of the substitute father-figure, Captain Hook, who of course continues the chain of substitutions by kidnapping Wendy "back," the better to threaten Peter. (Yes, it is indeed striking that in examining yet another intertext at work in *La place de l'étoile* we come across another Peter who, like Peter Schlemihl discussed above, has lost his shadow and who, like Raphaël, undergoes a fraternal split/doubling, in this instance through the Michael/John brother couple who compete with him for Wendy.) And of course Disney's father-figure, son-figure, and mother-figure often sang their way through their subconscious hostilities, as do far more consciously Modiano's corresponding figures in the theatrical scene.

And so, *La place de l'étoile,* by looping this frightening "Austrian corporal" back both to its own distinctive Oedipal confrontation and to those of its *Peter Pan* intertext, makes "Hitler as Captain Hook" function semiotically. Apropos, we should note that because this figure goes unnamed, even "Hitler"—for all its referential pull—remains a referent that is only indirect (insofar as this scene at least is concerned, since the novel does use "Hitler" elsewhere, for example 44), and so offers less purchase to history. Furthermore, "Hitler as Captain Hook" is instantiated by allusion not only to an already literary and cinematic (and so less referential) figure, but also to a highly fanciful literary and cinematic figure of pronouncedly ahistoric play, Captain Hook. And this semiotic functioning—as far as it goes—is as it should be, because that—as far as it goes—is how literature works. As Paul Ricoeur, no controversial critic à la Michael Riffaterre, would put it: "The referent of the text has become a function of the text" (Ricoeur, *Reader* 144). This reading would support the Riffaterrean contention that we can indeed read literary texts and their signs successfully within an exclusively literary frame of reference.

But does the success of this reading encompass as much as it can and should? On the one hand, even the super-charged referentiality of "*Sechs Millionen Juden*" might be argued to fall within the purview of Riffaterrean semiosis and not to require extratextual reference for understanding. That is because, in light of the text's references to Nazi concentration camps (for example 43-44), the "*Sechs Millionen Juden*" could be read to incorporate intratextually the essential point for the reader's understanding of the sign "Hitler," namely that it includes mind-numbing moral monstrosity. On the other hand, just as for historical texts based on massive extratextual reference to the Holocaust, even the simplest reportorial questions of the "who, what, when, where, why, how" of the matter lead only to a sense of compelling need to know ever more, so too it is hard to conceive of any reader—even one theoretically isolated from any historical knowledge of Hitler and the Holocaust—not resisting pure intratextual semiosis because of the unshakeable distraction created by such inevitable questions. "*Sechs Millionem Juden*" cannot *not* raise those questions in a novel that, as we have seen in the Introduction above, constantly compels the reader to sort out the historical from the fictional. Furthermore, Riffaterre maintains that semiosis is not only open to, but also requires, extratextual reference either to "another literary work or a text-like segment of the sociolect" (Riffaterre, "The Interpretant in Literary Semiotics" 41). But if as per Riffaterre's practice words have history of a literary sort (in etymologies, lexical evolution, and intertexts), all of the latter are far from being purely literary, and so they have history, period. So barring essentialist frontiers between literary and non-literary readings (frontiers made all the more problematic in texts like *La place de l'étoile* that satirize historical figures, that is, subject history to overt literary devices), then words have history in referents as well. (On this point, see Dunn 365, MacKenzie 52, Terdiman *Present Past* 192.)

Now, as indicated above, one can—properly—maintain that literary texts and historical texts have intentional properties: there being no difference between the material linguistic nature of literary texts and that of historical texts (consider for example seamless passages cribbed from history by Madame de Lafayette in *La Princesse de Clèves*), one can read a given text either as intending to be primarily literary or as intending to be primarily historical, and as a consequence get either a distinctive literary reading or a distinctive historical reading. (A less quick argument for how the intentionality of such texts guides their reading can be found in Philippe Lejeune's *Le pacte autobiographique*.) But it is precisely the very lack of material linguistic difference in intentional textual objects that keeps extratextual reference unavoidably in play as the reader scans and then recollects all the elements of a text. At the very least, extratextual reference comes into play as a trace lingering in the awareness of even the most disciplined, focused reader confronting the Holocaust, notwithstanding Riffaterre's postulate of a "radical erasure" (Riffaterre, "Undecidability" 110) brought about by the semiosis that bestows literary significance.

In short, then, so undeniably lingering is the referential, historical pull of "*Sechs Millionen Juden*" that the preceding semiotically adequate decoding becomes simply inadequate. Ferdinand Saussure, Emile Benveniste, and Roman Jakobson, even though pioneers of the structuralist inspiration to which Riffaterre is indebted, would doubtless agree with this and with any other more holistic understanding of the workings of literary language. Antoine Compagnon has reminded us (128-29) of the holistic character of the argument made by Jakobson writing famously about what he called linguistic functions, among which are included both the context or referent as well as the message itself, with emphasis on the latter viewed as characterizing language's poetic function but without denying a role to the referent. Jakobson in fact struck a cautionary note about excluding the referent from literature:

Toute tentative de réduire la sphère de la fonction poétique à la poésie, ou de confiner la poésie à la fonction poétique, n'aboutirait qu'à une simplification excessive et trompeuse. La fonction poétique n'est pas la seule fonction de l'art du langage, elle en est seulement la fonction dominante, déterminante, cependant que dans les autres activités verbales elle ne joue qu'un rôle subsidiaire, accessoire. (Jakobson 218)

Ferdinand de Saussure and Emile Benveniste have been shown to have compatible views (Vanoncini 330, note 2). Or to consider the matter from the perspective of effect rather than theoretical structuralist postulates, one can turn to Terence Cave's formulations on the relationship of life to literary texts:

In speaking for [literary texts], we can also, perhaps, in however mediate a form, speak for life, for the untidy, slightly alarming thing that hangs ghost-like in the air beyond the real presence of the text. The theology of such a proposition is suspect, scandalous even; it requires an act of faith beyond the call of critical duty. Yet if the ghost is laid, the superstition quashed, the power of literature must surely go. (Cave 12)

So instead of accepting Riffaterre's pronouncements that semiosis must eventually deny any pertinence to mimetic reference, we should consider a semiosis that would at least incorporate the irrepressible issue of how mimesis or the referent resists complete semiosis. Let us then consider not only the possibility of such a tension-ridden reading, the possibility of an inherent agon between mimesis and semiosis,[5] but also the possibility of that agon being incorporated into the semiosis.

The mimetic and the semiotic can be seen enmeshing each other in *La place de l'étoile* when we consider the context in which we find the Hitler segment introduced above. In the fourth chapter's opening paragraph that introduces the segment we read: "Vienne. Les derniers tramways glissaient dans la nuit. Mariahilfer-Strasse, nous sentions la peur nous gagner. Encore quelques pas et nous nous retrouverions place de la Concorde. Prendre le métro, égrener ce chapelet rassurant: Tuileries, Palais-Royal, Louvre, Châtelet" (*La place de l'étoile* 145). The geographical incoherence created by having a Viennese tramway lead to a Parisian métro will not obviously parse in an initial heuristic, referential reading, and so functions as a Riffaterrean ungrammaticality. But it might seem sensible just to attribute the incoherence to the narrator's psychological delirium, and in that way maintain a purely mimetic, "grammatical" reading. That might be acceptable, were it not for two considerations, the second (in textual sequence) and most categorical of which arises on the last pages of the same chapter 4 and so of the novel. There, as observed in Chapter 1 above, we find Raphaël resisting none other than the master of psychological readers, Herr Freud himself. At the very end Raphaël's text raises the possibility that all along it has in its entirety been "only" an imaginary psychoanalytic session with an imagined Freud, who is portrayed as insisting that Raphaël's narrative should be understood exclusively in terms of psychological dysfunction, that is, in mimetic, referential terms: "vous avez simplement des délires hallucinatoires, des fantasmes, rien de plus, une très légère paranoïa..." (*La place de l'étoile* 213). But Raphaël, we saw above in the preceding chapter, is having none of it, rejecting his own imagined Freud and the latter's psychological, more referential explanations in favor of an explanation both referential *and* literary: he insists that his account be evaluated by a figure called Louis-Ferdinand Bardamu. As seen in Chapter 1 above, that name of course conflates the referential Louis-Ferdinand Destouches, *nom de plume* Céline, the historic author of *Voyage au bout de la nuit*, with that famous novel's narrator Ferdinand Bardamu.

Moreover, there is another consideration (and the first in textual sequence) that opposes a reading of the beginning of the fourth chapter—and with it the Hitler segment—as an exclusively mimetic text. The initially incomplete list of Paris stations on the number 1 métro line (Tuileries ... Châtelet) had merely been suspended, concluding in fact with Raphaël's arrival toward the end of the book at another stop along the same line, la place de l'Étoile, the stop named in the book's title, and so a stop the mention of which brings completion to the novel by circling it back to its beginning. This is one of several indications that the bewildering chapter that initially appears delirious is actually a carefully structured literary artifact, that is, a semiotic device, but one making a fairly explicit point of incorporating referentiality, although only uneasily. Another indication of the uneasy relationship can be found on the second page of the novel's fourth chapter, which peremptorily illustrates the literary engaging the non-literary and holding it in tension, for the repeated list of métro stations metamorphoses this time into a list inclusive both of subway stations passing by in Parisian space and of giants of French literature passing by in literary time: "Tuileries. Palais-Royal. Louvre. Châtelet. L'exquise Mme de Lafayette. Choderlos de Laclos. Benjamin Constant. Ce cher Stendhal" (*La place de l'étoile* 146). To compound the literariness, the authors' names also progressively evoke evolutionary modes of narrating fictional reality that are found in their novels: in Gérard Genette's terms and respectively, heterodiegetic with zero focalisation, homodiegetic with variable internal (epistolary) focalisation, homodiegetic with fixed internal focalisation, and heterodiegetic with variable internal focalisation (see Genette, *Figures III* 206-9, 251-53).

In addition, the overt mimesis-semiosis tension reaches far beyond the scene portraying Hitler as Captain Hook. If it is in puns that language most succinctly and aggressively points to the inherent tension between its ability both to negotiate reference and to turn in on itself self-consciously and thus away from reference, we do well to recall the two-sentence paratextual pun that opens *La place de l'étoile* and that plays on the doubly sylleptic expression "place/place de l'étoile/Étoile," and so that infiltrates retroactively the title itself, an important agent of semiosis for the text. As explained above in Chapter 1, the pun's first sentence starts off with the most arresting referentiality for an informed French reader by mentioning June 1942. The first sentence's concluding question, moreover, asks for directions to la place de l'Étoile, the site of the Arc de Triomphe, an actual monument not only *of* history like the Louvre or Palais Royal, but also a monument explicitly *to* history, a monument whose *raison d'être* itself is history. But for all that, within the context of a Riffaterrean approach one plays down the allusion to dreadful history in an effort to reach necessary semiosis, trying to avoid highly variable, idiosyncratic reactions to the extremely charged reference. Semiotic focus may waver with the first sentence, then, but it prevails in the second and concluding sentence, because it is there that the pun itself, the play of language, closes and gives significance to the text. All successful puns work as self-referring artifices that highlight verbal play at the expense of any fixed referentiality, as does this one. So at the conclusion of the pun itself, semiotic considerations seem to carry the day decisively against referentiality. Countering that decisiveness, however, the next (paratextual?) line characterizes the pun as "(*Histoire juive*)." The pointed ambivalence at the heart of the French word "*histoire*"— "history" or "story"?—plunges the reader back into the issue of historic referentiality versus storied semiosis.

In keeping with that very ambivalence, retrospection suggests that the pun itself includes unnecessary historicity. Although piquant and resonant, the specific historic details ("*un officier allemand*" instead of for example "*un touriste étranger*" or "*un touriste*") seem at odds with what one would expect a pun to focus on, pure verbal play: would the word play not occur quite successfully and perhaps more cleanly with less specific historical allusions? So on the one hand the pun as it progresses sets up the reader to break away from referentiality, onto the terrain of its own ludic textuality; on the other hand, the initial impact of such detailed, powerful, and theoretically superfluous referentiality in the pun's opening sentence, while superceded, will be forgotten or denied only with difficulty, and not at all in the final word "*histoire*."[6]

For another and more important problem, the reader (or this reader at least) is left with insistent, profound unease at the thought of punning on the language of the Holocaust. It makes aestheticizing semiosis seem somehow indecent. If, however, the reader is not focusing on rejecting extratextual referentiality in favor of semiosis, it becomes easier to try to recuperate into the latter the former *as another element of semiosis*, using for example the terms of the matrix proposed in the chapter above. It will be recalled that the matrix involved a rootless French Jewish writer's guilt at being obliged to use the racism-tainted French language. That matrix can be seen to generate still another materialization, this time on a more autofictional level in a Jewish French novelist's dilemma when incorporating into his text historical references to French contributions to the Holocaust. The adequate representation of them being impossible, the writer produces "only literature," an artifact at least as woefully inadequate to its referents as an historical document would be, but all the more inadequate and even guilty because it absorbs into its aesthetic play words that yearn to capture monumentally horrible events that have absolutely nothing playful about them. So the "indecency" of the pun on the words "*place de l'*étoile" would be a proleptic Riffaterrean expansion[7] of the guilty use of language in the matrix.

Furthermore, we should recall that, beyond the title, the entire novel is choked with what can only be called an intentional hash of proper names (see Introduction) that leaves the reader no choice except to deal repeatedly (and often unsuccessfully) with the difficulty of trying to identify which names are purely imaginary, which historical, and which a cross between the two. In negotiating the simplest reading of the text, then, on page after page one cannot help but stumble over and over on the problem of referentiality in literature and the problem of literariness in history. Instead of the names' losing to literary significance their possible sociolexical meaning, in their sheer number and semantic uncertainty they repeatedly call attention to precisely the difficulty in determining those meanings. The fact that some of the names refers to moral monsters of history only intensifies the issue.

Consequently, comparing the preceding reading with Riffaterre's *dicta* that mimesis has no place in the transformative moments when literature signifies, that is, no place in semiosis, one can maintain that a Riffaterrean reading mindful only of the *dicta* does not do justice to the enduring post-heuristic tension between the referential and the semiotic that is clearly and variously expressed in Modiano's text. If a close consideration of language shows it to reflect inherently an unstable medium between us and direct contact with reality per se (unstable because, for one reason, the rapport itself appears to shift under scrutiny), one should in fact expect as well a literary text—a text allowing language most fully to explore itself—to address that barrier. So *La place de l'étoile* does.

Moreover, *La place de l'étoile*'s conflation of the silly, the nightmarish, the intertextual, and the historical in a Hitler as Disneyesque Captain Hook can be read to prompt a richer, tension-ridden version of semiosis that has a variety of thematic implications. For example, the striking image of Hitler in Modiano's text can with semiotic profit invite the reader into reflections on Hitler *qua* image, on Hitler the historical orator and politician appearing as image in documentary films and photographs, and imagined as image in various kinds of texts. Such reflections on Hitler as image are of a piece with the idea implied by, indeed incarnated in, Raphaël's portrait of him: Hitler had always in fact been an image of the sort expected of a consummate showman, one as compelling and constructed as any of Disney's. But the destructive impact of this particular showman has been so massive and mind-boggling that any attempt to capture his reality verbally must ultimately seem reductive to the point of veering toward what the reader in fact finds in *La place de l'étoile*, namely a cartoonish yet nightmarish caricature. So by means of this, *La place de l'étoile*'s most Hitlerish "Hitler"—the hallucinatory one screeching "*Sechs Millionen Juden!*"—Modiano communicates, indeed "semioticizes," forcefully and memorably the banal truth of language's poverty before reality. In other words, language's referential inadequacy can be seen to function as an element within this novel's semiosis.

Furthermore Hitler as image is but an element of this novel's dominant and larger theme of the power of image. That theme is most notably exemplified in the novel's saucy but enraged exaggeration of stereotypes of the Jew, for instance: "je proclamais inlassablement ma juiverie. D'ailleurs, mes faits et gestes allaient à l'encontre des vertus que l'on cultive chez les Français: la discrétion, l'économie, le travail. J'ai, de mes ancêtres orientaux, l'œil noir, le goût de l'exhibitionnisme et du faste, l'incurable paresse" (*La place de l'étoile* 17). The theme is anchored in the novel's references to for example Céline, Robert Brasillach, and Drieu la Rochelle, gifted writers who lent considerable literary power to stereotypical images that strengthened the ideological forces behind the Holocaust. Furthermore and quite apropos of this chapter's general argument, such is the tangle of history and literature that, as we read in Modiano's extended and reverential interview of the French journalist, writer, and intellectual Emmanuel Berl (1892-1976), literature not only imitates history, but there is no reason not to believe that it can also have an impact on history. Berl properly speculated about the impact of the anti-Semitic strain in the influential literature of the gifted writer Céline:

> Le plaisir de la parole ou de l'écriture n'excuse pas ce que ça peut, à ce moment-là, avoir de criminel. A Céline, naturellement, je suis prêt à pardonner. Mais, il y a peut-être eu des gens qui ont fait des dénonciations, qui sont coupables de la mort de juifs, et qui l'ont fait après avoir lu Céline—ils ne l'auraient pas fait sans lui. (Berl 128)

In short, and to begin sketching a broader conceptual horizon as a conclusion for this section, one of the shortcomings to be found in

Riffaterre's approach is that it usually does not take into consistent account what *La place de l'étoile* portrays as the unavoidable and lingering tension between semiosis and mimesis, in this argument's example the unavoidable tension between a novelistic Hitler and the Hitler of the Holocaust of history, or if we extrapolate to art in general, the unavoidable tension between the aesthetic and the political. A comment on the postmodern by Thomas Docherty seconds the point with an observation encompassing the postmodern in general, not just postmodern literature. Maintaining that the postmodern has been marked by a tension between a concern with the past-influenced present and a quasi-Nietzschean "actively forgetful" futurity, Docherty finds that that surface tension points to an:

> underlying tension between an attitude to postmodernism as an aesthetic style and postmodernity as a political and cultural reality; that is, it opens a question which had been debated before, on the proper relation between aesthetics and politics. The particular intimacy of the relation between the aesthetic and the political under the rubric of the postmodern is apparent even from the earliest engagements. (Docherty, "Postmodernism" 2-3; see Spanos for the same point regarding postmodern fiction.)

Much critical opinion has it, of course, that Modiano's work reflects the postmodern.

But Riffaterre, an exceptionally talented critic and theoretician who has long been fighting the worthy fight against naïve literary referentiality, has not worked thoroughly into his theory his own practical recognition of such tension, and specifically the tension between semiosis and mimesis (or as above p. 92, "double reading" or "double meaning"), a tension that, moreover, can be found *within* semiosis. In fairness, we need to recall once again that Riffaterre has sometimes argued against tension-free reading and has pointed to the enduring instability of texts. Asked in an interview about the advance of his theory of intertextuality over that of Yuri Lotman and Mikhail Bakhtin, he locates it:

> in the concept of mobility, of a constantly changing perception
> of the text which explains why a text never ceases to be active:
> the fact that a reader can never verify his interpretation, his
> perception of "significance" without rereading at the level of
> "meaning," a process that exposes him again to the same diffi-
> culties he encountered at first, to the same incompatibilities
> between the sociolect and text's idiolect that can be solved
> only at the level of significance. (Riffaterre, "Text" 116-17)

But at the end of the same interview, Riffaterre himself reintroduces the
principal problem about his theory when he asserts: "Texts are built so as
to be fully read, even though they may not lead us to this readily" (118).
In spite of the cautionary expression "not . . . readily," the totalizing
words "fully read," like his frequent expression "necessary reading," imply a textual univocity and fixity that strain against this less characteristic
assertion of textual "mobility." One may even wonder whether in his
case the tension within semiosis, a tension that he has slighted, is not
making subterranean protest via the tension in his pronouncements on the
mimesis-semiosis relationship.

Naturally, the topic of referential tension in literature extends
beyond a study of *La place de l'étoile,* and it merits general attention,
among other reasons because of what can be considered a common but
mistaken working assumption often made by teachers/scholars of literature in the heat of the professional fray: in discussions about the nature
and extent of referentiality in literature—as in discussions about the nature and extent of referentiality in language itself—one too frequently
presupposes an unassailable base-line experience of the very referential
reality by which to refute or support the referentiality of literature and/or
language. But Plato, it should be recalled—Plato, to whom the Western
philosophical tradition has been described by Alfred North Whitehead as
a series of footnotes (Whitehead 39)—found our experience of reality
itself problematic. So this section will conclude by recalling that the very
ground on which many of us resist or maintain referentiality in literature
and language has less referential certainty than usually presupposed, that
our confidence either way regarding referentiality in literature and language stands on uncertain terrain.[8] And is an awareness of that uncertainty not one of the artistically communicated effects of the métro

passage from Modiano's *La place de l'étoile?* Moreover, under the epistemological scrutiny prompted characteristically by postmodernist texts such as his, does the play between the presumably real referent and the textual imaginary not leave us teetering on referential ambiguity? This seems all the more likely, since there is ample critical opinion maintaining that ambiguity in fact constitutes a theme central to Modiano's entire oeuvre (see Morris *Patrick Modiano* [Berg], Bedner "Présentation," and Martine Guyot-Bender's and William VanderWolk's collection of essays, for which ambiguity set in the context of memory becomes an organizing concept). And in literature do the referent and the textual imaginary not shift back and forth toward each other without ever decisively fusing with or leaving each other? Is that movement not captured in the Parisian métro scene whose station stops shift toward remembered monuments of French literature only ultimately to return to the place de l'Étoile métro stop in Paris that is also the novel's title? Is such movement also not felt as a highly imaginative phosphorescent figure out of kiddy fiction shifts toward, without fusing with, an all too historic murderer of six million Jews, just as the novel's potpourri of proper names teeters between the referential and the fanciful? Appropriately—and to bring the argument about referentiality in *La place de l'étoile* back to its textual illustration—the peg-legged historical/fanciful "Hitler as Captain Hook" advances only by teetering between a "real" leg and a "fabricated" wooden leg, a teetering between the hypnotic lure of mimetic reproduction and the aesthetic experience of literary semiosis.

So in *La place de l'étoile* Modiano got the problem right in his unstable version of the back-and-forth of semiosis-mimesis,[9] and of the back-and-forth of literature and politics, especially of literature and the Holocaust.[10] And in so doing, he made his novel what could be called "just another footnote" to the first great modern novel, *Don Quixote,* the subject of which is a reader taken in by the referential power of outrageously literary romances and pastorals, even as *Quixote*'s reader is taken in by the referential power of the outrageously literary Don Quixote, a character—we should note—set in the political context of one of the many dress rehearsals for the Holocaust, the Spanish intolerance of Muslims and Jews, and the subsequent Inquisition.

III. The Aestheticizing Intertext

Just as the problem of extratextual literary reference has echoes far beyond just *La place de l'étoile,* the Riffaterrean preoccupation with resistance to such reference has echoes elsewhere, for example insofar as it can be seen as part of a general inclination going back at least as far as Kant to isolate aesthetic practice from so-called "real-world" issues such as politics and ethics (Erkkila 41-43). Such aestheticization presided over the very inception of the genre so central to the subtext of *La place de l'étoile* and thus to Modiano's oeuvre, namely the detective story. So now, as we did with Chamisso's *Peter Schlemihls wundersame Geschichte,* we will set out on an extended intertextual detour, this time to consider the foundational detective stories of Edgar Allan Poe. One objective will be to show again the rich pertinence of a Riffaterrean approach to *La place de l'étoile,* insofar as the aestheticizing insistence of this critic lines up well with the aestheticizing impulse of the detective story genre, the genre that yields the interrogation subtext of Modiano's novel. Moreover, Poe's ideology and texts will be shown to work as agents of repression, an impulse argued in the preceding chapter to explain the dynamics behind the figure of the Self/Brother of *La place de l'étoile.*

Poe, widely recognized as the founder of the detective-story genre (Dupuy 17), at the same time wrote pieces such as "The Poetic Principle," whose "notions of supernal Beauty, art for art's sake, pure poetry and poetic craft have played [a constitutive role] both nationally and internationally, in the emergence of nineteenth-century aestheticism, New Critical formalism, postmodern textuality" (Erkkila 44-45), and, I would specify, contemporary literary semiotics. So Poe wrote the three Dupin detective stories not only as the racist that we will see him to be, typical of nineteenth-century America, but as a racist emphasizing:

> what he calls "radical and chasmal differences between the truthful and the poetical modes of inculcation" (*Works* 14:272), [and whose] desire to distinguish and differentiate the aesthetic as a separate realm of activity, participates in, even as it seeks to surmount, an emergent scientific discourse of racial difference, purity, and distinction that grounds both

modern "white" subjectivity and Western aestheticism.
(Erkkila 66)

Consequently, two of Poe's founding detective stories, although owing a great deal to his and America's history of racism, repress those historic and political facts in a seductive aestheticism. Moreover and as we shall see, many famous critics have testified indirectly to the repressive power of Poe's texts by becoming dupes of, and participants in, the repression.

That Poe the man was a racist,[11] there can be little doubt. In his *The Narrative of Arthur Gordon Pym*:

> Pym is so outraged at the duplicity and savagery of the [black Antarctic] islanders (they pretend to befriend the party of white explorers whilst in reality scheming their massacre) that he condemns them as "among the most barbarous, subtle and bloodthirsty wretches that ever contaminated the face of the globe." Critics have seen in this and similar passages evidence that Poe was deliberately playing on Southern hysteria by suggesting that negroes [sic] were in reality a treacherous and hostile people; seen in these terms the concluding chapters are said to be an elaborate allegory on racial inequality and intolerance. (Hammond 123; see Beaver for an extensive treatment of *Pym* as racist allegory.)

Less egregious examples of Poe's racist pathology also thread their way throughout his oeuvre, as Toni Morrison mentions in her analysis of the studied absence of Afro-Americans in early American literature:

> It could never have occurred to Edgar Allan Poe in 1848 that I, for example, might read *The Gold Bug* and watch his efforts to render my grandfather's speech as something as close to braying as possible, an effort so intense you can see the perspiration—and the stupidity—when Jupiter says "I knows," and Mr. Poe spells the verb "nose." (Morrison 13-14)

Regarding Poe's romance pieces specifically, Joan Dayan has argued that they are inextricably bound with slavery and its radical dehumanization

("Romance and Race"). Similarly but apropos this time of Poe's detective fiction, Jon Thompson wrote that Poe's Auguste Dupin, appropriately titled "Chevalier," incarnates a romanticized ideology of rationalism that projects the aristocratic ideals of the antebellum South, ideals that assume racism of course (J. Thompson 48). That proposition harmonized with John Carlos Rowe's argument concerning Poe's entire oeuvre, that the writer's aristocratic notions "are finely interwoven into the fabric of his art" along with his sexism as well as his racism (Rowe 118).

To be sure, Poe's racism was consistent with his times. In a sobering study of Poe's "average racism" for his time, Terence Whalen reminds us that nineteenth-century America fought with itself not over the question of racism—in "dueling racisms" both abolitionists and slavers entertained demeaning racial stereotypes regarding slaves (Whalen 33)—but rather "just" over the question of slavery. That unfortunate distinction serves to underscore the extent to which Poe's work is coextensive with issues of his day. Roger Forclaz's book-length study *Le monde d'Edgar Poe* has amply demonstrated how much Poe's work was a product of his milieu, incorporating as it does more than that of any other American writer of his times popular topics such as exploration, travel in hot-air balloons, melancholia, consumption, being buried alive, and so forth. Consequently, one simply cannot read with adequate understanding, for example, many of Poe's stories of political satire, unless one draws upon knowledge of events contemporaneous with composition, and unless one keeps in mind how rabidly elitist and anti-democratic Poe was.[12] A good example of that occurs in "The Man Who Was Used Up," the eponymous General Smith being an imaginary vehicle to ridicule the often wounded and former officer, Vice-President Richard M. Johnson, Andrew Jackson's running mate (see Levine 438 and following pages). More pertinently to my argument, apropos of "The Murders in the Rue Morgue" which was first published in Philadelphia in 1841, Elise Lemire has documented how Poe's stay there from 1838 to 1844 probably intimated to him the major points of his story, namely the brutal violation and killing of white women in their bedroom by a powerful "ape" imitating his white master with a razor blade. She centers her argument on the Philadelphia race riots of 1838 that had been fed by notions of the conflation of Blacks with simians, especially orangutans, in strength, violence, and sexual hunger, by rage at thoughts of racial intermarriage, and by resentment of free Black entrepreneurship, the chief instrument of which was the barber's razor blade. The point, of course, is not the possible "sources" of Poe's story, but rather its subtle manipulation of reader reception by means of inflammatory, effective, but for all that, inexplicit allusions to history.

Nonetheless, in spite both of the incontestable and distinctive anchoring in his milieu both of Poe's works and of their reading, up until very recently[13] Poe's general critical reception would have him suspended outside of time and space (Forclaz 121). This is no accident. In fact, it represents a view with which Poe himself would probably have felt comfortable, since his insistence on "the poem per se" can serve as a prelude to contemporary textual, ahistorical criticism (Carlson 9). If one understands Poe's idea of Truth to tend to synonymy with history and referentiality, then as we saw at the beginning of this section, his "The Poetic Principle" adumbrates structuralist and poststructuralist principles:

> The demands of Truth are severe. She has no sympathy with the myrtles. All *that* which is so indispensable in Song is precisely all *that* with which *she* has nothing whatever to do [. . .]. *He* must be blind indeed who does not perceive the radical and chasmal differences between the truthful and the poetical modes of inculcation. He must be theory-mad beyond redemption who, in spite of these differences, shall still persist in attempting to reconcile the obstinate oils and waters of Poetry and Truth. (Poe, *Essays and Reviews* 76; emphasis in the original)

But for our understanding of repression at work in Poe's detective stories, even more important than Poe's critical reception and his own critical attitudes is the aestheticizing thrust of his detective stories themselves that repress the question of slavery. To begin with, the reader never "sees" the apparent subjects of the stories, the orangutan of "The Murders in the Rue Morgue," Marie Rogêt of the eponymous story, or the letter of "The Purloined Letter." We remain always at least one narrative remove from them because Dupin's method consists primarily of analyzing, not events, but texts and stories about events. As a result, the diegesis of actions in time and space gets swallowed up in the diegesis of analysis and in fact in the diegesis of the narration of analysis. That constitutes of course the tales' clear legacy to the detective story genre, what Todorov termed the "second story," the larger story of the inquiry after the crime. But the tales doubtless owe much of the impact that they had precisely to their exaggerated aestheticization. David Van Leer has drawn from the structure of Poe's tales the epistemological conclusion that: "The real interest in these tales is not who (or what) done it but what 'truth' and 'world' are, how they may be reconstructed, and what follows from that construction." Van Leer buttresses that conclusion with the following observation: "The fractured chronology of all three narratives shifts attention from the evidence to the manner of its discovery and interpretation, and general philosophical discussions both frame the narratives and interrupt (at times overwhelm) Dupin's explication of the crimes" (Van Leer 66-67). Earlier, Jacques Derrida of course had famously laid out another aestheticizing tactic of "The Purloined Letter." Pointing out that the trilogy begins in a library, Derrida quotes extensively from the opening pages of the third tale in order to elaborate that:

> Thus everything "begins" by obscuring this opening in "silence," the "smoke" and the "dark" of the library. The casual observer sees only the smoking meerschaum: in short, a literary setting, the ornamental frame of a story. On this border, negligible for the interpreter interested in the center of the painting and the interior of representation, it was already possible to read that the whole thing was a matter of writing, and of writing off its course, in a writing-space unboundedly open to grafting onto other writing, and that this matter of writing, the third of a series in which the "coincidence" between the first two is noticeable, breaks suddenly into the text with its first word "au troisième, No. 33. Rue Dunôt [...]". (Derrida, "The Purveyor" 102)

One of the principal effects of all these aestheticizing moves is of course to repress history. That effect is in keeping with the very locale of the three tales. The texts take barely disguised refuge in an ahistorical environment, an abstract, distorted "Paris" of misspelled French names and nonexistent geography, a "Paris" whose signified is less "a French historic place *at which*" and much more "a *refuge from* American historic placing," where narratives of ratiocination can reign with less risk of intrusions from messier, more troublesome narratives of history. Furthermore, Laura Saltz has shown how an inclination to repression thoroughly in-forms "The Mystery of Marie Rogêt." Based on the (at first) mysterious (apparent) murder of a young New Yorker, Mary Rogers, Poe's inconclusive, bewildering story—rewritten as more (and more correct) information followed the start of the writing—turns out to have in fact been about a botched abortion, a fact not directly acknowledged (that is, it was repressed) by the final version of the text:

> The buried abortion serves as a literary site for Poe's inquest into the related problematics of privacy and publicity, self and self-authorship—issues that are raised historically and existentially by controversies surrounding abortion in the 1840s. Poe conceals Marie's "concealment," consigning her terminated pregnancy to a narrative absence, a hidden realm inhabited by secret forms of sexual knowledge. Such knowledge is the unspoken subject of Dupin's ratiocinative investigations. In this view, the evasions and concealments of "Marie Rogêt" are not its flaws, but its structure and obsession. (Saltz 239-40)

From the three tales taken as a whole, moreover, Barbara Johnson has come away with a compatible impression, finding in their "digressiveness" a suggestion that the "true subject" is always being purloined, repressed (Johnson 110-11).

But history will out, even in literature. For Poe's three texts, it will do so in seemingly incidental details. For example, the would-be ahistorical "Purloined Letter," whose removal from history produces the entry "18--" in its first paragraph, is "still penetrated by history, for this date *follows* the French Revolution in a text that plays with the threat posed to the monarchy by a message stolen by a minister of state" (Rowe 123). More pertinently to the nature of the current discussion, history will out in its intertexts. Unless one takes an essentialist position on literary narrative, whereby the latter seals off absolutely its effects, dynamics, and interactions from other, putative "non-literary" kinds of narratives, literature can incorporate referents whose referential power strains against literariness. As was argued above regarding *La place de l'étoile,* one such narrative for contemporary Jewish writers would be the Holocaust. So too for a nineteenth-century apologist for American slavery—such as Poe—a similar narrative would be that earlier, other Holocaust, the original sin of the USA, which I am suggesting insists on being an intertext of much of Poe's fiction in spite of his detective stories' repressive tendencies. So in "The Murders in the Rue Morgue" for instance, the orangutan—etymologically in Malay "a human being of the forest"—can only "ape" civilized behavior in its efforts to be like its master; it needs to be strictly controlled and isolated for its own and society's well-being; and it savagely violates innocent white women when it is not so controlled. Such a character in the fiction of a defender of the USA's "peculiar institution" needs to be read as part of a still all too dynamic American racial intertext, if it is to be viewed in its semiotic richness.[14]

The opposition in "Rue Morgue" between on the one hand the orangutan (material and savage body) that decapitates, and on the other hand Dupin (spiritual and noble Reason) who glorifies the head, has been obvious enough. Only recently, however, have some critics started to argue a point that seems only a little less obvious, that American racism has articulated precisely that opposition in the polar terms of so called black and white races (see Rowe 128). That fuller opposition should have long been part of a general reading of "The Murders in the Rue Morgue," a reading attentive to the story's "ineluctable co-implication of Reason and race" (Barrett 164). But that had not been the case, the role of racism in Poe's stories having instead fallen into a telling critical gap.

That gap regarding Poe's racism surely owes a great deal to the general literary and critical gap regarding Afro-Americans so articulately exposed by Toni Morrison:

> We can agree, I think, that invisible things are not necessarily "not-there"; that a void may be empty, but is not a vacuum. In addition, certain absences are so stressed, so ornate, so planned, they call attention to themselves; arrest us with intentionality and purpose, like neighborhoods that are defined by the population held away from them. Looking at the scope of American literature, I can't help thinking that the question

should never have been "Why am I, an Afro-American, absent from it?" It is not a particularly interesting query anyway. The spectacularly interesting question is "What intellectual feats had to be performed by the author or his critic to erase me from a society seething with my presence, and what effect has that performance had on the work?" (Morrison 11-12)

But even when one leaves the realm of extratextual considerations and comes to more clearly and exclusively literary intertexts of Poe's detective tales, Poe criticism has shown remarkable resistance to the fairly obvious, if race is involved. For instance, one of the favorite fictions of period white readers being the "tragic mulatto" or "octoroon mistress," in 1838 (seven years before writing "The Purloined Letter") Poe may well have written a story with the borrowed premise of a woman "passing for white": "In 'Ligeia,' Poe signals [for the eponymous character] the same physiognomic traits as did taxonomists of color in the Caribbean and the South: hair, eyes, and skin" (Dayan, "Amorous Bondage" 130). Fictional white ladies, like the queen of "The Purloined Letter," sometimes had a secret to hide, an unspeakable and unspoken secret whose contaminating essence risked subverting all accepted sociopolitical structures. The secret of both fictional heroines was of course that of the United States themselves, namely that they were not as white as they had claimed themselves to be. By this reading of "The Purloined Letter," the movement of the letter-signifier brilliantly observed by Lacan also "purloins" out in the open even politics as signifier—politics, the very subject without which the story's monarchy-defending plot has no *raison d'être*. Once one entertains the possibility that the queen can be viewed as the borrowed figure of the mulatto trying to "pass for white," that is, once one recognizes in Poe's text still another example of the parallel and associative conditions of dependency, inferiority, and vulnerability routinely ascribed in nineteenth-century American fiction to women and African-Americans, one can then catch in the repressive aestheticizing tale overtones of its nonetheless penetrating if systematically muted racist melody. That melody contributes to the tale's compelling thematic dance of textual absence selectively dealt with in Poe criticism. Even the highly poetic "The Raven" is susceptible to a reading thickened by the subject of racism. Within the context of the Republic's original sin, the bird—black, seeking escape, forced into the poet's little room by a raging storm outside—more than suggests the situation of enslaved Americans of the middle of the nineteenth century. In such a reading, the third from last stanza, the polysemic "nevermore" takes on a meaning hardly intended by Poe, we can be certain, but more than possibly sensed by him and many others, a portent of spiritual doom:

> "Prophet!" said I, "thing of evil!—prophet still, if bird or devil!
> By that Heaven that bends above us—by that God we both adore—
> Tell this soul with sorrow laden if, within the distant Aidenn,
> It shall clasp a sainted maiden whom the angels name Lenore."
>   Quoth the Raven "Nevermore."

(See Erkkila, 60-67, for an extended analysis of "The Raven" in light of the socio-historical traumas of Poe's time.)

This critical repression of vital intertexts has not gone unobserved. Derrida himself has insisted on the need to see Poe's detective stories in the light of all their various intertexts, but he did not address Poe's racial intertexts himself. He reproached the most famous translation of Poe's stories into French, Charles Baudelaire's, and more pointedly the most famous French explication of "The Purloined Letter," Lacan's psychoanalytic masterpiece, for having failed to acknowledge what Derrida called below "framing," which would include intertextual play among the three tales:

> These reminders [of how Baudelaire's mistranslations obscured some of the interconnections among the three tales themselves], of which countless other examples could be given, make us aware of the effects of the frame, and of the paradoxes in the parergonal logic. Our purpose is not to prove that "The Purloined Letter" functions within a frame (omitted by the Seminar, which can thus be assured of its triangular interior by an active, surreptitious limitation starting with a metalinguistic overhand), but to prove that the structure of the framing effects is such that no totalization of the border is even possible. The frames are always framed: thus by some of their content. Pieces without a whole, "divisions" without a

totality—this is what thwarts the dream of a letter without division, allergic to division. From this point on, the seme "phallus" is errant, begins by dis-seminating, not even by *being* disseminated. (Derrida, "The Purveyor" 99; original emphasis)

So my purpose is not at all to suggest that historic and literary intertexts of American racism and slavery constitute the tales' final frame. Rather, as Lindon Barrett has put the matter apropos of "The Murders in the Rue Morgue":

> Emphatically, the contention here is not that "The Murders in the Rue Morgue" is about U.S. slavery or in any way *directly* about the position of Africans and African descendents in U.S. society. The point is that the "materiality of history," to borrow the phrase of John Carlos Rowe, directly impinges on the narrative by characterizing its exposition and celebration of extraordinary reason in widespread (international) racist formulations [by for example Emmanuel Kant and Georges Cuvier] proposing subordinate evolutionary, social, and intellectual positions to nonwhite peoples. Mental apprehension of the offending orangutan in many ways supplants the need for open declarations about race, or might in itself signal such a declaration. No dark-skinned person or persons need be singled out as guilty, and the reference to Cuvier [in the story as the dramatic factor revealing the identity of the killer] subtly and with calculated verisimilitude substantiates this knowledge. (Barrett 170; emphasis in the original)

My contention is both that historic and literary intertexts can readily barge into the tales' textual play, and that those intertexts *should* have more readily entered critical discussion of the tales, given Poe's racism in so much of his writing both fictional and non-fictional. From an intertextually comprehensive point of view open to historical narratives, they certainly should have been more available to discussion, as Joan Dayan has carefully documented. First of all, in the years before Poe started the Dupin series in 1844, he had been preoccupied with the 1831-32 Jamaican rebellion and the 1831 rebellion of Nat Turner

(Dayan, "Romance and Race" 97), whose deadly use of the broad ax finds a distinct echo in the orangutan's murderous slashing. Secondly, Edward Long, the pro-slavery historian whose work Poe had read and for which he either wrote or edited a favorable review, had propounded an analogy between African slaves and orangutans: "What is most striking and of course most infamous in Long's meditation [on the gamut of being from matter to spirit] is that the word *negro* calls up a disturbingly minute analysis of body parts and gradations of being, until finally he draws an analogy between the negro and the orangutan" (Dayan, "Amorous Bondage" 113). Moreover, Long had linked the two luridly, to the slaves' disadvantage:

> Edward Long discussed at length the "courteous, tender disposition" of the orangutan, debasing black women in the process. Long tells his readers that orangutans "sometimes endeavour to surprize and carry off negroe women into their woody retreats." He then turns to these negroes [sic], to whom he grants not a trace of affectionate feeling, describing them as "libidinous and shameless as monkies, or baboons" (II 360, 364, 361)." (Dayan, "Amorous Bondage" 119)

Even from an intertextually more restricted point of view that would prefer to consider not historical texts but only Poe's literary production, another text by Poe, "Hop-Frog," involves orangutans as human beings, moreover in a situation no less grizzly than that of "Rue Morgue." In the tale, an outraged dwarf, after persuading an abusive king and his seven ministers to let themselves be disguised as orangutans by means of tar and flax and then be chained, kills them by setting them on fire. And yet, to my knowledge, few if any of the very famous explicators of Poe have been open to these historical and literary intertexts, and as Claude Richard's list of those critical giants shows, the explicators (Poulet, Bachelard, Ricardou, Todorov, Genette, Barthes, Lacan, and Derrida [Richard 1]) comprise a Who's Who of structuralist and poststructuralist critics: "In the history of Poe criticism, however, as in T. S. Eliot's *From Poe to Valéry*, the French response to Poe has served as a kind of aesthetic purifier, cleansing Poe's face of the marks of race and history to save him for the transcendence of art" (Erkkila 69). The point becomes even more intriguing in light of Uri Eisenzweig's position, based on an observation by Frank Kermode, that the detective story is inherently racist (Eisenzweig 243 and following pages).

Several conclusions can be drawn from this consideration of Poe's detective stories. In respect to the way in which the latter are read, we can concur with critics such as John Carlos Rowe that until recently too much Poe criticism repressed significant historical racial intertexts, a tendency in conformity with the aestheticizing tendencies both of Poe himself and of his detective stories. It appears, then, that aestheticizing repression has been at work both at the very inception of, and in the critical reception of, the detective-story genre. The repressive quality of the critical reception has been especially noteworthy in France, and so it is that quality to which Modiano and the literary world that formed him were presumably exposed.

In respect to the literary legacy of the detective stories as it impacts *La place de l'étoile,* we can see how the interrogation subtext and the entire novel that it guides (the two of which borrow the basic narrative structure of the detective story of analysis) do not borrow merely the preoccupation with interrogation. They also borrow the extreme repression characterizing the telling and reading of Poe's tales, in their resistance to divulging even their own questions, as well as to divulging the crime guiltily driving both the subtext and the novel, the death of the Brother. This helps to explain further how *La place de l'étoile,* and indeed Modiano's entire oeuvre, remain at war with themselves, as on the one hand and in their indirect debt to Poe they repress the memory of the crime against the Brother (a sibling tale that resonates with the story both of the Afro-American Holocaust and of the Jewish Holocaust), while fighting on the other hand the repression of memories of racism, like that of Poe's detective tales and many of their critics. In that regard, it helps to recall that through intermediaries Modiano borrowed on the one hand from Poe's founding, aestheticizing detective stories, but on the other, quite different hand Modiano borrowed more directly from the hard-boiled versions of the detective story such as Hammett's stories. The latter let loose the "gorilla" in the guise of the "hard-boiled detective" who wars against aestheticization by anchoring the text in the sociolect with its stories of the socio-political violence of urban graft, Prohibition, the Depression, and so forth.

IV. Human Awareness Functioning Variously: The Historic, the Aesthetic, and the Moral

Reading *La place de l'étoile* à la Riffaterre, one sees how Adelbert von Chamisso's *Peter Schlemihls wundersame Geschichte* acting as primary intertext, and how the interrogation scene acting as subtext, work as unconscious agents helping to give organicity to the difficult text. Modiano's baffling novel can then be parsed semiotically as a verbal construct in which the sememes of rootlessness, guilt, and artistic yearning fuse in its matrix. What fuses them is a Jewish-French writer's/narrator's dealing in post-Holocaust France with his repressed anxieties over fraternal murder-suicide enacted linguistically and historically on both personal and mass scales.

However, if one reads *La place de l'étoile* in a Riffaterrean way more practical than rigorously theoretical, that is, in a way more open to referentiality straining against literariness, the result is an even richer semiosis. Moreover, powerful references to French collaboration with the Holocaust and to historical figures that were involved, for instance Adolph Hitler, not only enrich a semiotic reading of *La place de l'étoile*, they also seem inevitably to invoke the moral vista against which the politics and history played themselves out. Certainly that is the impression testified to by sophisticated readers of various backgrounds and interests, such as Martine Guyot-Bender and Myriam Ruszniewski-Dahan (see the Introduction). For another instance Gerald Prince, persuaded that "[t]hrough memory, with all its tricks and traps and uncertainties, the past refuses to be left alone" in Modiano's texts (Prince, "Re-Membering Modiano" 39), comes away from Modiano's texts knowing that "something happened":

> The story line repeatedly dissolves: narrative modes of organization are not adequate to the discontinuity of the past, memory, life (cf. *Livret de famille* 156), and the narration—elliptical, hesitant, wandering—breaks up into bits and pieces (cf. *Livret de famille, De si braves garçons*) and presents quite a story without quite telling one. The self is not illuminated. The quest comes to no end. The past is not recaptured (Modiano's masterful use of tenses only underlines the elusiveness

of what was, what has been, and what is). The riddle can't
be solved. But something happened. (Prince, "Re-Membering
Modiano" 43)

In light of the preoccupation with the Holocaust in *La place de l'étoile*
and in light of the echoes of that tragedy throughout the oeuvre, the
something attested to by Prince may safely be presumed to have been
bad. And in Colin Davis's opinion, the allusions made to the Collaboration and anti-Jewish racism by Modiano's novels exert "unremitting
moral pressure" on his readers (Davis 676). So Modiano, in masterfully
producing a fiction that compels reading and that invites substantial reflection about it and its art, in masterfully raising at the same time the
most substantial, compelling questions about the difficulties created by
the textuality that surrounds and perhaps constitutes us to a significant
degree, has produced in *La place de l'étoile* a novel that leaves us with
the feeling that all those issues arise in a moral universe that we can and
should still ponder. *La place de l'étoile* coextensively stimulates reflections both aesthetic *and* moral, textual *and* historical, reflections that engage us distinctively as a species.

The moral component of that perspective in turn offers additional reasons for the odd success of Modiano's outrageous first published novel. And of course an explanation of Modiano's success has
been a goal of this study all along. The personal intensity, the repression
of memory, and the moral connection prompted by traumatic fratricide
within a Collaboration-obsessed work reflect Modiano's obsessions, but
they have of course special and tragic historic and political significance
in France, where they have patent parallels with official amnesia about
the fratricidal betrayal of French Jews by their French compatriots to the
Nazis. So we have additional, moral support for Henri Rousso's claim
(see Introduction) that a reason for Modiano's extraordinary success is
that his personal obsessions as a writer struck an all too responsive
chord in the French body politic. It should be noted, however, that obsessions arising from fratricidal urges and acts have more than passing
moral significance and interest for societies and readers outside of
France as well, as is demonstrated by the diversity of myths dealing
with the internecine family. Consider for example Cadmus's progeny
and Adam's: Cadmus who "forgot" to continue the search for his ab-

ducted sister and who—serpent-slayer later become serpent—sowed the serpent's teeth that sprang into fratricidal warriors, Cadmus who founded the city ruled by Laius the would-be murderer of his son Oedipus, Cadmus the political forebear of Oedipus who was more successful at dealing death within the family than his father and who subsequently and no less successfully released both the repressed truth of the two crimes and the murderous drives of the mutually destructive Polynices and Eteocles; Adam the father of murderous Cain and the forebear of Noah who cursed his son Ham and their descendants, Adam the ancestor of Abraham ready to kill Isaac and of Isaac's quarrelling sons Jacob and Esau, and of the jealousy-torn sons of Jacob.

But even these assertions of moral considerations that apparently sit uneasily with Riffaterrean resistance to powerful mimesis can be seen to effect another semiotic loop. That happens first and simply if we reflect on the implications of the very Devil's presence in *Peter Schlemihl*. As a sign of course, the Devil incarnates most overtly the moral question of right and wrong, and so the Devil-marked intertext from Chamisso arguably makes a subtle and indirect contribution to the moral tone of *La place de l'étoile*'s enhanced semiosis. The semiotic loop also occurs through the subtext. The subtext's debt to the detective story contribute the same moral tone as the intertextual Devil, but in a way a bit more abstract than that of the primary intertext: "The interest in the thriller is the ethical and characteristic conflict between good and evil, between Us and Them. The interest in the study of a murderer is the observation, by the innocent many, of the sufferings of the guilty one. The interest in the detective story is the dialectic of innocence and guilt" (Auden 147).

Furthermore, as we have seen above regarding the knight-errant side of Chandler's Marlowe, detective novels of the "hard-boiled" school insistently weave moral questions into the fabric of their plots (Tani 24 and following pages; Margolies 84). In short, *La place de l'étoile*'s debt to *Peter Schlemihl* and to detective stories of whatever stripe entails a moral message. The text's own focus on one of the great crimes of history could do no less. Notwithstanding the incontestable aesthetic, semiotic power of *La place de l'étoile*, that power is in fact contested morally within the novel's pages, much as in Modiano's later *Livret de famille* (1977), where the would-be purely musical broadcast of a former agent of the Holocaust who is hiding in Switzerland has its aesthetic, ahistoric perfection contested by dim but discordant voices:

> Le principe de l'émission, qui consiste à diffuser des pièces musicales sans commentaires, est déjà révélateur. Il s'agit d'atteindre le plaisir esthétique sans partage, sans présentation historique. Mais parfois, un "grésillement" vient rompre la "netteté de son cristalline" (*L.F.*, p. 125) de l'émission et le narrateur croit discerner des voix qui appellent au secours, comme si la perfection, la propreté cachaient quelque chose. (Salaün 20)

Finally, since this has been a study based on a linguistic/semiotic approach, much the same conclusion could be reached by heeding etymological hints. We should observe that to re-call/*re-appeler* (and Raphaël's fancied psychoanalytic self-interrogation with Freud is an exercise in imaginary re-call), to re-present/*re-présent-er* (all language and literature do both), and to re-proach, *re-proch-er*, (to raise issues of guilt, as *La place de l'étoile* insists on doing both covertly and overtly), are all three essentially to re-flect, going from present to past, from a here to a there (*re-appeler*, *re-présent-er*, *re-proche-er*). And if one accepts that human awareness is fundamentally the attempt to compare a here to a there, then memory (a temporal here-to-there), literary representation (a semiotic here-to-there), and guilt (a deontological here-to-there) may all three be viewed as human re-flection functioning variously. In that light and in large measure, Modiano succeeds also because in his work the historic, the semiotic, and the moral find themselves in each other and complement each other, to the delectation of us readers of literature for whom awareness at its best is a convergence of the historic, the semiotic, and the moral.

But to give Riffaterre his large due and to acknowledge that delectation is not always the best path to understanding, and to avoid the erroneous impression that such issues of literary criticism are easily settled, we should recall that Riffaterre's mimesis-resisting attempt to focus exclusively on what makes literature work *qua* literature has as noble a critical antecedent as possible:

Aristotle makes some mention of the processes and products of art in [various] aspects—and art has at some time in later history been treated as exclusively or essentially inspiration, pleasure, instruction, symbol, cure, and so through the long list—but the great accomplishment of Aristotle's philosophic method as applied to the arts is to separate and distinguish the other aspects under which a thing may be considered (treating them in appropriate contexts and sciences) from the problem bearing on the constructions and productions of art that are consequent simply to their being works of art. Aristotle's treatment of tragedy in the *Poetics* is the first attempt to consider poetry as art without concern for the educational, therapeutic, moral, and political affects of poetry, which were central to Plato's treatment and which Aristotle takes up in the *Nichomachean Ethics* and the *Politics*. (McKeon xxix)

◆ ◆ ◆

Chapter 3

The Riffaterrean Reading of *La place de l'étoile* as a Template for the Oeuvre

The preceding chapters offer a detailed and exclusive focus on *La place de l'étoile,* a focus that had initially been justified in large measure by the opinion of some Modiano scholars (see above, p. 17) that *La place de l'étoile,* in spite of its specific perplexing qualities, can be viewed usefully as representative of Modiano's oeuvre. In order to justify retrospectively that foundational proposition, the following pages will offer selected examples of ways in which the conclusions derived from the above study of *La place de l'étoile* can serve as a critical template for an approach to subsequent novels by Modiano.

Attention will first focus on Modiano's second and third novels, *La ronde de nuit* (1969) and *Les boulevards de ceinture* (1972), because together with *La place de l'étoile* they make up a trilogy, and so they can be regarded as necessarily having a tight connection with Modiano's first novel. Attention will then shift to Modiano's next two novels, *Villa triste* (1975) and *Livret de famille* (1977) in order to show how the Riffaterrean template derived from *La place de l'étoile* can be used to highlight a decisive turning point that marks in various ways and in various degrees the rest of the oeuvre to follow. That turning point takes place when the Mother/Whore of the subtextual interrogation scene takes on the qualities of the Loving Woman. Finally, *Vestiaire de l'enfance* (1989) and *Accident nocturne* (2003) will be considered as examples illustrating especially noteworthy incarnations of the Loving Woman.

I. *La place de l'étoile, La ronde de nuit,* and *Les boulevards de ceinture:* A Trilogy

In any overview of Modiano's oeuvre, one should begin by ac-knowledging what upon even brief reflection becomes obvious, namely that the first three published novels, *La place de l'étoile, La ronde de nuit,* and *Les boulevards de ceinture* form a tightly interwoven trilogy. To begin with, like *La place de l'étoile,* the other two texts are emphati-cally fantasy-driven, to such an extent that trying to sort out narrative instance from narrated story in each of them takes mental acrobatics. As a result of the intradiegetically fantasy-driven nature of these narratives in their entirety, a caveat is in order: in order to remain faithful to impor-tant impressions "experienced" by the narrators of both texts, analysis often has to treat characters and incidents as if, within the fiction, they had existence. Nonetheless, as with the analysis of *La place de l'étoile,* the assumption throughout the following treatment of *La ronde de nuit* and *Les boulevards de ceinture* will be that the characters and events are the fantasies of the imaginary narrators. So *La ronde de nuit* recounts in the first person, as do all of Modiano's novels except *Une jeunesse,* a story that because of historic and narrational aporias can be considered imaginary intradiegetically vis-à-vis the already imaginary narrator, but the narrative instance stands extradiegetically to the imagined intradi-egetic story itself. In other words, the aporias are imaginary at another level within the already fictional narrative: on the first fictional level we have an imaginary narrator who on a second fictional level now imag-ines, now remembers a story, with no clear distinction as to which of the latter processes is which (see for example Doucey 33-34, 37). Apparently (so little is categorical in Modiano) the narrator of *La ronde de nuit* is musing as he imagines himself sitting on a bench in front of 3 bis, square Cimarosa. Since a map of Paris shows a rue Cimarosa but no square Cimarosa, even the narrative site itself takes us epistemologically to Modiano's characteristic *tertium quid,* where imagination and recall dramatically conflate. The narrator's fantasy/memory would then spin out his activities and reflections, as willy-nilly he narrates himself into becoming a double agent in the face of conflicting demands from two father-figures. The first is Henri Norman or "le Khédive,"[1] the head of a Collaboration auxiliary police force cum corrupt trading organization, and the second Lieutenant Dominique, the head of a Resistance cell. The fact that the narrator's final paragraph recounts what will ostensibly be his own inevitable death indicates, however, that fantasy makes it impossible to sift out the contributions of memory.

Along similarly fantasy-driven lines, the narrator of *Les boulevards de ceinture* searches for his vaguely criminal father but knows nothing about him, having apparently met him only briefly when he himself was seventeen. The narrator is reduced to imagining him indirectly, through his own detailed knowledge about Collaboration figures contemporary with his father: "Je me penche sur ces déclassés, ces marginaux, pour retrouver, à travers eux, l'image fuyante de mon père. Je ne sais presque rien de lui. Mais *j'inventerai*" (*Les boulevards de ceinture* 76; my emphasis). He does so while apparently sitting much like the narrator of *La ronde de nuit,* only this time in a cabaret:[2]

> Oui, toutes ces choses imprécises appartenaient au passé. J'avais remonté le cours du temps pour retrouver et suivre vos traces. En quelle année étions-nous? A quelle époque? En quelle vie? Par quel prodige vous avais-je connu quand vous n'étiez pas encore mon père? Pourquoi avais-je fait pareils efforts, alors qu'un chansonnier racontait une "histoire juive," dans un cabaret qui sentait l'ombre et le cuir, devant d'étranges consommateurs? (*Les boulevards de ceinture* 129)

And these "memories" may well be the result of the narrator's compulsion to prowl around Paris with a lively, open imagination: "Il suffit que je frappe du talon sur certains points sensibles de Paris pour que les souvenirs jaillissent en gerbes d'étincelles" (90); "Plus tard, je marcherai à travers cette ville et elle me paraîtra aussi absente qu'aujourd'hui. Je me perdrai dans le dédale des rues, à la recherche de votre ombre. Jusqu'à me confondre avec elle" (175).

So within that fanciful context the story opens with his then imagining himself in the time period of a photograph that is said to have been taken during the Collaboration years, and that is said to contain an image of his father and the latter's two war-time associates. Even the ontological status of that photo within the fiction is uncertain. On the one hand, the beginning of the text suggests that the photo had been found by chance at the bottom of a drawer (*Les boulevards de ceinture* 14), leaving the impression that it was probably the narrator who found it. On the other hand, the last page of the text indicates that Grève, the barman at the Clos-Foucré, had been in possession of the photo and that he gave it to the narrator (180). In either case, the narrative gambit enjoys a pronounced literary status, insofar as—in Nettelbeck's and Hueston's terms—it is "*si peu original, si 'nouveau roman'* " (*Patrick Modiano* 50).

Regarding the trilogic character of the three narratives, it is not only prevailing fantasy that ties the three novels tightly together. There is in addition a considerable number of textual details, thoroughly listed by Bruno Doucey (10-12, 41), that argue for the three novels' constituting a trilogy. To begin with and at the simplest level, all three novels share the primary setting of France's shameful Collaboration years of 1940-44, a primacy abandoned in the fourth novel, *Villa triste,* and only intermittently evident thereafter. Even when the subsequent novels do lend a significant role to the Collaboration years summoned up from the past, the narrators' perspective is more securely anchored in the present time of narration, for example concerning *Rue des boutiques obscures,* in which an amnesiac detective narrator in 1965 investigates retrospectively the elusive Collaboration period in order to remedy his current loss of memory.

The three texts tie themselves to each other on two other levels, both subtle but both symbolically powerful, as Doucey indicates. First, they follow what could be sketched as a geographical line of attempted escape, in that *La ronde de nuit*'s opening locale lies at a short distance from the central la place de l'Étoile, where the action described in the first novel concluded; and the primary scenes of *Les boulevards de ceinture*—as the title itself indicates—take place on the ring of Paris's peripheral boulevards, toward which the narrator of *La ronde de nuit* described himself as fleeing at the end of his account. Second, in tension with the thrust toward linear escape, all three titles denote circularity, and thereby connote how at their end the narratives, by returning to their own beginnings, fail to break out into either a sense of resolution or a certain history. Finally, in a set of partial overlaps, the first two novels share several secondary characters, while the narrator of the second novel refers to himself as the son of the historic swindler Alexandre Stavisky

(1886-1934) and the narrator of the third novel refers to himself as Serge Alexandre, another designation for Stavisky.[3]

Considering the two novels in light of the above Riffaterrean reading of *La place de l'étoile* will bring out common structures that underlie the triad. To begin with, we can recall that, as argued in Chapter 1 above, the Riffaterrean "matrix" of *La place de l'étoile* arises from the conjunction of the sememes of rootlessness, guilt, and artistic questing. As we shall see, that conjunction manifests itself in the triad (and indeed the oeuvre), although of course subject to varying emphasis now on one of the sememes, now on another. And within the sememes themselves, sememes being only a bundle of semes, emphasis can similarly be expected to shift.

Regarding the matrix's rootlessness, let us consider *La ronde de nuit*'s variously named narrator. He imagines himself largely in the Paris of World War II, shuttling his person and his allegiances between the Collaborationist right bank and the Resistance left bank. In the former locale he is dubbed with unsuspecting descriptive appropriateness "Swing Troubadour," in the latter dubbed with unsuspecting gender-bending appropriateness "La Princesse de Lamballe." This rootlessness (or what he calls his "*goût du mouvement*," *La ronde de nuit* 41) also erupts in his imagining himself at different points in the narrative driving around Paris with an odd couple that he chooses to adopt (the child Esmeralda and the blind giant Coco Lacour), and at the end in his hurtling toward Paris's periphery in an attempt to avoid assassination at the hands of the Collaborationist chief, le Khédive. Moreover, his sense of rootlessness expresses itself chronologically in his occasionally fancying himself as having lived in the nineteenth-century. Most importantly, that sense has a patently psychological dimension, as will be suggested below in a discussion of his uncertain identity.

As for the matrix's guilt, it comes directly to the fore in this second novel at those moments when Swing Troubadour recalls his mother's shameful prediction: "Je revis le visage de maman. Elle se penchait vers moi et, comme chaque soir, avant d'éteindre la lumière, me glissait à l'oreille: 'Tu finiras sur l'échafaud!' " (*La ronde de nuit* 46-47); when he calls up images of the betrayed members of the resistance: "Vous vous souvenez de toutes les gentillesses qu'ils ont eues pour vous. L'un d'eux vous lisait les lettres de sa fiancée [. . .] . Un autre connaissait le nom de toutes les étoiles. Le REMORDS" (53-54); and when he recalls his doctor's scornful prediction: "Le médecin me disait qu'avant de mourir chaque homme se transforme en boîte à musique et que l'on entend pendant une fraction de seconde l'air qui correspond le mieux à ce que fut sa vie, son caractère et ses aspirations [. . .] . VOUS, mon petit gars, ce sera le bruit d'une poubelle que l'on envoie dinguer la nuit dans un terrain vague" (60). Finally, the matrix's artistic questing morphs into the narrator Swing Troubadour's spending much of his time hunting in Paris's *hôtels particuliers* for art objects that will be appropriated for le Khédive (39).

Another clear element of the template that *La place de l'étoile* offers for a reading of the triad and the rest of Modiano's oeuvre is the interrogation subtext à la Riffaterre. So powerful a role does this element play in Modiano's imagination that he entitled even his extensive 1976 interview with the intellectual, journalist, and writer Emmanuel Berl (1892-1976) *Interrogatoire,* in spite of the unflattering, vaguely criminal implications of "interrogating" Berl, whom the interview clearly shows Modiano to admire and respect. As one might expect for Modiano's first novel after *La place de l'étoile, La ronde de nuit* is impacted powerfully by the previous subtext. Indeed, the latter novel opens with the second most prominent character, the policeman le Khédive, putting a series of questions to the most prominent character, the narrator. That interrogation leads up to the question that will reoccur throughout the narrative, and around which the action will evolve, the question of the identity of La Princesse de Lamballe: "Êtes-vous entré en contact avec celui qu'on appelle 'La Princesse de Lamballe'? Qui est-il?" (*La ronde de nuit* 16). The subtext further permeates the text in the frequently repeated references to, and fragmentary descriptions of, a brutal and ultimately fatal interrogation. It takes place at the salon of Le Khédive's headquarters on square Cimarosa, during one of the two major reoccurring scenes, an evening's events at the salon on the one hand and on the other the narrator's outing to the Pré Catalan in the Bois de Boulogne with Esmeralda and Coco Lacour, the fugue-like alternation of which scenes takes up much of the book. Appropriately, there appear figures recalling the original subtext's cast of characters, the weak Jewish Father, the strong Nazi Son, and the Mother/Whore. But *La ronde de nuit* psychologically displaces those characters from *La place de l'étoile* respectively into the collaborating and so Nazi-like father-figure of le Khédive who addresses the narrator as "*mon fils*" (31) and repeatedly as "*mon petit,*" into the weak Jewish son-figure of the narrator who—in one of his multiple identities—claims to be the son of the murdered Jew, Alexandre Stavisky (137), and into the various mature and thus maternal women present for the salon's orgy.

Much of Modiano's subsequent work is marked also by the dual/split Self/Brother of *La place de l'étoile,* a presence that would nuance our understanding of his postmodern tendencies, making the decentered self encountered throughout his oeuvre a site at which the postmodern and the autofictional are one for him. Regarding *La ronde de nuit,* this duality/split is adumbrated in the opening scene at Le Khédive's salon, during which pronoun usage suggests that the narrator has difficulty in articulating his identity. Only after the first seven pages does he even begin to incarnate himself verbally in any direct way, finally making cautious reference to himself at the end of a string of examples of the indefinite French pronoun *on.* At that point, first the narration moves through three examples of the formal sense of *on,* "one": "Un carnet jaune acheté rue Réaumur. Vous êtes étudiant? a demandé la marchande. (On s'intéresse aux jeunes gens. L'avenir leur appartient, on voudrait connaître leurs projets, on les submerge de questions)" (*La ronde de nuit* 18-19). Then the narrative makes an ambiguous use of *on,* (which of course even though indefinite can be used to refer to the first person), in a way that could refer either to all those in the salon or just to the narrator: "On ne voit rien dans cette pénombre" (19). Then the narrator ever so discretely makes his own first reference to himself, starting an extensive string of examples of the same pronoun to describe "the one" who will betray the lieutenant: "On s'efforce d'oublier ses yeux bleu-noir [ceux du lieutenant] [. . .] " and so on (19). It takes two more pages before the narrator finally declare himself as a *je:* "Coco Lacour fumait son cigare. Esmeralda buvait sagement une grenadine. Ils ne parlaient pas. C'est pour cela que *je* les aime" (20-21; my emphasis). Tellingly, the rest of the page introduces a *vous,* a *nous* along with a not necessarily compatible *notre,* and a *tu,* the imprecise reference of which imposes rereading and reflection in the effort to sort them out:

> Coco Lacour, Esmeralda, ces noms *vous* suffisent comme me
> suffit leur présence silencieuse à mes côtés [. . .] . *Je* suis leur
> ange gardien. *Nous* viendrons chaque soir au Bois de Bou-
> logne pour mieux goûter la douceur de l'été [. . .] . Rien n'a
> changé ici, depuis *notre* enfance. Te rappelles-*tu*? *Tu* jouais au
> cerceau le long des allées du Pré Catalan. (21; my emphasis)

The *nous* ("nous viendrons chaque soir au Bois de Boulogne") is used as part of a reference to what will be the frequently mentioned evening spent together at the Bois by Coco Lacour, Esmeralda, and the narrator, and so here it designates Coco Lacour, Esmeralda, and the narrator. But Esmeralda being only a child and so too young to have shared the narrator's childhood, and Coco Lacour being a mature adult and so too old to have done the same, and in fact as the reader learns much later, Esmeralda and Coco Lacour never having existed in the first place even within the fiction (146), the *notre* of "*notre enfance*" is troublesome. At the very least, this and similar pronominal usage communicates the narrator's split personality and duality of feelings (see Doucey 59).

But in light of the discussion of the Self/Brother in Chapter 1 above and the peculiar pronoun usage in *La place de l'étoile,* the shift in reference marked by *notre* also evokes ever so slightly the suppressed memory of the Brother. It is conceivable that the *tu* could be construed simply to be an example of the narrator referring to himself, had it not been momentarily muddled by the odd "*notre enfance*" that follows the ordinary self-reference found in the *Je.* Similar pronoun vacillation can be seen to occur elsewhere, as for instance if one compares the shifting *vous* and *on* of pages 52 that settles into just a *vous* on page 53 with the certain *vous* of page 54, and then with the unstable mix of *vous, je, tu,* and *nos* on pages 60-62. In fact the text subtly harks back to—and so emphasizes—the problem by repeating on page 61, with one shift in tense, two of the key sentences from page 21: "Te rappelles-tu? Tu joues au cerceau sur les pelouses du Pré Catalan."

This difficulty in articulating self-identity and the hint at dual/ split identity blossom in the fertile ground of the clearly precarious identity of a narrator who declares himself both to be the twentieth-century son of Stavisky and to carry the identity papers of the nineteenth-century Maxime de Bel-Respiro (*La ronde de nuit* 146), who conjures up secondary characters who too have doubled identities (Doucey 56), who accepts both that his Resistance persona be named the feminine "Princesse de Lamballe" (*La ronde de nuit* 106) and that his traitor persona be described as the equally feminine "donneuse" (92), and who on occasion recalls the kaleidoscopic Raphaël Schlemilovitch himself: "Me plaçant une dernière fois devant le miroir de Venise j'y rencontrais le visage de Philippe Pétain. Je lui trouvais l'œil beaucoup trop vif, la peau trop rose et finissais par me métamorphoser en roi Lear" (141); "Qui suis-je? [Marcel] Petiot? [Henri] Landru?" (149). There is no surprise then that this psychological "double agent" finds himself playing/imagining the role of political double agent who works for both the Collaborators and the Resistance, even as he spends the narrative shuttling in fact or imagination between Paris's Collaborationist right bank and its Resistant left bank.

But just as in *La place de l'étoile* when Raphaël, having first become the brother of Des Essarts-become-Lévy and then having killed his brother Lévy, only to be killed by a Lévy who resembled him like a brother, in *La ronde de nuit* the same fratricidal/suicidal impulse can be spotted at work. For a dramatic instance, the starkly polar antagonists, Le Khédive and the man whom he will torture and execute, the resistance Lieutenant Dominique, momentarily fuse into one: "Le Khédive et le lieutenant ne font qu'une seule personne [. . .] " (73). This momentary fusing of executioner/executed may be seen to move toward becoming part of a pattern by reasserting itself shortly thereafter in slightly different terms, when the narrator describes himself as both the betrayer Judas and the betrayed Jesus (98). And pattern it turns out to be, if one is to judge for instance from the narrator's frequent and haunting representations of Coco Lacour and Esmeralda: they are the objects of loving yet homicidal urges on the part of the narrator (22 and 70), and for all the intensity of his love-hate relationship with them, he will doubt (26) and, as we just saw, eventually deny their existence (146), because he comes to admit that they are none other than he: "Je suis cet aveugle roux et cette minuscule petite fille vulnérable" (26). So like Raphaël Schlemilovitch, Swing Troubadour does indeed appear to "swing" on an identity fault line marked by a fratricidal/suicidal quality, a fault line sketched in pronominal instability. Furthermore, the fault line's reappearance brings to light yet another element bonding the first three novels as a trilogy: at the end of their narratives all three the narrators imagine pushing themselves into self-destructive situations, a coincidence surely arising from the guilt that hounds the autofictional narrators.

Let us now turn to a consideration of how *La place de l'étoile,* understood in its Riffaterrean reading, can serve as a critical template of discovery for the third novel in Modiano's triad, *Les boulevards de ceinture.* The latter too reveals the Riffaterrean matrix at work. For instance, we see the narrator engaged in a quest for art, quite literally in that when living briefly with his father in Paris at the age of seventeen he made some money by hunting for unsuspected rare editions to sell at a high price (*Les boulevards de ceinture* 87-88). And on much the same superficial note, exactly as for Raphaël Schlemilovitch, part of his artistic creativity was to write in books forged and outrageously provocative dedications, of the following sort: "Je vendis un Maurras 500 000 francs, grâce à cette petite phrase: 'Pour Léon Blum, en témoignage d'admiration. Et si nous déjeunions ensemble? La vie est si courte… Maurras' " (88). And also just as was the case for Raphaël, his narrative shows him questing after art in his striving to write, doing so sometimes most modestly, as for instance when he writes "true revelations" for *C'est la vie,* a Collaborationist, salacious rag of a weekly directed by Jean Muraille with an eye to blackmail (133), and sometimes less modestly, as when he declares himself to be a novelist and author of published novellas, significantly two (39-40, 50), matching both in number Modiano's own publications at the time of publication of *Les boulevards de ceinture* and in age Modiano's own age of twenty-seven at the time of publication.[4] But much more pertinently, his entire text constitutes a verbally imaginative quest, an artistic quest for an inaccessible father, in order to create a father verbally out of details dredged up from the world that his father knew in the past.

Regarding the next element of the Riffaterrean matrix, rootlessness characterizes the life that the narrator, aged seventeen at the time, and his father had spent together before the father disappeared from the son's life for the second time, having apparently first abandoned him as an infant: they would spend the nights wandering around Paris at night on foot and by car, always residing only briefly at one address after another (*Les boulevards de ceinture* 61-2, 81, 89-90, 92). Those perambulations resume ten years later when the narrator finds his father at the Clos-

Foucré, an inn on the outskirts of Paris: desperate to query his father, he cannot address him directly in the presence of the other characters, their only exchanges occurring tentatively as he ambles along with his father on the way back to the latter's lodging. And of course there is the point at the heart of all that movement, psychological rootlessness:

> Rien n'a changé. Après dix ans, je vous retrouve pareil à vous-même: épiant la porte d'entrée du salon, comme un rat effarouché. Et moi, je me retiens au bras du canapé, à cause de la housse glissante. Nous aurons beau faire, nous ne connaî-trons jamais le repos, la douce immobilité des choses. Nous marcherons jusqu'au bout sur du sable mouvant. (152)

And since the three elements of the matrix are not just points on a list but rather facets of a single dynamic, the third facet—guilt—imbricates itself into this life of criminal and disgraceful writing and of movement-inducing anxiety. In fact, so strongly does the guilt function in a semiotic reading of this text that it becomes reasonable to wonder counterintuitively if, in Serge's act of literary creation within the fiction, guilt did not generate imaginatively the criminal behavior, instead of vice versa. To be sure, the narrative has the father like the son knowing the guilt that could derive from forging, and in the father's case the narrative shows him almost "knowing" a lynching as a result of his being caught trying to sell a forged rare stamp (*Les boulevards de ceinture* 84-86). But guilt suffuses the text most thoroughly and most profoundly because of the scene in which the absentee father, shortly after meeting his teenaged son, is said to have almost killed him by pushing him in the back as they waited for a metro car coming into the station. It is at this point that *La place de l'étoile* as a template for *Les boulevards de ceinture* has excep-tional value, for in light of the Riffaterrean reading of the first novel the metro scene of the third novel—central to the text thematically, dramati-cally, and physically (it covers pages 96-105 in a text of 166 pages)—can be seen to generate the organizing subtext of this third published novel, a subtext that, consistent with its trilogic unity with *La place de l'étoile,* involves an interrogation.

When we take a Riffaterrean approach to the murderous metro scene, the third novel's subtextual parallels with the first stand out: the crime is obviously one of deadly family antagonism; the interrogation to which the attempted murder leads is inconclusive and marked by repression, since the police chief—even though clearly sensing what happened (*Les boulevards de ceinture* 101-2)—has no success in persuading the narrator to expose the truth; and the odd, gap-associated number four appears again when policemen—inexplicably three in number since only two suspect figures are involved, the son and the father (103)—suddenly burst into the room (as did the four nurses in *La place de l'étoile*) in order to join the fourth policeman, the chief. Although *Les boulevards de ceinture*'s number four in itself may seem to hark back only tenuously to the repression at work in Modiano's original interrogation, there is good reason for maintaining that repression is at work throughout the entire episode. First, starting with the episode's very first sentence, it sets itself under the sign of repressive resistance, as the reluctance behind the words *quoi qu'il m'en coûte* indicates: "Maintenant je vais en venir, quoi qu'il m'en coûte, à l''épisode douloureux du métro George-V' " (96). Second, the fruit of repression, a striking gap like the one explored above in Chapter One, opens up in the middle of the narrative describing the events of the metro scene: in one sentence we read that the narrator was pushed in the back as the car entered the station, but in the very next sentence we read that he is stretched out on a station bench, being congratulated for having had a narrow escape (98). Between the push and the congratulations, there lies a gap for the reader: did the narrator in fact not fall on the tracks?; did he fall but somehow manage to make it back up to the platform before the cars passed by, or is the gap another diegetic aporia due just to the imagined nature of the event? Only two pages later is the gap attended to and imperfectly at that, when we read that someone designated by the impersonal pronoun *on* apparently caught him just as he was losing his balance: "'Heureusement qu'on vous a retenu'" (100). But even assuming that the narrator was indeed pulled back, the gap lingers on in the obvious question: was the *on* who pulled him back, the father or a stranger?

In retrospective reading, these three essential Modianesque subtextual elements—familial antagonism, interrogation, and repression or gaps—can be seen to reappear elsewhere in *Les boulevards* as parts of kaleidoscopic visions, or if one prefers as motifs reconfigured through Freudian displacement, helping to weave the seemingly disparate fantasy fragments into a harmonized, organic textos. Consisting of sixteen blocks of narrative, this novel deals with eight main scenes: 1) the narrator's observation of a photograph representing his father and his two associates, Muraille and Guy Marcheret, a crude, bullying former legionnaire, both of whom come to life out of the photograph and invite Serge to dinner at the country inn appearing in the photograph; 2) the narrator's very first and surprising meeting with his absentee father when the narrator was a seventeen-year old student in Bordeaux; 3) the metro/interrogation scene; 4) a second dinner with his father and associates; 5) a brief description of the narrator's own new routines with his father's associates; 6) the wedding ceremony and reception for the marriage to Marcheret of the flighty and dissolute Annie Muraille, Jean Muraille's daughter; 7) the narrator's and his father's flight from the reception and subsequent arrest in Paris; and 8) a return to the present, with the narrator again observing the photograph. Of all these scenes, the two most thoroughly influenced by the common subtextual elements are the longest scene, that is the two dinner scenes taken as a whole, and the scene that constitutes the basic subtext for *Les boulevards de ceinture,* the metro/interrogation scene.

In the dinner scenes the familial antagonism behind the metro scene manifests itself in the relationship between the father and his two "musketeer" brothers (*Les boulevards de ceinture* 23), a fraternal trinity prefigured by the text's very opening sentence: "Le plus gros des trois, c'est mon père" (13). During the first dinner scene Marcheret will cruelly twist and hold the father's cheek for minutes at a time (18), and during the second he and Muraille will insult and humiliate him (58, 60). As for the interrogation motif, the exchanges between the narrator and Muraille are opened by a series of fourteen abrupt and disconcerting questions, questions disconcerting at least for the wary, insecure narrator (37-40). At a later point, Muraille and Marcheret give the narrator the impression of being policemen leading away his father in handcuffs (120). But in keeping with the role reversals arising from unstable identity (see below), the narrator himself would like to become the interrogator, and thereby explicitly evokes the interrogation motif. Speaking of his father and possible trial evidence, he says: "On voudrait *interroger* les personnes qui l'ont connu mais leurs traces se sont effacées avec les siennes. Sur ce qu'a été sa vie, on ne possède que de très vagues indications souvent contradictoires, deux ou trois points de repère. *Pièces à conviction?*

un timbre-poste et une fausse légion d'honneur" (134; my emphasis). This desire to interrogate would be in keeping with his having wanted to become a policeman (42) and his keeping a file on his father's gangster associates (32, 65-76).

And the gap of repression opens up during the dinner scenes, in the unexplained and unexplored inability of the son to confront his father, to put to the latter all the questions haunting him: does the seemingly oblivious father in fact recognize him after ten years of absence?; why did the father need to abandon him twice?; and the ultimate but unarticulated question that ties antagonism, interrogation, and repression together, for what strange reason did the father apparently try to kill his own son? Tormented by the questions that he would like to pose (for example 60-62), the narrator has to face not only *"l'habileté avec laquelle il [son père] éludait les questions gênantes. Ne m'avait-il pas déclaré un jour: 'Je découragerais dix juges d'instruction'?"* (61). He also and more importantly has to confront—unsuccessfully—his own mysterious refusal to confront the truth. After accompanying his father up to the gate outside the latter's lodging near the Clos-Foucré, he finds himself on the brink of what he calls a possible chance of a lifetime to get answers, only to become peculiarly unable to make the leap. He yields to the power of his own psychological resistance: "Nous étions à quelques mètres de la grille et j'attendais l'instant où il me serrerait la main pour prendre congé. Ensuite, je le verrais se perdre dans l'obscurité et je resterais là, au milieu de cette route, dans l'état d'hébétude où l'on se trouve après avoir laissé passer l'occasion, peut-être, d'une vie" (62). The verbs in the conditional, in addition to reinstating clearly the primacy of imagination, show that even when the narrator fantasizes about hearing answers to his questions, his repressive impulses will not let him fantasize possible answers. This will be distinctly echoed in the psychologically blocked ending of the metro/interrogation scene: "Après l'événement regrettable du métro, j'aurais souhaité une mise au point entre nous. Impossible. Il m'opposait une telle force d'inertie que j'ai préféré ne plus insister" (*Les boulevards de ceinture* 104).

And since we saw that this triad of subjects—familial antagonism, interrogation, and the gap of suppression—functions in *La place de l'étoile* against a backdrop of slippery identity, in the two main scenes of *Les boulevards de ceinture* the characters are caught up suitably enough in a riot of exchanged roles. In addition to the exchanges just mentioned above regarding the role of interrogator, there is of course the most important example of role reversal for the son, the one that occurs in the metro scene when the father tries to kill the son. The narrator can be considered to be working from an Oedipal framework, since he has an affair with Sylviane Quimphe, mistress of the musketeer and substitute father-figure, Muraille (*Les boulevards de ceinture* 122). As a result of that framework he would have found it normal for a son to try to kill his father. But role reversals are such here that he finds *rien d'exceptionnel* in his father's trying to kill *him* (151), a reversal much like the one that reappears in the dinner scenes where the son yearns to play a protective fatherly role for his father instead of the usual opposite (109). But that particular reversal itself gets reversed back to the typical Oedipal antagonism, when the narrator entertains thoughts of killing Muraille (132), the principal associate/substitute for the father. Not incidentally, he would do so by attacking him from the back, as his father had done with him. This Muraille-father substitution later reasserts itself in a "signature way" at the wedding scene, when Muraille, who wears a signet ring like the father (17), pushes the narrator in the back (157-58), resurrecting the central memory of the narrator's feeling in his back a hand wearing a signet ring, as he was pushed from behind into the path of the metro car, the sensation that proved for him the father's guilt. Along the same internecine lines, the two "musketeer brothers" plan to (and will) betray the father, that is, plan to have him executed in the camps as a Jew (for example 132, 174-78). Unsurprisingly, since the text is the imagined account of an imagined narrator, all the roles and the role reversals are his. All along, his imagined search for the father has of course been his search for his own identity, for himself. Abandoned victim, in his fantasy he comes to confront himself as policeman and suspect become one:

> Pendant plusieurs mois, j'ai effectué des filatures à titre bénévole. Je devais suivre les personnes les plus diverses et consigner leur emploi du temps. Combien de secrets émouvants ai-je découverts au cours de ces randonnées... Tel notaire de la Plaine Monceau, vous le surprenez à Pigalle en perruque blonde et robe de satin. J'ai vu des êtres insignifiants se transformer d'un instant à l'autre en créatures de cauchemar ou

> héros de tragédie. Les derniers temps, j'ai cru devenir fou.
> Tous ces inconnus, je m'identifiais à eux. C'était *moi* que je
> traquais sans relâche. (*Les boulevards de ceinture* 149-50;
> emphasis in the original)

In addition to these prominent parallels, there is a wide variety of seemingly incidental parallel details that make clear the thoroughness with which the metro/interrogation scene and dinner scenes reconfigure each other kaleidoscopically and textually pull each other into semiotic unity. Most of these parallels deal with locale. For example, the metro/interrogation scene started with the father's keen interest in "*la Petite Ceinture, ligne de chemin de fer désaffectée qui fait le tour de Paris*" (*Les boulevards de ceinture* 96). Aside from the obvious echo of the locale of the dinners and wedding on the *Les boulevards de ceinture* encircling Paris, there is also in the word "*désaffecté*" the less obvious but far from less affective echo of the abandoned dwellings taken over by Muraille and his crowd (27-28), a state more significantly resonant with the son's abandonment by his father, and with Collaboration France's abandonment by moral leaders. Similar echoes of the desolate outer belt resonate in the beginning of the second paragraph of the metro/interrogation scene:

> Ce dimanche 17 juin, nous avions suivi la Petite Ceinture à
> travers le XIIe arrondissement. Non sans mal. Vers la rue de
> Montempoivre, elle se raccorde avec le chemin de fer de Vincennes et nous finissions par nous y embrouiller. Au bout de
> trois heures, étourdis par ce dédale ferroviaire, nous prîmes la
> décision de rentrer à la maison en empruntant le métro. (97)

Aside from both the dinner and the metro/interrogation scenes taking place in the summer (64), both also take place in a south-westerly location in relation to Paris, the dinners on the edge of the Fontainebleau forest in Seine-Marne (27), the exploration in the twelfth arrondissement near the bois de Vincennes. (In addition, the metro taken, Vincennes-Neuilly (97), is marked by forests at both ends.) Insofar as the concept of locale can embrace interior settings, one can see as well how the police interrogation room with its calendar and photograph on the wall (102) was transformed into the calendar- and photograph-equipped bar (13-14) where the narrator will be interrogated and will begin his own tentative interrogation.

Once on the look-out for such kaleidoscopic reconfigurations, one suspects in retrospect that the name of the inn where the dinners and wedding take place, Clos-Foucré, owes something phonetically to the establishment in front of which the father and son climb into the police wagon on their way to the interrogation, Fouquet's (*Les boulevards de ceinture* 99). That would be in keeping with Jean Ricardou's theory of *scripturale création* whereby writing, in for instance the imagistic and homophonic quality of its words, generates the vision of its fictional world, instead of vice versa:

> Loin de se servir de l'écriture pour présenter une vision du monde, la fiction utilise le concept de monde avec ses rouages afin d'obtenir un univers obéissant aux spécifiques lois de l'écriture. A la réaliste banalisation qui prétend trouver dans le livre le substitut d'un monde installé, l'expression d'un sens préalable, s'oppose ainsi le déchiffrement créateur, tentative faite, à partir de la fiction, pour éclaircir cette vertu qui, inventant et agençant les signes, institue le sens même. (Ricardou, *Problèmes* 25)

Speculation along those lines raises the possibility that the frequent and compulsive walking that marks this narrative contributed to the generation of the name of the character Marcheret. Furthermore, given the interpenetrable identities of Modiano's characters, Marcheret's being an orphan (70) would seem to be in topical debt to the status of the narrator, who mentions no mother and is twice abandoned by his father. In a more detailed parallel concerning Marcheret, his status as a former legionnaire given to drunkenness and his (self-declared) status as a Turkish citizen (30) picks up the closing details of the metro/interrogation scene, where, as his father slipped away not to be seen by the narrator for another ten years, the narrator had to deal with a drunken former soldier from Russia who ended his military career in Turkey (104-5). When in the imagined narrative the father reappears, there reappears in his wake the drunken military figure with a connection to Turkey, Marcheret. Along similar lines, the name "Muraille" may owe some of its genesis first to the physical *dédale* (96) of the abandoned belt railroads (96) that for the narrator ringed Paris, then to the physical *dédale* posed for him by the streets of Paris itself (175), and finally to the psychological *dédale* posed for him by the ring boulevards, all three acting like so many confining walls or *murs*.

We can close this demonstration of the functioning of the metro/ interrogation subtext in *Les boulevards de ceinture* by considering two of its results. First of course, in viewing the text from the outside of the fiction, that is, as a reader comparing two novels by the author Patrick Modiano, one observes in both of them very similar semiotic dynamics à la Riffaterre. But a second result, one not to be overlooked, is that the work of the metro/interrogation subtext underscores the imaginary process for the imaginary narrator *within the fiction*, as he compulsively reconfigures verbal material in his effort to construct a father imaginatively. His reconfigurations, in their compulsiveness, lay bare his desperate emotional and psychological needs. And the two results, the extra-fictional and the intra-fictional, come together in this text's hint at its own status. When the narrator names the metro/interrogation scene, he literally quotes the name: "Maintenant je vais en venir, quoi qu'il m'en coûte, à 'l'épisode douloureux du métro George-V' " (96), citing the scene here and on two other occasions (124, 151) as if it already had had an earlier verbal status. Because of the way subtexts work, it had in fact had that earlier verbal status in the preceding scenes. So his punctuation allues to what the text is doing throughout on both the extra- and intra-fictional levels: it is quoting itself. This observation of writing quoting itself in *Les boulevards de ceinture* is of a piece with numerous seemingly incidental but arguably self-conscious details found in the novel's attention to writing, details that will touch the different yet identical figures of the subtext triad, the policeman-perpetrator-victim. Thus, regarding the policeman, throughout the interrogation scene the text indicates insistently how its exchanges were being typed out by a police clerk (101, 102, 102-3) even as we read them. The preoccupation with writing touches the father in his own compulsive writing (about *la Petite Ceinture* no less, 96-98), and the substitute father-figure's newspaper, Muraille's *C'est la vie,* covers what goes on within the Parisian beltway. And of course, as indicated above, the narrator is drawn to writing in a variety of ways. In short, in spite of readers' urges to make mimetic sense of the text, and in spite of the narrator's painful desire to impart referential validity to his imaginings, there is no breaking free from the tension slyly intimated by the name of Marcheret's house, "*la 'Villa Mektoub'* " (25), still another intra-fictional citation set off from the text, we should note, this one meaning in Arabic, "it is [only] written."

II. The Oeuvre Evolves

The conclusion that Alan Morris draws from his analysis of Modiano's oeuvre (up through *Un cirque passe* of 1992) is that in it Modiano pursued "a lengthy—and largely successful—quest for personal exorcism" (Morris, *Patrick Modiano* [Berg] 205). The evolutionary process notwithstanding, Morris does emphasize the oeuvre's considerable homogeneity: he finds constant the themes of remembrance, identity, time and the past, along with characterization that produces shadowy, ghost-like presences, all set within a world view that is essentially bleak and characterized by inescapable, profound ambiguity (Morris, *Patrick Modiano* [Berg] 205-6). Still, Morris does establish that, because of success in purging personal demons, Modiano's cathartic impulse lessens along the way. This implies then that the oeuvre progressively becomes less compulsive, less hallucinatory, and less tormented. So in the pages that follow we should expect that the Riffaterrean reading of the compulsive, hallucinatory, and tormented *La place de l'étoile* will provide a less useful template for the oeuvre than it did for the other two works of Modiano's opening triad, a group for which Cau's description of the first piece obtains: "Ce livre, comme un chat fou de douleur, va te bondir au visage et te griffer jusqu'au sang. De cet assaut tu porteras les marques et l'on dira, en voyant ton visage labouré: 'Ce type-là a dû lire *La Place de l'étoile*. Il n'est que de voir ses cicatrices' " (Cau 3). But less useful is far from being useless, especially if the compulsions, hallucinations, and torment can be shown to find different, less "clawing" avenues of expression.

With *Villa triste,* the tone of the Modianesque narrative takes an important and sharp turn, perhaps because romance—even if it may be, as we shall see, imagined by the imaginary narrator—can so greatly change so many things. And with romance comes a "*Modiano deuxième manière*," one for whom women will assume a far more central (and positive) role (Nettelbeck and Hueston, *Patrick Modiano* 74, 111).

Toward the end of *Villa triste* the narrator, known to readers only under the admittedly false name that he attributes to himself, that of an alleged Russian count Victor Chmara, relates that he had in the course of a walk on Paris's rue de Castiglione read in the provincial paper *Le Dauphiné* an obituary announcing the suicide of Dr. René Meinthe. His account goes on to assert that he then had stopped to sit in a garden off the Louvre (*Villa triste* 185-89). His words would have us surmise in retrospect that this newspaper item had prompted the recollections that make up the entire account preceding the reading of the obituary. As we shall soon see, however, this putative narrative instance poses a considerable problem.

The account preceding mention of the obituary covers the early nineteen-sixties when as a fearful eighteen-year-old Chmara fled the risk of involvement with France's Algerian war and with France's accompanying civil strife, the period of *L'Organisation de l'Armée Secrète*'s terrorist resistance against France's giving up Algeria as a colony. During that Franco-French strife reminiscent of the Franco-French strife of the Collaboration/Resistance years, he had fled Paris in order to spend a summer in Haute-Savoie, on the border of a lake on the border of Switzerland in a psychological state bordering on paranoia (19-20). There he met two individuals uncertain in their own border condition: René Meinthe, a whimsical homosexual and non-practicing practicing physician who regularly slipped over the border to Geneva with no explanation, possibly because of involvement with the OAS; and Meinthe's close friend, Yvonne Jacquet, both a "mobile model" who shuttled from country to country but who never seemed to model and a marginal actress working with a no less marginal but dissolute production company, while she benefited from a mysterious source of income and hovered on the border between privileged youth and the onset of unwelcome middle age. Meinthe's and Jacquet's putative Savoyard world was no less uncertain a border condition: "Ici la végétation est composite, et on ne sait plus si l'on se trouve dans les Alpes, au bord de la Méditerranée ou même sous les Tropiques" (13). With each of the three characters perched precariously on personal borders in a site of uncertain borders, they were destined for each other: "En somme, nous étions faits pour nous rencontrer et nous entendre" (74). Chmara narrates that upon meeting Yvonne, he instantly fell in love, plunging into that other border condition between the real and the imaginary called romance: "Elle marchait vers notre table, une écharpe verte en mousseline nouée autour du cou. Elle me souriait et ne me quittait pas des yeux. Quelque chose se dilatait du côté gauche de ma poitrine, et j'ai décidé que ce jour était le plus beau de ma vie" (31). We should observe that this particular border condition is symbolically evoked throughout the narrative by the attention paid to the narrator's monocle, required for his split vision bordering between clarity and obscurity. Or if within the Oedipal atmosphere of the oeuvre one prefers to consider the punishment visited upon Oedipus, the border vision is a half castrated vision that results from regarding a mother-figure with an only initially successful desire to possess.

So great is the transforming power of romance for the narrator, that the dark melancholy language of the previous three novels, while keeping its form, finds in this novel new mysterious senses that shift to more positive sonorities. For instance, when reflecting on the name that Meinthe had given to his villa, the narrator discovers how the word "*triste*" had come to mean something other than "sad," something richer and better, something that too, as the emphasis below suggests, springs from a threshold, border experience:

> Et sur le portail de bois blanc écaillé, Meinthe avait inscrit maladroitement à la peinture noire (c'est lui qui me l'a confié): VILLA TRISTE.
>
> En effet, elle ne respirait pas la gaieté, cette villa. Non. Pourtant, j'ai d'abord estimé que le qualificatif "triste" lui convenait mal. Et puis, j'ai fini par comprendre que Meinthe avait eu raison si l'on perçoit dans la sonorité du mot "triste" quelque chose de doux et de cristallin. *Après avoir franchi le seuil de la villa*, on était saisi d'une mélancolie limpide. On entrait dans une zone de calme et de silence. L'air était plus léger. On flottait. (175-76; my emphasis)

So the very title itself, which is of course the shorthand summary and identity of the narrative, signals an undermining of Modiano's earlier disturbing language, a move that for a verbal artist is tantamount to an undermining of his work's earlier world-view. Moreover, we shall soon see that this nod in *Villa triste* to language's ability to generate meaning independently of its usual objective reference hints at the work of another example of Jean Ricardou's *scripturale creation* (Ricardou *Problèmes* 26). And it is of course an indirect illustration of what Riffaterre emphasizes as the inherent mimetic shortfall of the literary use of language. In a symbolic reprise of the semantic and world-view shift by the oeuvre, the final paragraph of *Villa* triste breaks out from the constricting torment of the circles of his first three novels, by lingering over the sight of a piece of circular baggage that the narrator, significantly, leaves behind (*Villa triste* 212).[5]

Raphaël, Swing Troubadour, and Serge Alexandre never know the magic of romance, and so they never express, and indeed seem incapable of, a romantic response to a woman. In significant measure, that should be attributed to the emotional grip held over them by the nexus of tormenting elements illustrated in the Riffaterrean reading of their narratives. That is not to suggest that individual elements of the nexus do not haunt the narrator of *Villa triste* too. On the contrary, like the rest of Modiano's narrators, he knows them all, but to different degrees, without the intensity experienced by his earlier peers, and without the elements' tight mutual reinforcement. Apropos of the Modianesque nexus, Chmara knows rootlessness quite well, for instance as a self-described *apatride* (132, 171) living out of different hotel rooms remembered as having "l'odeur même de l'inquiétude, *de l'instabilité, de l'exil* et du toc" (174; my emphasis), and he knows the artistic quest, insofar as he tries to resurrect verbally both Meinthe and Yvonne, and insofar as he had claimed in his youth to be a writer (142-43). But he does not seem burdened by particularly substantial feelings of guilt that would tie in tightly with the rootlessness and quest: in spite of criminal literary forgeries (130, 195), he admits to feeling blameworthy only for a trifle, namely leaving a hotel without advance notice (54-56). And what is especially noteworthy, unlike his predecessors he does not try to kill anyone. Absent the foundational guilt, a reading of his account cannot yield the tight Riffaterrean matrix to be found in the tales of Peter Schlemihl and his three Modianesque counterparts. Doubtless because of the guilt missing in the narrator, a lack determined both from his view of himself and from his

projecting vision of the world around him, the final element of the Riffaterrean nexus—the subtext involving the dual/split Self/Brother—has
its weakest hold on this narrator. True, throughout his account, the narrator, Yvonne, and Meinthe unsuccessfully "interrogate" each other; there
are repeated references to police (for example 19, 22, 55, 58, 188), and
even to two juries (80 and following pages, 198); and Yvonne, slightly
older than the narrator, with licentious friends and suspect funds (in fact
being called a whore at one point, 129-30) does easily fit the part of
Mother-Whore to Meinthe's Father[6] and to the narrator's Son. But unlike
previous configurations of the subtext Family, this one does not have
Jewishness touch Father or Mother, and there is little sign of the haunting, guilt-inducing Brother lurking behind a narrative gap. In another
indication of the switch of Modiano's themes and images to the more
emotionally benign, even prenatal memories, previously the tormented
"recollections" of the Collaboration and the Holocaust that distinguished
the narrators of the first three published novels, while occasionally
touching Victor Chmara, become predominantly comical: René (that is,
the "Re-born") Meinthe carries on the theme of prenatal memories, insisting however that they are those of Queen Astrid of Belgium, with no
sense of menace or horror whatsoever.

In spite of this novel's low emotional register of the elements
highlighted by the Riffaterrean template, there is value in considering
Villa triste from a perspective opened up by that template. In Chapter 1
above, we saw how an odd usage of personal pronouns in *La place de
l'étoile* pointed to a gap in the Family subtext, a gap born of suppression
induced by a guilt-ridden sense of fratricide. As a result, the reading of
La ronde de nuit above was more open to resonances of a similar gap in
an otherwise puzzling sequence of personal pronouns. Likewise, when
one reads *Villa triste* sensitive to pronoun usage, an interesting critical
by-way opens up. One observes that, as was the case with Swing Troubadour, the narrator initially goes on for several pages before committing
himself to a clear verbal incarnation in a *je,* and in fact Chmara's delay
continues for the entire first chapter. The slowness of this commitment,
coming only after extended use of an imprecise *nous* and an equivocal
on, suggests that the narrator is gradually imagining himself into his
story. Encouraged by this narrational curiosity to suspect that personal
pronouns may again play a revealing role, this reader found that through-

out the narrator's account of his relationships with Yvonne, he uses the formal *vous* whenever he quotes himself speaking to her (for example *Villa triste* 37, 65), even though for her part she is usually cited as using the familiar *tu* in speaking to him (35, 97, 115, and so forth, but see 67). Also to be noted, Meinthe and the narrator regularly interact on the very correct level of a mutual *vous*. And yet, on two different narrative occasions, both of them highly imaginative scenes passed off as essentially memories, the narrator uses *tu* for his companions (50, 185).

The first of the latter occasions occurs toward the third chapter's conclusion, an account of an orgy at the home of the director of a film in which Yvonne had appeared. While the description of details from the orgy plays itself out realistically enough without getting graphic, the narrator's description of Yvonne abruptly lapses into hallucinatory textuality. First of all, the depiction is set under the sign of the book. The narrator indicates that in the spirit of the orgy Yvonne and he had sex, but in keeping with the narrator's emotional modesty, they slip away from the others to have sex only with each other and in privacy: it is a solitary library to which they repair.[7] In fact, the narrative leaps from a brief description of the library—consisting of all (!!!) the books from the French detective collection le Masque—to a postcoital description of Yvonne's naked, sleeping body (*Villa Triste* 48). In the dark library, variously illuminated by the moon, a night light, an aquarium, and a lantern covered with patterns and images, Yvonne's body becomes a playground for the fantastic. It alternately changes colors, it is inscribed with passing tattoos, it consists only of parts, or it is cut in half (48-50). But fantastic shapes start their play over her body by assuming the configuration of *un loup* (48), that is, of a mask, which harks back to the books and suggests the dynamic of verbal generativity that is at work here.

In telling confusion, the passage and chapter conclude with the narrator's puzzled observation that when in memory he evokes this scene, it is in the context, not of the story of an erotic or physical experience, but rather in the context of an imagined pre-war Berlin associated with the director of an unfinished film (*Villa triste* 50). The presumed memory of the Haute-Savoie erotic encounter is contaminated and overpowered by a reconstruction of a fanciful Berlin that is linked with an unfinished movie, that is, the "memory" of the encounter morphs into the play of imagination and open textuality. It is at that point that the *tu* appears:

> Et moi, quand j'évoque cette nuit-là, j'avance entre les maisons massives du Berlin d'autrefois, je longe des quais et des boulevards qui n'existent plus. De l'Alexander-Platz, j'ai marché tout droit, traversé le Lust-Garten et la Sprée. Le soir tombe sur les quatre rangées de tilleuls et de marronniers et sur les tramways qui passent. Ils sont vides. Les lumières tremblent. Et *toi*, *tu* m'attends dans cette cage de verdure qui brille au bout de l'avenue, le jardin d'hiver de l'hôtel Adlon.
> (50; my emphasis)

That the narrator uses the emotionally charged *tu*, a charge strengthened by its rarity for him, only after free, arbitrary aesthetic association overpowers attempts at mimesis, allows us to detect here a hint at the actual status of his entire account's "memories": the Yvonne of the *tu,* the one who has the most intimate and personal relationship with him, is in fact very much, and almost explicitly acknowledged as, an element woven into, and spun out of, free aesthetic creation. In other words, and as we shall soon see, she is in considerable measure the product of *la scripturale création.* The more restrained and mimetic passages that make up most of the book would then be his verbal fantasies taking on (circularly) a deceptive referential cast as they thicken in a web of references, as language itself tends to do.

A similar state of narrative affairs obtains in the passage where *tu* is used to designate René Meinthe, a passage for which there is no satisfactory mimetic explanation. In it the narrator recounts his "observations" of Meinthe, but he does so unobserved himself, as well as unmentioned and uninvolved in the action, like an improbable camera invisible to the characters involved. His passage describes Meinthe the night of his suicide (see *Villa triste* 15-18, 51-53 119-22, 182-87), as if the narrator had somehow been on hand to gather an abundance of specific details. The proposition is highly unlikely, for as Alan Morris has pointed out, in this scene as in others there are substantial chronological inconsistencies. For Morris this suggests that "traditional chronology has *intentionally* been discarded," and indeed it raises the possibility that the narrated events are entirely imagined (Morris, *Patrick Modiano* [Berg] 69-70; emphasis in the original), prompted by Chmara's reading Meinthe's obituary while on a bench near the Louvre. With that mimesis-challenging background, we can consider the second *tu* passage. It reads as follows, marked as was the *tu* passage involving Yvonne by the play of darkness and light: "Nous voici rue Marlioz. La villa est au coin, là-bas, à gauche. Je la vois. Et je *te* vois qui marches d'un pas encore plus lent que tout à l'heure, et qui pousses d'un coup d'épaule le portail de bois. *Tu t*'es assis sur le canapé du salon et *tu* n'as pas allumé l'électricité. Le lampadaire, en face, répand sa clarté blanche" (*Villa triste* 185; my emphasis). So here too, thanks to the chronological inconsistency demonstrated by Morris, we can say that it is only in a scene showing clear tension with referentiality that the affect signaled by *tu* arises.

Here too, then, *la scripturale creation* may be understood to be at work. I would propose as one possibility that the narrator, having read the newspaper account of Meinthe's suicide, gives his imagination up to verbal associations, from which much of his story would then spin itself out. That proposition results from focusing on details such as the following, found in one of the sentences from the reported newspaper account: "Selon un témoignage, il aurait passé quelques moments au *Cintra*, 23 rue *Sommeiller*" (*Villa triste* 186; my emphasis). Le Cintra, the bar named in the newspaper story, bears the name of something to drink, specifically the Portuguese wine *cintra*. This word may be seen to set up a series of drinking associations that become key details that become imaginative kernels that become incidents that eventually weave themselves into story text. So for example, one of the details added to the narrator's expanded version of events is that Meinthe ordered a glass of port (53), a patent association readily made because of the cited name of the bar, but one perhaps facilitated by the similarity of the street name (*Sommeiller*) to *sommelier,* a wine steward. That the verb *sommeiller* also brings us into the realm of napping, of the nether world of consciousness between wakefulness and sleep, does nothing to weaken the point of subtle verbal association on the borders of awareness. Moreover, the word *Meinthe* finds visual and sonorous likeness in *menthe*, which is linked within the text itself to other drinks, the alcoholic *diabolo menthe* and the non-alcoholic *tilleul-menthe* (49, 206), the latter an infusion of linden and mint leaves that too involves the concept of drinking, which points us back to the proposed originary bar scene. That non-alcoholic example too teases with elusive associations beyond the non-alcoholic, until one recalls that some of the more complex wines can have linden aromas. In addition, it seems too much a coincidence that Chmara imagines the initial locale of his story to be a *pension de famille* called *les Tilleuls*. In another linking of the alcoholic and non-alcoholic, he subsequently leaves "The Linden Trees" in order live with Yvonne in her hotel, *l'Hermitage* (54), a name that happens also to be that of a red wine of Southern France. Equally consistent with this proposed compulsive verbal repetitiveness, the site of another of the major scenes, the orgy, is *Villa les Tilleuls* (39).[8] Tightening up even further the self-referential web of associations, when Yvonne is evoked fantastically as seen above, she is dreamily held within a cage of chestnut trees and *tilleuls* (50).[9] In retrospection, then, there is no surprise in realizing that the narrator, when imagining himself confronted with the need to come up with a non-French alias, imagines himself blurting out *Chmara,* an Arabic word for alcohol and the only name under which the reader knows him. In addition, the Portuguese associations of *Cintra/cintra* would also help to explain why the Jewish narrator, in order to explain his odd paranoia regarding France's Algerian war, recalls not the plight of Jewish refugees in his native France during World War II, but rather the plight of Jewish refugees in Lisbon at that time. Nor are those Portuguese associations without relevance to the fact that one of the major events of the book, the awarding to Yvonne of *la coupe Houligant,* ends at night with dancing to *Avril au Portugal* (110). Notably, in the description of Chmara's one and only neck tie, the *Cintra/cintra*'s verbal compulsiveness—an originary textual subconscious behind the apparent mimesis—even offers a quick literal and metaphorical peek at its own fixation and how it works: "cravate bleu nuit semée de fleurs de lys qu'un Américain m'avait offerte et au revers de laquelle étaient cousus les mots: 'International Bar Fly' " (25). So the sewed-in words inscribed on the tie "loop" us back to the opening bar scene while writing Chmara enduringly and emblematically into it; but significantly, it is all hidden on the underside.

As a measure of the intricacy of detail with which the verbally associative web grows, the narrator, imagining Meinthe being drawn to le Cintra by what is described as a visual whirlwind of the green and red of bottles of alcohol (*Villa triste* 52), imagines Yvonne first coming into his life under those same colors (27-28). Similarly, imagining Meinthe in the originary scene passing by a movie house showing *La dolce vita,* the narrator will make of Yvonne a movie actress, and he will, as indicated above, involve her and himself in an orgy with the film production company, and at one point they pass by a fountain and try to push each other into it (113), actions reminiscent of Fellini's movie. The sense of textual self-referentiality becomes denser still with the description of the film in which Yvonne had played a role before Chmara imagined himself meeting her (64-65), for the summary of *Liebesbriefe auf der Berg (Lettre d'amour de la montagne)* announces what little plot there is to *Villa triste:* the character played by Yvonne winds up at the end with the ski instructor, as in *Villa triste* Yvonne herself will do with the former ski-champion Daniel Hendrickx, running off with him on the last pages without any warning to the narrator.

None of all this is meant to imply that for *Villa triste* all or even most of its textual production can be explained by *la scripturale création* alone—few if any worthy literary texts benefit from readings based on univocal explanations, least of all rich, elusive, and allusive texts like Modiano's. If one compares a reading focusing on key words à la Ricardou with a reading à la Riffaterre, one quickly sees that, while sharing a structuralist inspiration, the first reading emphasizes literary production in the structures of the writer's imagination, and the second emphasizes literary production in the structures of the reader's imagination. Nonetheless, given the complexity of Modianesque literary production voracious in its sources and means, the clarifying value of the two structuralist approaches, however different they are, is considerable, and in fact those approaches can be seen to work in parallel ways. For instance, within this novel Ricardou's *la scripturale création* spills over into the intertextual creation so important to Riffaterre. To observe that, one need do no more than to recall the work of the French novelist and *Académicien* (and fascist sympathizer intolerant of Jews) Paul Morand, whose work Modiano of course knows (see for example Berl 110). The title of one of Morand's novellas, *Le prisonnier de Cintra,* which involves a suicide, while introducing intertextuality into this reading also thickens the resonances of the *Cintra/cintra* of the originary bar scene by hinting at a possible semiotic motivation behind the Meinthe's suicide. Still another of Morand's novellas, *La folle amoureuse,* deals with a Spanish woman who becomes the mistress of a Russian nobleman, only eventually—like Yvonne vis-à-vis the putatively Russian Chmara—to be separated from him. The fact that the end of this latter novella proposes a fantastic reincarnation of the nineteenth-century mistress as a twentieth-century participant in the Spanish civil war cannot help but raise the question whether René Meinthe, that other re-born (*re-né*), does not owe to intertextuality something of what he insists is his own reincarnation, that as the woman Queen Astrid of Belgium (*Villa triste* 190).[10]

And naturally there are examples of still other sorts of textual production, but à la Riffaterre. For instance, in Modiano's intertext-suffused oeuvre one can only expect that Chmara's repeated and emphatic references to the lake, which eases his paranoia by acting as a concrete reminder of his easy access to Switzerland, activates within *Villa triste* the textual pull of one of France's best known poems, Alphonse de Lamartine's "Le lac."[11] Literally muffled echoes from the recitation of the poem become an explicit part of the narrative (199), and of course the poem, like *Villa triste,* concerns itself with problems of reconstructed or "echoed" time as reconstructed or "echoed" in voices, and with a love doomed to an unhappy end: thus both the novel and the poem to which it harks back raise issues of their own textual production.

One final point can be made about the usage of *tu* in *Villa triste.* Distinctive as it is, it links Meinthe and Yvonne together in an unusual affective closeness. A reader mindful of the familial implications of pronoun usage in *La place de l'étoile, La ronde de nuit,* and *Les boulevards de ceinture* cannot help but be struck by the hints found in *Villa triste* that in the narrator's imagination the two characters, so emphatically portrayed as inhabiting an uncertain marginality, share an equally uncertain family marginality: Chmara decides that, even though they are unrelated and from very different social backgrounds, they had known each other "*depuis toujours*" (76), that they have something to hide about their relationship (for example 78), and he adds that Meinthe, with no particular consistency, declares himself to be both *marraine de guerre* (77) and brother for Yvonne (168). The suppressed Brother-figure and the guilt that accompanies it have little or no role in this novel's use of personal pronouns, but thanks to the curiously sibling-like René-Yvonne pair, troublesome echoes of that guilt, while muted almost to silence, seem still to be on the borders of awareness in this story about being distracted by the liberation of romance while living fearfully on a border. But troublesome echoes notwithstanding, with *Villa triste* love has emotionally filled for a while what we have been calling the oeuvre's gap.

Those dim echoes of guilt do however come close to expression in Modiano's next novel, the highly autofictional *Livret de famille.* My discussion will linger only briefly over this novel, since for my purposes it can be considered primarily as a complementary companion piece to *Villa triste.* But *Livret de famille* is unique in this regard: it is the first published novel in which Modiano names and identifies his much mourned brother Rudy (in chapters 8 and 14 of *Livret de famille* 111-12, 209), an important fact for this entire study that maintains that suppressed irrational guilt over Rudy's death during their childhood plays a seminal role in Patrick's oeuvre. In chapter 9 of *Livret de famille,* hard on the heels of this groundbreaking development for the oeuvre, the narrator Patrick creates what is an excellent metaphor for the way in which the suppressed feelings about the brother make themselves known in the early oeuvre but only barely. He describes (123-27) how at night, all alone at twenty during a brief sojourn in Lausanne, he would scan his radio dial with the greatest of care, "millimeter by millimeter" (123). One night he happened to stumble onto a program that gripped him in an unexplained hypnotic spell. Broadcast only at night and only for the short, unusual span of twenty minutes, "Musique dans la nuit" became an obsession for him. Playing a variety of only the briefest of pieces, the "elegantly dry" program with no commentary (124-25) was presented by two quite different, vaguely antagonistic, voices, that of Robert Gerbauld, grave and nasal, and the other, that of Jean-Xavier Curtine, sharp, metallic, almost feminine. Sometimes, but only sometimes, the narrator believed he could make out a third, barely perceptible voice trying in vain to break through the music and feeble overlaid background voices in order to communicate either a cry for help or an indistinct message:

> Etait-ce parce que mon ouïe s'affinait, mais je crus discerner
> un léger grésillement sous le flot de la musique. Je supposai
> d'abord qu'il s'agissait des bruits de parasites que l'on entend
> lorsqu'on capte un poste étranger, mais j'eus bientôt la certi-
> tude que c'était le murmure de plusieurs conversations entre-
> croisées, murmure confus d'où se détachait parfois une voix

> qui lançait un appel au secours ou un message indistinct,
> comme si plusieurs personnes profitaient de cette émission
> pour échanger des messages entre elles ou se retrouver à tâ-
> tons. Et comme si leurs voix, vainement, tentaient de percer
> l'écran de la musique. (125)[12]

Furthermore, in a reprise of the theme, one night, in spite of the narrator's observation that the presenters' voices customarily did not offer
commentary, one of them breaks out into precisely that, in order to express his impression of the music having communicated an indirect cry
for help or an indistinct message of grief:

> —Chers auditeurs—sa voix [celle de Gerbauld] avait un trem-
> blement inaccoutumé—l'œuvre que nous venons d'entendre
> me va droit au cœur. Cette musique ressemble à une plainte
> d'outre-tombe, c'est un long cri d'exil. . .
>   Un silence. Gerbauld reprit, la voix de plus en plus
> altérée:
>   —Le compositeur a certainement voulu traduire ici
> l'impression qu'il avait d'être le dernier survivant d'un monde
> disparu, un fantôme parmi les fantômes. (126)

But these passages, for all their metaphoric accuracy in intimating what
this study views as the ghostly voice in the oeuvre, do not establish in
Livret de famille as a whole the overriding, anguished, and tormented
tone heard in the first three novels. One handy measure of that is that the
narrator Patrick does *not* try to kill anyone, which makes him like Victor
Chmara of the companion piece *Villa triste* and unlike the trio of
Raphaël, Swing Troubadour, and Serge Alexandre. True, he does at one
point entertain the preliminaries of a murderous fantasy (84-85), but the
preliminaries do fully realize themselves. I would propose then that this
failure of fantasized murderous hostility to erupt into fullness and a fortiori into action suggests that *Livret de famille* continues in the happy effects of romance seen in *Villa triste*. In fact *Livret de famille* shows very
concretely the happy effects of romance, namely marriage and the birth
of a child. Mention of the newborn opens and closes the text like a new

talisman, working as an encapsulating, successful counter to the almost articulated guilt and to the angry hostility theretofore generated by it.

So the oeuvre has evolved under the influence of the Woman, who no longer functions exclusively as the Mother/Whore of the opening trilogy. Henceforth the oeuvre will be influenced variously by her role as Lover. Under the positive inspiration of the Woman as Lover, the central interrogation scene in which she, the Father, and the Son/Brother appear will become less a site of psychological anguish, and more a generative source of detective stories like traditional—but inconclusive—whodunits, the clearest examples being *Rue des boutiques obscures* (1978) and *Quartier perdu* (1984). In these novels a spirit of artistic play displaces the anguish found in the triad (see for example O'Keefe "The *Odyssey* and Signs to the Rescue").

Appearing in the midst of the various Modianesque detective stories, *Vestaire de l'enfance* (1989) offers a good illustration of how an application of the findings of the Riffaterrean reading of *La place de l'étoile* can cast an intriguing if uncertain light on the evolution of the Woman in subsequent novels. It happens that the narrator Jean Moreno/ Jimmy Sarano represents the last of Modiano's very explicit dual/split narrators, preceded by the *La place de l'étoile*'s kaleidoscopic Raphaël Schlemilovitch, *La ronde de nuit*'s Swing Troubadour/Princesse de Lamballe, *Rue des boutiques obscures*'s Guy/Pedro McEvoy/Jimmy Pedro Stern, and *Quartier perdu*'s Ambrose Guise/Jean Dekker. We can argue that one possible reason for the identity of Modiano's tortured narrators becoming subsequently less fissional is a new dynamic in the relationship of the subtext's four personae (the Father, Mother, Son, Brother), a dynamic that will allow love to counter guilt.

Identity, so much a product of memory, is everywhere in Modiano's work as unstable as uncertain memory can make it. But in *Vestiaire de l'enfance* the conditions are right for especially unstable identity, in that the narrator is especially aggressive in filtering out time and place, markers through which memory tries to organize itself. He focuses on time primarily in its mythological dimensions, for example: "Le seul passé qui m'intéresse, et dont j'ai découvert les traces, semble mythologique [. . .]" (*Vestiaire de l'enfance* 40-41). And the characters that he describes live, as he himself does, a life resistant to reflection (for example11-12), a dizzying life set in an indeterminate everywhere that is nowhere geographically, linguistically, and culturally (for example 133-34), a life perched on an uneasy fault line outside of time, between on the one hand the immobility of transparent timelessness (for example 17, 42-43, 65, 151) and on the other hand a cyclical round of repetitions, as for instance in scenes (35, 83), situations (62-63, 66, 73, 127-28, 141), and names (40, 71-72).

One of the results of this breakdown in memory and so in identity is a bold, barely coherent conflation of identities across genders and across the roles of the subtextual Family. For all its boldness here, however, transgendering is nothing new in Modiano's work, having early on expressed itself at times overtly, witness Swing Troubadour/la Princesse de Lamballe and René Meinthe/la reine Astrid of *Villa triste,* at times more covertly, witness Edmond of *De si braves garçons* who as a student had played a woman in a school play, and who later as an adult had a role in a play the title of which explicitly rephrases the earlier situation, *Mademoiselle Moi* (*De si braves garçons* 175-76). But *Vestiaire de l'enfance* marks the first time that the possibility arises for the Modianesque narrator that the Brother (a child) as representative of guilt can become the Woman as representative of love. For the already doubled narrator Jean/Jimmy, the guilt-producing Child (*Vestiaire de l'enfance* 50-51, 98, 109-20), incarnated this time in la petite Marie, does her own doubling, in her case across time and with the Woman, incarnated by the apparently same Marie as an adult, with whom the narrator eventually sleeps (68-69). The affect of the latter incarnation of the persona co-opts that of the former, love countering guilt, thereby countering for a decisive, final time the radical sundering of identity under the goad of guilt. Furthermore, the gender switch from a masculine Brother/Child is facilitated in French by "Marie" being both a female's given name and a frequent component of a male's given name. True, the abandonment of the Brother as self/twin was first explicitly proposed by Jean Dekker/Ambrose Guise in the earlier *Quartier perdu*: "Il n'y avait plus de place ici, désormais, pour ce Jean Dekker dont on allait retrouver les fiches d'hôtel à la Mondaine. Il fallait que je laisse ce frère jumeau derrière moi [. . .] " (*Quartier perdu* 181). But it is in *Vestiaire de l'enfance* that the break is realized: the Child "twin brother" Marie is subsumed for the narrator in his embrace of the Woman Marie. This delirious but yet only barely coherent breakdown of identity doubtless reflects accurately enough Modiano's own chaotic sense of his identity: "je suis moi-même un tissu vivant de contradictions et de bâtardise. Mi-Juif mi-Flamand, une moitié de moi-même persécute, dément ou corrige l'autre, dans un jeu antagoniste où tout se mélange et s'interpénètre…" (Modiano, in Ezine 23). Moreover, in the three novels that in quick succession followed the publication of *Vestiaire de l'enfance* (*Voyage de noces* [1990], *Fleurs de ruine* [1991], and *Un cirque passe* [1992]), the transgendering continued, in that they show a reconciliation of feminine-masculine psychic poles (see Kaminskas's "Modiano's Female Trilogy"). In fact, the transgendered confusion hinted at in *Vestiaire de l'enfance* will eventually reappear decisively in Modianesque narrators becoming female on two subsequent occasions, *Des inconnues* in 1999 and *La petite bijou* in 2001.

But the positive inspiration of the Woman as Lover can flag, such that the Mother/Whore side reasserts itself, as for instance in the unsettling portraits of women's criminality and whorishness à la Série Noire, for example in *Une jeunesse* (1981), *Dimanches d'août* (1986), and *Un cirque passe* (1992). But be her inspiration generally positive or generally negative, the Woman usually disappears from the life of the narrator in either case, her absence thereby maintaining a trace of the emotional pain caused by the gap or void left in the Family by the Brother's death. For instance, nearly from the start of *Voyage de noces* Ingrid Teyrsen, the focus of the narrative, indubitably establishes herself as a protective, loving maternal figure in the narrator's life:

> Elle m'a pris le bras à cause de la rue en pente. Le contact de son bras et de son épaule me donnait une impression que je n'avais ressentie encore, celle de me trouver sous la protection de quelqu'un. Elle serait la première personne qui pourrait m'aider. Une sensation de légèreté m'envahissait. Toutes ces ondes de douceur qu'elle me communiquait par le simple contact de son bras et par ce regard bleu pâle qu'elle levait de temps en temps vers moi, j'ignorais que de telles choses pouvaient se produire, dans la vie. (*Voyage de noces* 39)

But in spite of her dominant role of Mother as Loving Woman, through her own suicide she will on the last page of the narrative become for the narrator a powerful siren of suicide, thereby evoking for the reader of the oeuvre the remorse-ridden gap that plagued the fratricidal/suicidal Self/Brother: "Ce sentiment de *vide* et de remords vous submerge, un jour. Puis, comme une marée il se retire et disparaît. Mais il finit par revenir en force et elle ne pouvait pas s'en débarrasser. Moi non plus" (*Voyage de noces* 158; my emphasis).

But little if anything being definitive in the work of Modiano "the king of ambiguity," the Woman can still—at least momentarily—evolve from the Mother/Whore to the Loving Woman, infusing a novel by Modiano with positive, tender eroticism, as is the case in his latest (as of this writing), *Accident nocturne* (2003). The novel relates in hindsight the narrator's frustrating search as a young man for the beguiling Jacqueline Beausergent, whose car had accidentally sideswiped him. That negative introduction suits her at first, since she can be read to reincarnate the hostile Mother/Whore: hostile of course because of what she did with her car, maternal in her reassuring touch (for example 11-12), whorish because she at first appears to be the "kept woman" of a *brun massif* (for example 12, 18, 23-25, 26-27), and because the narrator associates fur coats such as hers (for example 10) with whores (13). But his text concludes with his account of his finally having found her, and in spite of the violence of their first encounter, and in spite of her subsequent elusiveness and apparent disrespectability, he had finally discovered her to be innocent, open, and tender toward him, as indicated by her language and her reassuring Ingrid-like touch: "'Mais non, je n'ai rien à cacher... La vie est beaucoup plus simple que tu ne le crois...' Elle m'avait tutoyé pour la première fois. Elle me serrait le bras [. . .] " (*Accident nocturne* 147). His closing paragraph relates the thinly veiled erectile thrust of an elevator that, as she whispers in the narrator's ear, lifts them to an apartment where they will sleep and be together—but only temporarily, since the mature narrator is offering merely a melancholy retrospective that looks back down the years following her subsequent and unexplained disappearance from his life as a youth.

By way of summary, then, the four figures constituting the subtextual Family of *La place de l'étoile*'s Oedipally strident theater scene can be seen first to dominate the opening trilogy of Modiano's oeuvre, and then under the influence of erotic love to undergo an evolution, primarily in the figure of the Mother/Whore. That evolution will waiver, now producing a positive figure, now a negative figure, but eventually if not permanently subsuming in love the guilt created by the death of the Brother.

◆ ◆ ◆

Conclusion

This study opened by pointing to the puzzle posed by Modiano's incontestable success, which got its start with the controversial *La place de l'étoile*. That puzzle provided the reason, more accurately of course the excuse, to choose consciously a similarly controversial critical approach, that of Michael Riffaterre, for a reading of *La place de l'étoile*. The intent was to suggest, in harmony with the critical overview offered in the Introduction, that Modiano's oeuvre is richly available to a great variety of approaches. Moreover, the hope is that my own pleasure at recalling and building upon so much sophisticated, insightful scholarship already written about or pertinent to Modiano's work has been apparent enough to be the more decisive explanation of why readers and scholars have consistently spent time with his books, and why they will continue to do so.

As another justification of my study, and as another explanation of Modiano's success, the road followed led to several interesting byways, such as questions of literary referentiality and the role of several famous intertexts, byways that I hope were ventured on with something at least suggestive of the mix of finesse and acuity that they deserve. But in the belief that a good conclusion points beyond the work that it ends, I would like to have my study end by pointing to byways that it must be content only to identify, not to pursue.

The Riffaterrean approach identified reading problems, problems that eventually led to a consideration of guilt. That of course should come as no surprise in a discussion of a post-Holocaust work written by a Jewish Frenchman haunted on the one hand by the memory of his father's (and so prenatally, his) barely surviving the Nazi scourge, Albert Modiano having twice narrowly escaped being sent to the camps, and on the other hand by the memory of his father's having on one of those occasions escaped that very scourge only through his comfortable contacts with shady Parisians collaborators. Father and son were would-be victims of a Holocaust advanced by the Collaboration, only to have survived because of help from the Collaboration: a sure-fire formula for an introspective writer's being haunted by guilt, a formula compounded by the childhood tragedy of a sibling's death. What in the process of this analysis did however come, if not as a complete surprise then as an unexpected recognition for this reader, was the resulting hint that, if Modiano is as important a writer as many critics are coming to find, great first-person narratives may necessarily tend to an exploration of guilt.

In a phenomenological exploration of confession, Paul Ricoeur, building on Immanuel Kant's reflections on human consciousness, tries to verbalize the near instinctive sense of guilt behind such texts as Kafka's fictional meditations on a priori guilt and Paul's seventh verse in the epistle to the Romans ("Once I was alive apart from law; but when the commandment came, sin sprang to life and I died"). Ricoeur keys on the symbiotic relationship between freedom and evil:

> In a first stage of reflection, I say: to affirm freedom is to take upon oneself the origin of evil. By this proposition, I affirm a link between evil and liberty, which is so close that the two terms imply one another mutually. Evil has the meaning of evil because it is the work of freedom. Freedom has the meaning of freedom because it is capable of evil [. . .] .
> (Ricoeur, "Guilt" 229)

But human freedom of course is inconceivable outside of awareness, and awareness—Ricoeur comes to suggest—*necessarily* leads to guilt; awareness *means* guilt:

> But in placing myself before the consequences of my act, I refer myself back to the moment prior to my act, and I designate myself as he who not only performed the act but who could have done otherwise. [. . .] But the awareness that one could have done otherwise is closely linked to the awareness that one *should* have done otherwise. It is because I recognize

my "ought" that I recognize my "could." (Ricoeur, "Guilt"
230; original emphasis)

Nor is Ricoeur's point to be taken only within the confines of rather rare-
fied ethical reflections within the confines of philosophy. For example,
the poet W. H. Auden has reflected ethically from within the confines of
detective fiction, the genre that as we saw profoundly marks *La place de
l'étoile* and that can readily be seen to mark the rest of the oeuvre, and
the genre that certainly is one of the literary genres—if not *the* literary
genre—that best exposes the most widespread practices of reading. In his
reflection Auden used a different context and different terms to make the
same point as Ricoeur about the radically guilty character of human
choice and consciousness:

> I suspect that the typical reader of detective stories is, like my-
> self, a person who suffers from a sense of sin. From the point
> of view of ethics, desires and acts are good and bad, and I
> must choose the good and reject the bad, but the *I* which
> makes this choice is ethically neutral; it only becomes good or
> bad in its choice. To have a sense of sin means to feel guilty at
> there being an ethical choice to make, a guilt which however
> "good" I may become, remains unchanged. (Auden 158)

I propose then that, seen in this light, Modiano's novels, in their intricate,
initially rambunctious, subsequently delicate exploration of narrative
awareness tinged unerringly with guilt, give rise to the question whether
most great first-person narratives, starting with the anonymous *Lazarillo
de Tormes* and proceeding on up through masterpieces such as Goethe's
Die Leiden des jungen Werther and Camus's *La chute,* do not necessarily
veer to the issue of guilt.

   Moreover, in light of the preceding reflections by Ricoeur and
Auden, Modiano's texts can be seen to probe human identity astutely,
precisely because of their concern with guilt-producing events such as
the French Collaboration with Nazi agents of the Holocaust. That is perhaps just another way of saying that, throughout the ages, it has been in
pondering the horrific extremes of some of our conduct that we get a
penetrating glimpse of the astonishing freedom that defines and identifies

us. Is it, then, a mere coincidence that in French literature, a literature in which one of its historically operative words—*moral*—means both "mental" *and* "ethical," and in which *la conscience* can mean either "awareness" or "conscience," is it a coincidence that in such a literature the theme of guilt characterizes many of its defining texts, texts throughout the centuries generative of major literary currents in France and generative of renown outside of France? One thinks immediately of the *Chanson de Roland,* perhaps *the* foundational text of French literature, key moments of that *chanson de geste* being first Roland's and Olivier's debate over guilt for the annihilation of the rear guard and then the epic's concluding test of Ganelon's guilt; one thinks of Renaissance Rabelais's carnavalesque rejection of guilt, distilled into the solitary and singular Thelemite rule *Fais ce que voudras;* there is of course the towering seventeenth-century masterpiece *Le Cid,* the two main characters of which anguish in exquisite neo-classical cadences over the necessarily guilty choice of duty either to love or to family; of course, Jean-Jacques Rousseau's eighteenth-century *Les confessions* is nothing if not the fruit of a paranoid compulsion to sound and exculpate a guilty conscience, as exemplified in the famous episode of *le ruban volé;* it is to guilt that the eponymous hero of Victor Hugo's *Hernani,* the play that was French Romanticism's official "coming out," owes his characteristic inability to act on vengeance and love, making him a Rodrique *manqué;* and Jean-Paul Sartre's *Les mouches* represents one of the twentieth century's existentialist attempts to define choice against the imperatives of guilt. Moreover, with the theme of guilt we will find ourselves back at the issue raised by Guyot-Bender and Ruszniewski-Dahan, namely ethical considerations in literary works such as Modiano's, considerations that contemporary critical discourse too often slights. The point to be taken is that although we certainly are semiotic and aesthetic beings who look for literary understanding and pleasure, we are not exclusively semiotic and aesthetic beings, remaining also ethical beings who lessen the value of literature if we overlook the ethical issues woven into it.

And finally, the sweep of the byways ventured upon invites a final, equally sweeping question. Even a cursory reading of Modiano's oeuvre will show that, like Raphaël Schlemilovitch, all of his narrators and the majority of his characters are clearly neurotic, in fact as neurotic as the "Modiano" of the media. Could it be that Modiano's oeuvre should be taken as a hint that we are all neurotic; indeed, and to circle back to a term emphasized in the opening of this study, that we are all outrageous? Could it be that the deliriously neurotic Raphaël Schlemilovitch, because of his boundless powers of imagination and concomitant (or more accurately, constitutive) powers of narrative re-creation, is another incarnation of Everyman? One could do worse than to let Paul Tillich suggest that the answer might well be in the affirmative:

> The history of human culture proves that again and again neurotic anxiety breaks through the walls of ordinary self-affirmation and opens up levels of reality which are normally hidden.
>
> This however brings us to the question whether the normal self-affirmation of the average man is not even more limited than the pathological self-affirmation of the neurotic, and consequently whether the state of pathological anxiety and self-affirmation is not the ordinary state of man. (Tillich 67)

◆ ◆ ◆

Notes

Introduction

1. *The French Review* has graciously given permission to reproduce in this introduction and in chapter 1 various sections from my article: "Hard to Swallow: A Not-So-Postmodern Reading of Patrick Modiano's Postmodern Oeuvre" (O'Keefe "Hard to Swallow").

2. See especially Anne-Marie Obajtek-Kirkwood's *L'Occupation "rêvée" de l'"autre vie" de Patrick Modiano* and Baptiste Roux's *Figures de l'Occupation dans l'œuvre de Patrick Modiano*. Annie Demeyère's *Portraits de l'artiste dans l'œuvre de Patrick Modiano* is especially useful for identifying historical cinema, entertainment, and sports figures. Roland Brasseur's *Je me souviens de* Je me souviens, a book of notes on Georges Perec's *Je me souviens*, happens to be informative also about a number of factual references throughout Modiano's oeuvre, references that appear in *Je me souviens* as well.

3. In its most obvious sense the title refers of course to Paris's most famous intersection, la place de l'Étoile, now officially called la place Charles de Gaulle. Ironically, the switch is all too bitterly appropriate, since de Gaulle was the chief architect of the myth of universal French resistance that displaced the history of, for instance, Vichy's criminal imposition on Jews of a place where the star of David had to be worn.

4. In these pages, the expression "Modiano's novels" will refer exclusively to the following texts (in their order of publication): *La place de l'étoile, La ronde de nuit, Les boulevards de ceinture, Villa triste, Livret de famille, Rue des boutiques obscures, Une jeunesse, De si braves garçons, Quartier perdu, Dimanches d'août, Remise de peine, Vestiaire de l'enfance, Voyage de noces, Fleurs de ruine, Un cirque passe, Chien de printemps, Du plus loin de l'oubli, Dora Bruder, Des inconnues, La petite bijou,* and *Accident nocturne.*

Modiano being Modiano, however, there are serious problems in deciding on the best designation for these texts. For an example, some of these novels were not announced as "*romans*" on their title page. So the original Gallimard edition of *Les boulevards de ceinture* had "*récit*" on the title page, only to become "*roman*" on the published-works list to be found in the subsequent *Une jeunesse*. *De si braves garçons* had neither "*roman*" nor "*récit*" on its title page, only to be pronounced a "*roman*" on the published-works list to be found in the book that followed it, *Quartier perdu*. Similarly, *Dora Bruder*, Modiano's personal account of how his investigations into the Holocaust victim Dora Bruder led to his writing *Voyage de noces*, was originally published in Gallimard's *Edition Blanche* series with no indication of genre. However, it was listed as *roman* on Modiano's publication list figuring in his very next work *Des inconnues* (1999). So as Annie Demeyère proposes (165-66), *Dora Bruder* can be read either as a highly personal historic document or as fiction.

The problem is not only serious, it is also interesting. The repeated and detailed interplay between fiction and autobiography in all of Modiano's texts has created the possibility that the confusion arises because of the resulting unusual nature of Modiano's work. Neither "*roman*" nor "*récit*" may be totally appropriate. Thierry Laurent prefers "autofiction," even though he acknowledges that the term should apply properly only to the apparently more strictly autobiographical fictions, *Livret de famille*, *De si braves garçons*, *Remise de peine*, and *Fleurs de ruine* (Laurent 9-12). Akane Kawakami's highly informed analysis of Modiano's oeuvre makes a case for reading many of Modiano's books as "*romans*," but for reading others like *Livret de famille* as "autofictions" (Kawakami 106-8). For reasons to be made clear in the following pages, I will take a position closer to Laurent's while continuing to use the word "novel." That usage happens to be the current practice of Modiano's publishers, Gallimard and Seuil.

Furthermore, such shorthand on my part excludes books by Modiano like *Catherine Certitude* that are distinguished by their appropriateness as reading material for children, and others books such as *Memory Lane* that complicate questions of textuality by consisting of both text and corresponding illustrations. The latter kinds of book are, to be sure, integral, fully representative components of his work, but they raise additional issues not directly raised by his other, more numerous and more critically discussed novels.

5. The point was given initial if dismissive authority by the no less famous novelist Michel Tournier: "on pourrait faire un seul livre de tous ses ouvrages réunis" (Michel Tournier, quoted in "Autour des prix," *Les Nouvelles*

Littéraires [23-30 November 1978] 3, by Warehime, "Originality and Narrative Nostalgia" 335). Consider also, for instance: "La lecture du nouveau Modiano: *Un cirque passe* [1992] confirme l'impression de l'amateur: Modiano n'a pas trouvé de second souffle, capable qu'il est de reproduire à la puissance X le roman de 'Cette période de l'adolescence qu'on ne retrouvera plus, où les choses sont encore incertaines...' [Madeleine Chapsal, *Lire* 120 {septembre 1985}, 58] et le roman d'une ambiance: celle du laxisme moral, souvent dans un Paris surimprégné de souvenirs de l'Occupation. La récurrence des thèmes ne peut qu'être encore une fois soulignée: enquête sur l'identité du narrateur ou des personnages, passage à l'âge adulte à l'aide d'individus louches fournissant un argent volé, comme la récurrence des motifs: balades en ville, arrêts dans les cafés, la couleur rouge, la jupe et le pull-over..." (Breut 103). Warehime disagreed with this negative view of the oeuvre as a *roman-série*, and many are the critics who concur with Warehime. See for instance Nettelbeck and Hueston, "Anthology as Art, Modiano's '*Livret de famille*,' " and *Modiano, pièces d'identité*, Jules Bedner ("Présentation"), and Manet van Montfrans.

On the other hand, it has been possible for careful and quite enthusiastic readers of Modiano to conclude by means of no less telling details that, happily, all his novels do comprise the same, single book. Witness Jean-Claude Joye, who finds that the individual "parts" of this "*seul et même livre*" (114) all come to show that the search for identity driving them all never succeeds and must always be left in uncertain suspense. In that, Joye discovers universality: "cette universalité est celle de la communauté fantasmatique qui unit les hommes sans qu'ils le sachent et qui fait de chacun un être à la recherche perpétuelle, essoufflante, débilitante même de son ou plutôt de ses Moi successifs et fugitifs, mais aussi un être en quête des projections sans cesse renouvelées et souvent contradictoires d'une introuvable identité" (Joye 115).

6. "*La place de l'étoile*, cette place du cœur vers quoi chez Modiano tout converge et d'où tout rayonne" (Bersani, "Agent double" 81).

7. "On peut [. . .] y voir, du moins sous une forme symbolique, certains des éléments fondamentaux de son art futur [. . .] " (Nettelbeck and Hueston, *Patrick Modiano* 22-23).

8. "*La place de l'étoile* contains many of the elements that characterize Modiano's later work, from the creation of a fraudulent, dangerous, and dizzying world, the artful mixing of historical and fictive characters, and the protagonist's ambition to be a writer, to the hero's fundamental alienation and stubborn concern with origins and identity and his obsession with events from a past (in Schlemilovitch's case World War II and the Holocaust) that

is paradoxically both dead and alive. Yet the novel's amalgamation of savage buffoonery and poignant tragedy as well as its exploitation and explosion of the resources of fiction are pursued to a degree that is perhaps unique in Modiano's work" (Prince, "Patrick Modiano" 148).

9. "We would like to show that beneath the polemical style of this novel (and in symbiosis with its extratextual origin or intent), there is another (and more important) narrative significance that confers an existential dimension to *La place de l'étoile* and provides the reader of Modiano's novels with what is perhaps the fundamental paradigm of his *imaginaire* or inspiration as a writer" (Daprini 193). For Daprini, "the basic topos underlying Modiano's novels [is] the expression of transcendental and existential homelessness" (Daprini 198).

10. "*La place de l'étoile*, roman étonnant qui malgré son allure si particulière contenait en germe toute la thématique de l'œuvre à venir" (Bedner, "Patrick Modiano" 50). Bedner sees the stranger first announced in *La place de l'étoile* as the unifying theme running throughout Modiano's oeuvre.

11. "Trop souvent opposé à sa 'seconde période,' *La place de l'étoile* contient pourtant non pas en germe, mais sous la forme de l'excès, de la débauche de sens, toutes les problématiques suivantes" (Demeyère 236).

12. See for example: "*La place* represents Modiano's most experimental, difficult and angriest work. Nothing else Modiano has written expresses such raw adolescent rage in such a derisive manner" (Dickstein 146).

13. But Bruno Doucey for one would disagree. His study of Modiano's second published novel, *La ronde de nuit,* maintains that this work is more representative of the oeuvre than *La place de l'étoile*. "Mais *La ronde de nuit* peut être, à plus d'un titre, considéré comme le premier véritable roman de Patrick Modiano car il porte en lui, avec plus de profondeur que *La place de l'étoile*, les germes de l'œuvre à venir. *La ronde de nuit* est, au sens musical du terme, une 'ouverture': il introduit les thèmes, les éléments narratifs, les obsessions qui deviendront les ferments de son univers romanesque" (Doucey 11).

Chapter 1
A Riffaterrean Approach to *La place de l'étoile*

1. Some of the material that follows had been initially presented in the form of papers at different meetings of the University of Cincinnati's Romance Languages and Literatures Conference: "Riffaterrean Subtext as Guide to Patrick Modiano's Oeuvre" (May 1999); "A Semiotic Reading of Narrative

Ungrammaticalities in Patrick Modiano's *La place de l'étoile*" (May 2000); "Killing the Self/Brother in Patrick Modiano's *La place de l'étoile:* 'Avaler des lames de rasoir,' or The Dilemma of a Jew Writing in French" (May 2001); "The Referent in Literature: the Example of the Word 'Hitler' in Patrick Modiano's *La place de l'étoile*" (May 2003).

2. For arguments maintaining variously that Riffaterre's approach is not self-consistent, that his premises and/or terminology are faulty, see for instance (in chronological order, but with no claim to being an exhaustive list) Hardy, Dragoş, Fish (59-66, 87), Culler (79-99), de Man, Blanchard, Freadman, Walker, Vanoncini, Goyet, MacKenzie, and Compagnon (127-28). By my reading of Riffaterre and of these critics, the best formulations of shortcomings to be found in Riffaterre's approach come from the readily accessible Culler and Goyet, and from the less readily accessible Blanchard, de Man, and Freadman. Riffaterre has of course attempted to answer such objections. For instance, against Culler's accusatory question of why so many good critics have failed to find Riffaterre's one necessary reading, Riffaterre retorts that, in the face of what he terms "ungrammaticalities," those critics "look to the sociolect for linguistic reassurance when the text rattles them," that their "flight," their "attempt to cling to a linear rather than intertextual reading, undoes the text" (Riffaterre, "The Making of the Text" 69, note 7). That retort seems less than convincing in our contemporary critical ethos, one that can safely be characterized as highly sensitized to the intertextual and as resolutely resistant to the referential or sociolectic. For another retort, see Riffaterre's 1981 interview in *Diacritics.*

3. Among his many, many bravura performances there is his reading of Arthur Rimbaud's poem "Fêtes de la faim" (Riffaterre, *Semiotics* 76-80). For a teacher's appreciation of the practical value of applying Riffaterre's approach to a poem, see A. W. Lyle's "Practical Criticism à la Riffaterre." To see how useful Riffaterre's approach can be for novels, see Irwin Howard Streight's "A Good Hypogram Is Not Hard to Find." But for a far from favorable view of Riffaterre's approach, see Cid Corman's "Semi-Idiotics: Some Riffs on Riffaterre." And for a list of Riffaterre's work up to 1996, consider William Nelles's "Michael Riffaterre: A Checklist of Writings through 1996."

4. These are not the only terms used by Riffaterre to describe features and processes central to his approach. In fact sometimes he uses the same term for overlapping features and processes: "Riffaterre's terminology [. . .] is not entirely consistent and it is not always easy to separate his use of *hypogram, paragram* or even *matrix* rigorously from each other" (de Man 25, note 10). De Man based his comment on Riffaterre's work up to 1979, prin-

cipally his 1971 collection of essays *Essais de stylistique structurale*, and his two subsequent books *Semiotics of Poetry* (1978) and *La production du texte* (1979). All that work, which deals primarily with poetry, uses the word "hypogram" for one of the primary unifying factors in poetry, as later work (for example "La trace de l'intertexte" [1980], "The Making of the Text" [1985] and *Fictional Truth* [1990]) uses the words "intertext" and "subtext" for unifying factors in larger texts.

5   Opening homodiegetically with fixed internal focalization (see Genette, *Figures III* 206-9, 251-53), the text leaves its narrative instance unclear until its very last pages, complicating the understanding of that instance by characterizing itself slightly earlier as a biography (*La place de l'étoile* 115). The validity of this characterization is subject to challenge, both because Raphaël oddly does not describe his account as what would have been the more accurate "autobiography," and because he had initially undermined for his text the very value of the term "biography," through his early penchant for declaring himself at the drop of a name the author of instant, improbable biographical texts. His opening pages have him penning seemingly overnight studies of the historical writers Maurice Sachs, Drieu la Rochelle, and Robert Brasillach and bringing to press "Les Confessions de [the completely imaginary] Jacob X" (24). The groundwork for postulating the distinct possibility that Raphaël may have all along been imagining himself as an analysand of Freud's is laid only toward the end of the narrative. In the highly phantasmagoric fourth and final chapter the febrile young Jew describes himself as wandering on Vienna's Franz-Josefs-Kai (168), a detail that is picked up in the text's concluding passage, in which Raphaël's Freud announces: "mes infirmiers vous ont ramassé cette nuit sur le Franz-Josefs-Kai et vous ont conduit dans ma clinique de Potzleindorf" (213). One could easily maintain that this imagined scene (imagined, because Freud—who died in 1939—appears in Raphaël's post World War II account) is no more or less determinative narratologically than any of the other fantastic scenes that comprise the fourth chapter, were it not for the Freud figure's commenting on elements of Raphaël's account that had occurred much earlier: "Himmler est mort, comment se fait-il que vous vous rappeliez tout cela, vous n'étiez pas né [. . .]" (214). The analepsis allows the inference that from the start Raphaël may have been imagining himself addressing an imagined Freud. But inferred and no more this conclusion must remain: in the absence of supporting indications in the first three of the four chapters, it remains equally plausible that the text, which becomes progressively more and more fantastic, merely drifts in its fantasy from being an imagined "biography" to becoming an imagined session of psychoanalysis. Modiano

is then no less "king of ambiguity" (Morris 209 [Berg]) in his narrative instances than in all the other aspects of his art. But as we shall see, inferring an imagined psychoanalytic session as the narrative instance of *La place de l'étoile* can be critically productive.

6. "It is not easy to convince one's self of the second great change that takes place in the dream-thoughts [or latent dream content] through the agency of the dream-work. I refer to that process which I have called the dream *displacement*. It manifests itself by the fact that what occupies the center of the manifest dream and is endowed with vivid sensory intensity has occupied a peripheral and secondary position in the dream-thoughts, and *vice versa*. This process causes the dream to appear out of proportion when compared with the dream-thoughts, and it is because of this displacement that it seems strange and incomprehensible to the waking state. In order that such a displacement should occur it must be possible for the cathexis to pass uninhibited from important to insignificant ideas—a process which in normal conscious thinking can only give the impression of 'faulty thinking.'

"Transformation into expressive activity, condensation, and displacement are the three great functions which we can ascribe to the dream-work" (Sigmund Freud 749).

7. Gérard Genette defines "paratext" as follows: "paratexte: titre, sous-titre, intertitres; préfaces, postfaces, avertissements, avant-propos, etc.; notes marginales, infrapaginales, terminales; épigraphes; illustrations; prière d'insérer, bande, jacquette, et bien d'autres types de signaux accessoires, autographes ou allographes, qui procurent au texte un entourage (variable) et parfois un commentaire, officiel ou officieux, dont le lecteur le plus puriste et le moins porté à l'érudition externe ne peut pas toujours disposer aussi facilement qu'il le voudrait et le prétend" (Genette, *Palimpsestes* 9). In his later *Seuils* he will use the term *péritexte* to designate some of the ground that he initially covered with *paratexte* (*Seuils* 7-11).

8. To appreciate the extent to which doubling penetrates even the smallest details of Modiano's novels, one should read Stephen Steele's succinct but far-ranging study of Modiano's proclivity to use addresses that include *bis*, that is, addresses that are doubled. Steele will conclude his comments on this doubling by stressing, as will this study eventually, a passage from the last page of Modiano's *Chien de printemps* (121). Steele reads the passage as bringing to light "a *je* deprived of time and place haunted by an equally deprived other" (Steele 13). My reading, while different in emphasis, will be compatible with Steele's.

9. See "L'antisémitisme social français au miroir de la littérature des XIXe et XXe siècles" by Paul Catrice. Catrice points to such examples in an effort

to argue that French hostility to Jews has been due not just to religious prejudices but also to reactions against perceived abuses of finance and capitalism.

10. The suspicion comes closer to conviction if one chooses to turn to extra-textual, biographical information: the young Modiano had "swallowed" obsessively the anti-Jewish literature found in his own father's perverse library (Nettelbeck and Hueston, *Patrick Modiano* 6).

11. Coming from Brecht's exile poems of 1934-36, the ballad addresses the anti-Jewish discrimination of the Nuremburg Laws, particularly here "the concept of 'Rassenschande,' or Disgracing the Race, for non-marital sexual relations" between Jews and non-Jews; the poem was first published in Moscow's *Das Wort* in August of 1937 (Brecht 560). The biographical appropriateness for Modiano should be noted, in that the Marie of the poem is a non-Jew who has sex with a Jew (and for which she is victimized), just as Modiano's mother was a non-Jew married to Modiano's Jewish father. Another thing to be noted is a detail from the ballad that perhaps also helped to motivate this reference in Modiano's text. The ballad's fourth stanza includes the line, "Im Hemd, um den Hals ein Schild, das Haar geschoren" ("In a shirt, around the neck a sign, the hair shorn"), a line that anticipated what after the liberation of France at the end of World War II the French would do to French women who had had German lovers. The pungent irony of the French borrowing from the Germans the punishment visited upon women for loving "the enemy" sits well with the rejection throughout Modiano's oeuvre of official France's facile, hypocritical moral and political posturing after the defeat of the Nazis.

12. The identification with the rabbinical father-figure of the *morceau de bravoure* tightens when Lévy-Vendôme bids farewell to Raphaël in these terms: "On me reverra d'ici quatre-vingt-cinq ans jour pour jour, avec des guiches et une barbe de rabbin. A bientôt. Je vous aime" (*La place de l'étoile* 144).

13. Not surprisingly in light of the repeated references in *La place de l'étoile* to *A la recherche du temps perdu,* the latter appears to have provided a model of such a structure by closing on—or more properly by refusing to close, thanks to—a narrative helix (see Ricardou, *Nouveaux problèmes du roman* 133-39).

14. *Pièce/*"patch" also typifies the moral wrenching that Modiano manages to impart both overtly and subtly to his dazzling textual and verbal play, here because of the ghastly implications of the star of David "patch" imposed on French Jews.

15. It also anticipates the facility with which many of Modiano's subsequent characters will change names and procure false papers and passports, quick to adopt new personae with the aplomb of accomplished thespians. In addition, the practiced reader of Modiano cannot help but be sensitive to the resonance of the site of the action, *"une chambre aux murs blancs"* (walls that are "white" and/or "blank," in any event unadorned): among the prototypical sites in all of Modiano's texts figure rooms that have been stripped bare. Among other such Modianesque sites one finds cars, train stations, cafés and hotels with a more than usual transitory air, and strangely vacant streets through which the narrators roam, all these sites for a variety of reasons (usually involving memories or intimations of missing people) communicating under Modiano's pen an intense feeling of "blankness" or absence.

16. See for instance Dupuy (17 and following pages) for a traditionally historical approach to Poe's primacy, Knight (39 and following pages) for an ideological approach, and Tani for a more genre-based approach. But not every critic agrees about the privileged status of Poe's three stories: "Next to some subordinate motifs, we find all together in this [other] story the three elements that constitute the detective novel: first, the murder, or the series of murders, at the beginning and its solution at the end; second, the innocent suspect and the unsuspected criminal; and third, the detection, not by the police but by an outsider, an old maid and a poet; and then fourth, the extraordinarily frequent, though not obligatory, element of the locked room. The story is entitled 'Das Fräulein von Scuderi' ('Mlle de Scuderi'). Its author is the German romantic E. T. A. Hoffmann. It appeared in 1818, almost a quarter-century before E. A. Poe's 'Murders in the Rue Morgue,' with which, according to previous opinion, the history of the detective novel begins" (Alewyn 73).

   Of course, one should recognize as well that "detective novel" and "crime fiction" are neither synonymous nor synchronous. For example in his book *Form and Ideology in Crime Fiction,* Stephen Knight uses *The Newgate Calendar Stories* to show that crime fiction without detectives predates the modern detective-version of crime fiction. He proposes that the Newgate crime fiction reflects an organic, Christian world-model to which eighteenth-century society continued to aspire, whereas detective fiction reflects a bourgeois, Romantic world in which subjectivism, rationalism, and individualism prevail.

17. Occasionally the misnomer "schizophrenic" is used to describe such a personality. But the term "schizophrenia" applies to a delusional split between the mind and reality, whereby for example one hears non-existent voices,

and which is often characterized by paranoia. The psychological disorder of split or multiple personalities is not understood here to mean "schizo-phrenia."

18. Charles Rycroft offers the hypothesis that the same sort of doubling may penetrate even the act of reading detective stories: "In her article 'Detective Stories and the Primal Scene' (1949) [Geraldine Pedersen-Krag] suggests that [the popularity of detective stories] arises from their ability to re-awaken the interest and curiosity originally aroused by observation of the primal scene [. . .] . It is possible to draw a deduction from this hypothesis which Pedersen-Krag does not herself explicitly make. If the victim is the parent for whom the reader (the child) had negative Oedipal feelings, then the criminal must be a personification of the reader's own unavowed hostil-ity towards that parent. The reader is not only the detective; he is also the criminal" (Rycroft 114).

19. Which is not to say that Modiano's characteristic ambiguity does not grip his texts' use of detective stories. For a thorough demonstration of that, see Alan Morris's *Patrick Modiano* (Rodopi, 104-12).

20. In light of the plural, fraternal identity, moreover, Modiano's switching the dates of his and his brother's birth enables the inference that Patrick was born as a published author by taking Rudy's place.

Chapter 2
Referentiality in *La place de l'étoile:* Challenging Riffaterre and Aestheticization

1. See David Lehman's *Signs of the Times: Deconstruction and the Fall of Paul de Man* for a hostile, tendentious account of deconstruction and for a comprehensive review of the debate that ensued from the discovery follow-ing de Man's death that, among other examples of reprehensible conduct, he had written anti-Jewish articles for a collaborationist Belgian newspaper during World War II.

2. For a view of all literary theory and even of "literature" itself as an occulta-tion of ideological and political value-structures, see Terry Eagleton's *Lit-erary Theory*.

3. See also Lyle: "the distinction between literary and non-literary language, a distinction that Riffaterre maintains in his latest contribution (*Intertextual-ity,* p. 57; cf. *Text Production*, p. 1) is difficult to sustain: he provides us

with no definition of everyday discourse against which literariness or po-
eticity can be measured" (Lyle 247).

4.   " 'What we [Peter and his lost boys] need is just a nice motherly person.'
     'Oh dear!' Wendy said, 'you see, I feel that is exactly what I am.'
     'It is, it is,' they all cried; 'we saw it at once' " (Barrie 97).

5.   Jeffrey S. Walker, in doing a Riffaterrean reading of a text no less difficult
     than Modiano's *La place de l'étoile,* namely Ezra Pound's *Cantos,* too has
     found that Riffaterre's approach does an injustice to literary texts by down-
     playing mimesis in the mimesis-semiosis dynamic. Against Walker's under-
     standing of Aristotle on mimesis, Riffaterre maintains that mimesis is
     subsumed or transfigured by semiosis, and he does not accept that both can
     work more fully together, and indeed can both signify. At a crucial moment,
     however, Walker locates the foundation of his argument in Pound's inten-
     tions regarding the *Cantos* (Walker 52), a critical move that in the face of
     contemporary resistance to the "intentional fallacy" weakens the appeal of
     his argument. But these pages propose that, with a focus just on the power
     of the sign "Hitler," Walker's conclusions if not his method can be corrobo-
     rated. That same focus on "Hitler," however, will also show how Rif-
     faterre's already productive approach can be used even more productively.

6.   On this point, Riffaterre would probably—even if in tension with some of
     his own *dicta*—agree: "La surdétermination de la mimésis, il faut le sou-
     ligner, est inséparable d'un défi à la référentialité: c'est le calembour, ou du
     moins l'appartenance du même mot à deux codes incompatibles, qui assure
     la coexistence de la représentation et du verbalisme, d'une référence suppo-
     sée aux choses sous les mots et d'une référence évidente des mots à une
     donnée verbale. Le [sic] poéticité du texte se situe au double sens, dans la
     coïncidence, au même point, du sens propre et d'un sens contextuel qui
     s'excluent mutuellement. Oxymore maximum [...]: plus le texte se dit
     tourné vers le réel, plus le scandale éclate de la dérivation à partir des mots"
     (Riffaterre, *Production* 273).

7.   "[L]'*expansion* [. . .] transforme les constituants de la matrice en formes
     plus complexes, processus habituellement combiné à la conversion: les
     éléments transformés sont tous modifiés par un même facteur, un marqueur
     mélioratif, par exemple, ou un marqueur péjoratif' (Riffaterre, "L'Illusion
     référentielle" 101; emphasis in the original).

8.   But those who attack referentiality in literature have a widely recognized
     paradoxical problem. Christopher Prendergast, in his book that deliberately
     records the tensions created by his alternating defense of and assault on lit-
     erary referentiality, succinctly expresses the paradox that "places logical
     constraints upon the attack on mimesis and representational discourse gen-

erally, in that any such attack is obliged, as a condition if its intelligibility, to adopt the very categories of the object it attacks" (Prendergast 18).

9. Antoine Compagnon finds similar tension when he considers literary theory's main concerns (which he categorizes as *le monde, l'auteur, le lecteur, le style, l'histoire, la valeur*), arguing that in the end no critical theory can avoid points at which it will be found to oppose itself logically. Although insisting on the impossibility of not using a critical approach, Compagnon eventually finds in each critical approach a logical polarity or tension, which he chooses to call *perplexité:* "Comme Gargantua qui ne sait s'il doit rire ou pleurer quand un fils lui est né mais que sa femme en est morte, nous sommes condamnés à la perplexité" (Compagnon 281).

10. Martine Guyot-Bender has argued that the undecidability of Modiano's texts about the Holocaust constitute one of the ethical dimensions of his oeuvre, in that it creates obstacles for those who would make myths out of the Holocaust (Guyot-Bender 97; see the Introduction above). Furthermore, and in testimony to the undeniable referential power of *La place de l'étoile,* baffling and unsettling though this novel is, it was instrumental in changing the very way France views its recent history (see the discussion of the work of the historian Henry Rousso in the Introduction above).

11. The rabidity of his racism remains the subject of considerable dispute. While generally eschewing in print the radical position that slavery was good in itself, Poe has been charged by some critics with writing anonymously in 1836 an emphatically proslavery book review in *The Southern Messenger,* for which he worked at the time. One striking passage from that anonymous review reads as follows:

> Our theory is a short one. It was the will of God it [physical and moral difference due to race] should be so. But the means—how was this effected? We will give the answer to any one who will develop the causes which might and should have blackened the negro's skin and crisped his hair into wool. Until that is done, we shall take leave to speak, as of things *in esse,* in a degree of loyal devotion on the part of the slave to which the white man's heart is stranger, and of the master's reciprocal feeling of parental attachment to his humble dependent, equally incomprehensible to him who drives a bargain with the cook who prepares his food, the servant who waits at his table, and the nurse who dozes over his sick bed. That these sentiments in the breast of the negro and his master, are stronger than they would be under like circumstances be-

tween individuals of the white race, we believe. (Poe, "Slavery" 271)

Other critics argue that while Poe may have edited the review, he did not write it. To consider representative sides of the debate, see Rosenthal and Dayan ("Romance and Race") who affirm that Poe wrote the review, and Whalen who affirms that he did not.

12. I suspect that Riffaterre would riposte that satiric texts full of examples of what he calls the "direct relationship of words to things" (Riffaterre, *Production* 2), as opposed to the textual circularity of literary semiosis that forecloses its language's direct relationship to reality, can have many literary elements, can be "literary discourse," without for all that achieving literariness, a "unit of significance" all the components of which contribute to semiosis: "phrases, sentences, words can be found anywhere, everywhere, that present some aspects of literariness. They are sensed as literary, or as giving their context, their verbal environment, a literary flavour [. . .] . These components, however, are not in themselves sufficient to create literariness" (Riffaterre, "Text" 109-10). It seems fair to wonder, however, how "direct" *any* language's relationship to reality can be, if all language is figuration. Moreover, there will certainly be varying degrees of "directness" across any range of texts. So literary satire would seem to pose a problem for Riffaterrean literariness, unless one commits to an essentialist view of literariness, and so unless one presumably identifies beforehand the threshold beyond which, or the invariant dynamic thanks to which, a range of literary texts with progressively more and more "semioticized" political and social elements at one sudden point stops being "mere" satire possessing only "aspects of literariness."

13. See Kennedy and Weissberg on how recent attention to the issue of race in Poe has challenged ahistorical criticism in his regard.

14. If one accepts Poe's orangutan as a coded black African, then in his description of the orangutan we may well have an example of the banal projection of guilt away from the perpetrator and onto the victim: "a ferocity brutal, a butchery without motive, a *grotesquerie* in horror absolutely alien from humanity." In fact and to the contrary of Poe's intent, his words would seem an all too often apt description of the American slavery that Poe advocated.

Chapter 3
The Riffaterrean Reading of *La place de l'étoile* as a Template for the Oeuvre

1. Insofar as the phantasmagoric quality of *La ronde de nuit* manifestly confronts the reader with problem of referentiality, it is interesting to note that, against a backdrop of many historical secondary characters, there exist tight historical parallels between the pair Henri Chamberlin and Pierre Bonny, and the narrative's pair Henri Normand and his cohort in crime Pierre Philibert. But those parallels are tugged back from the security of simple referentiality into the "smoke" of semiotic imagination by, among other devices, Normand's having as a nickname the name of a brand of cigarettes, "le Khédive" (*La Ronde de nuit* 87).

2. In *Livret de famille* Modiano will offer a slightly different version of this procedure apparently dear to his narrators. Describing a writing project that he had undertaken in the course of his story, the narrator (Patrick, no less) says:

    > J'avais décidé du titre définitif: "Les Vies d'Harry Dressel," ce que m'avait dit Jansenne m'incitant en effet à penser que Dressel avait eu plusieurs vies parallèles. Je n'en possédais pas la preuve et mon dossier était bien mince, mais je comptais laisser aller mon imagination. Elle m'aiderait à retrouver le vrai Dressel. Il suffisait de rêver sur les deux ou trois éléments dont je disposais, et je parviendrais à restituer le reste, comme l'archéologue qui, en présence d'une statue aux trois quarts mutilée, la recompose intégralement dans sa tête. (*Livret de famille* 185)

    See also *Voyage de noces* 50-56, in the course of which pages the narrator will question his need for documentation to write a biography of a suicide victim, only to conclude that he needs none, content to "remember" (56) her past.

3. This overlap in for instance proper names and situations from one of Modiano's novels to another will continue in subsequent works—and will argue for the need to view the oeuvre as an evolving whole—but in the subsequent works there will be far fewer instances of the overlap. As another example of what we find here, we can consider that in *Livret de famille* (1977) the narrator will regularly meet a contact in front of a bar on rue des Boutiques Obscures (*Livret de famille* 148), the street name that will become the title of Modiano's novel subsequent to *Livret de famille*. On the other hand, although fewer in number and intermittent, the later overlaps can be quite

substantial, as when for instance la Petite Bijou, a secondary character from *De si braves garçons* (1982) becomes the narrator and subject of the novel *La petite bijou* (2001).

4. The narrator claims to have been seventeen when he first met his father (*Les boulevards de ceinture* 76), and the events he subsequently recounts are said to have taken place ten years later.

5. This abandonment of the circular on the last pages of the novel is not enough to dissuade Alan Morris that the circle haunts *Villa triste,* as it did the three novels that preceded it (Morris, *Patrick Modiano* [Berg] 71]). But even if one stresses the suggestive power of *Villa triste*'s concluding with the image of a circle left behind, Modiano's sense of torment over constricting circles will clearly not leave him completely, since they will come back forcefully with the images of circle-spinning spiders and forever turning merry-go-rounds in *Dimanches d'août* (1986).

6. If one does not insist that each of Modiano's texts limits itself to the borders set by its own title and physical pages, then Meinthe's status as father is subsequently strengthened: in Modiano's next novel, *Livret de famille,* the narrator Patrick Modiano writes that at his baptism when he was five years old, one of his substitute godfathers was named "Minthe" (*Livret de famille* 114). So if one accepts that Modiano's autofictional imaginary ties all his novels together in textual unity, then this phonetic duplication of Meinthe's name not only reinforces the perception of Meinthe as father-figure, but it also helps to tie *Villa triste* and *Livret de famille* together in a special way, a point of value for my argument below, that *Livret de famille* should be read as a pendant to *Villa triste*. It continues what began in *Villa triste,* to wit, the oeuvre's first interlude from the psychologically racking consequences of the guilt that in the first three published novels binds together the themes identified in the Riffaterrean matrix and subtext.

7. See Bruno Tritsmans's article for the role of the library in *Villa triste* as an element in that novel's portrayal of "*une forte érosion des pouvoirs de la littérature de dire le monde et de ressaisir le temps*" (Tritsmans 123).

8. Beyond what can be described as the usual associative play of *la scripturale création,* this associative interpenetration of drinks and places is strong throughout Modiano's imaginary, and on occasions quite explicit. The associations work both from drink to place, and from place to drink, for example: "Il versa la Marie Brizard dans des verres étroits et quand je goûtai cette liqueur, elle se confondit avec les satins, les ivoires et les dorures un peu écœurantes autour de moi. Elle était l'essence même de cet appartement"; "Le mot 'Portugal' avait aussitôt évoqué pour lui l'océan vert, le so-

leil, une boisson orangée que l'on boit à l'aide d'une paille, sous un para-
sol" (*Rue des boutiques obscures* 143, 172).

9. For the reader of Modiano's oeuvre, finding in the next novel, *Livret de
    famille*, the scene where the narrator mentions a competition named *le
    Tilleul d'or* (130), the question arises retrospectively whether the *Cintra/
    cintra/menthe/tilleul-menthe/tilleul* chain did not play its part in generating
    Villa triste's major chapter, which focuses on a competition, the odd "ele-
    gance competition," *la Coupe Houligant*.

10. A reading of *La folle amoureuse* leaves one wondering if the novella did not
    creep into Modiano's creative imagination in still another way. The epony-
    mous loving madwoman, Escolastica, needs orgasm with her lover to enter
    into contact with reality, to become a person, to acquire an identity:

    > Dès qu'il le satisfaisait, cet être sans poids spécifique prenait pied
    > sur le réel. Le prince était le pôle magnétique nécessaire à l'autre
    > pôle, au rétablissement d'un circuit humain. L'orgasme, serviteur
    > exigeant, mais fidèle, ramenait à la surface de l'âme folle un sens
    > commun, d'habitude son ennemi. Intervertissant l'ordre naturel,
    > Escolastica, extatique, pétrie, humectée, servie, s'abandonnait à la
    > raison.
    > —Dis-moi, qui tu es?
    > —Je suis toi, répondait-elle.
    > —Mais quand tu n'es pas moi?
    > —Je ne suis pas. Je suis vide. Je ne suis rien.
    > (Morand, *La folle amoureuse* 36)

    For all the raw sexism of Escolastica's coming to identity, its startling ex-
    plicitness (as explicit here as Morand's explicit hostility to Jews elsewhere,
    for instance in his novel *France la doulce*) may well have struck a respon-
    sive chord with Modiano's own fixation on the subject of identity. And be-
    cause of Modiano's habit of carrying over details from one novel to the
    next, one has to ponder the fact that if *La folle amoureuse* does indeed func-
    tion as an exceptionally subtle intertext for *Villa triste,* Escolastica's dra-
    matic words above, "*Je ne suis rien,*" could be a source for the opening line
    of *Rue des boutiques obscures,* which will use those identical words.
    Moreover, her saying to a man, "*Je suis toi*" could be connected to the gen-
    der-switching that will be seen to affect Modiano's narrators more and more
    as the oeuvre moves on. Whatever the source of the expression "*Je ne suis
    rien,*" the feeling and idea behind it will go on to influence deeply more
    than just the narrator of *Rue des boutiques obscures,* also reappearing in
    Dora Bruder (11) and *Accident nocturne* (116, 119).

11. This is not the only text by Lamartine that can be seen influencing a text by Modiano. For a consideration of the impact of Lamartine's *Raphaël* on *La place de l'étoile,* see O'Keefe "Patrick Modiano's *La place de l'étoile.*"

12. Modiano will return to a similar metaphor two novels later, in *Rue des boutiques obscures* (146-47), where the narrator gets to listen to barely perceptible overlapping voices coming from ghost-like characters apparently using an unassigned telephone number to communicate with each other.

◆ ◆ ◆

Bibliography of Works Cited

Agulhon, Maurice. "Paris." *Les lieux de mémoire*. Ed. Pierre Nora. Vol. 3. Paris: Gallimard, 1997. 4589-622.

Alewyn, Richard. "The Origin of the Detective Novel." *The Poetics of Murder*. Ed. Glenn W. Most and William W. Stowe. San Diego: Harcourt, Brace, Jovanovitch, 1983. 62-78.

Amette, Jacques-Pierre. "La Piscine." *La Nouvelle Revue Française* 240 (décembre 1972): 104-6.

Arendt, Hanna. Introduction. *Illuminations*. By Walter Benjamin. Ed. Hanna Arendt. New York: Schocken Books, 1969. 1-55.

Assouline, Pierre. "Modiano, lieux de mémoire." *Lire* 176 (mai 1990): 34-46.

Auden, W. H. *The Dyer's Hand and Other Essays*. New York: Random House, 1962.

Avni, Ora. *D'un passé l'autre: aux portes de l'histoire avec Patrick Modiano*. Paris: Editions L'Harmattan, 1997.

Aydelotte, William O. "The Detective Story as Historical Source." *Dimensions of Detective Fiction*. Ed. Larry N. Landrum, Pat Browne, and Ray B. Browne. Bowling Green, Ohio: Popular Press, 1976. 68-82.

Barrès, Maurice. *Les déracinés*. Paris: Emile-Paul, 1922.

Barrett, Lindon. "Presence of Mind: Detection and Racialization in 'The Murders in the Rue Morgue.' " *Romancing the Shadow: Poe and Race*. Ed. J. Gerald Kennedy and Liliane Weissberg. Oxford: Oxford UP, 2001. 157-76.

Barrie, J. M. *Peter Pan*. New York: Charles Scriber's Sons, 1950.

Barrot, Olivier. *Pages pour Modiano*. Monaco: Éditions du Rocher, 1999.

Barthes, Roland, et al. *Littérature et réalité*. Paris: Editions du Seuil, 1982.

Beaver, Harold. Introduction. *The Narrative of Arthur Gordon Pym of Nantucket*. By Edgar Allan Poe. Harmondsworth, Middlesex, England: Penguin Books, 1975. 7-33.

Bedner, Jules. "Patrick Modiano: visages de l'étranger." *Patrick Modiano*. Ed. Jules Bedner. Atlanta: Rodopi, 1993. 43-54.

———. Présentation. *Patrick Modiano*. Ed. Jules Bedner. Atlanta: Rodopi, 1993. 1.

Berl, Emmanuel. *Interrogatoire par Patrick Modiano*. Paris: Gallimard, 1976.

Bersani, Jacques. "Patrick Modiano, agent double." *La Nouvelle Revue Fran-*
çaise 298 (1 novembre 1977): 78-84.

———. "Patrick Modiano: *La place de l'Étoile*." *La Nouvelle Revue Française*
189 (septembre, 1968): 334-35.

Bertens, Hans. *The Idea of the Postmodern*. New York: Routledge, 1995.

Blanchard, Marc Eli. "Up against the Text." *Diacritics* 11.3 (1981): 13-26.

Bradbury, Malcolm. "Modernisms/Postmodernisms." *Innovation/Renovation*.
Ed. Ihab Hassan and Sally Hassan. Madison: The U of Wisconsin P, 1983.
311-27.

Brasseur, Roland. *Je me souviens de* Je me souviens: *notes pour* Je me souviens
de Georges Perec. Bordeaux: Le Castor Astral, 1998.

Brecht, Bertolt. *Bertolt Brecht Poems: 1913-1956*. Ed. John Willet and Ralph
Manheim with the co-operation of Erich Fried. New York: Methuen, 1976.

Breut, Michèle. "*Un cirque passe*: un tour de passe-passe romanesque." *Patrick*
Modiano. Ed. Jules Bedner. Atlanta: Editions Rodopi B.V., 1993. 103-17.

Carlson, Eric W. Introduction. *Critical Essays on Edgar Allan Poe*. Ed. Eric W.
Carlson. Boston: G. K. Hall and Co., 1987. 1-34.

Catrice, Paul. "L'antisémitisme social français au miroir de la littérature des
XIXe et XXe siècles." *Revue de Psychologie des Peuples* 22.3 (septembre
1967): 248-81.

Cau, Jean. Préface. *La place de l'étoile*. By Patrick Modiano. Paris: Gallimard
(Édition Blanche), 1968. 3-5.

Cave, Terence. "Distinctively Ungrammatical." Rev. of *Text Production*, by
Michael Riffaterre. *The Times Literary Supplement* 4224 (March 16, 1984):
278.

Chamisso, Adelbert Von. *Peter Schlemihls wundersame Geschichte*. Stuttgart:
P. Reclam, 1960.

———. *The Wonderful History of Peter Schlemihl*. Trans. Frederic H. Hedge.
The German Classics. Vol. 5. New York: The German Publication Society,
1913. 343-400.

Chandler, Raymond. *Stories and Early Novels*. New York: Library of America,
1995.

Chasseguet-Smirgel, Janine. *Pour une psychanalyse de l'art et de la créativité*.
Paris: Payot, 1971.

Cima, Denise. *Les images paternelles dans l'œuvre de Patrick Modiano*. Ville-
neuve d'Ascq: Presses Universitaires du Septentrion (Thèse à la carte),
1998.

Coenen-Mennemeier, Brigitta. "Le philtre magique." *Patrick Modiano*. Ed.
Jules Bedner. Atlanta: Rodopi, 1993. 55-71.

Compagnon, Antoine. *Le démon de la théorie: littérature et sens commun.* Paris: Éditions du Seuil, 1998.

Corman, Cid. "Semi-Idiotics: Some Riffs on Riffaterre." *Origin: Fifth Series* 5.4 (1984): 72-84.

Culler, Jonathan. *The Pursuit of Signs: Semiotics, Literature, Deconstruction.* Ithaca, New York: Cornell UP, 1981.

Daprini, Pierre B. "Patrick Modiano: le temps de l'Occupation." *Australian Journal of French Studies*: 26.2 (May, August 1989): 194-205.

Davis, Colin. "Disenchanted Places: Patrick Modiano's *Quartier perdu* and Recent French Fiction." Ed. Monique Streif Moretti et al. *Il senso del nonsenso: scritti in memoria di Lynn Salkin Sbiroli.* Napoli: Edizioni Scientifiche Italiane, 1994. 663-76.

Dayan, Joan. "Amorous Bondage: Poe, Ladies, and Slaves." *Subjects and Citizens: Nation, Race, and Gender from* Oroonoko *to Anita Hill.* Ed. Michael Moon and Cathy N. Davidson. Durham: Duke UP, 1995. 109-43.

———. "Romance and Race." *The Columbia History of the American Novel.* Gen. ed. Emory Elliot. New York: Columbia UP, 1991. 89-109.

Demeyère, Annie. *Portraits de l'artiste dans l'œuvre de Patrick Modiano.* Paris: L'Harmattan, 2002.

Derrida, Jacques. *De la grammatologie.* Paris: Les Éditions de Minuit, 1967.

———. "The Purveyor of Truth." Trans. Willis Domingo, James Hulbert, Moshe Ron and M.-R. L. *Yale French Studies* 52 (1975): 31-113.

Descombes, Vincent. "Les embarras du référent." *Modern Language Notes* 101 (September 1986): 765-80.

Dickstein, Juliette. "Inventing French Jewish Memory: The Legacy of the Occupation in the Works of Patrick Modiano." *Paradigms of Memory: The Occupation and Other Hi/stories in the Novels of Patrick Modiano.* Ed. Martine Guyot-Bender and William VanderWolk. New York: Peter Lang, 1998. 145-63.

Docherty, Thomas. "Postmodernism: An Introduction." *Postmodernism: A Reader.* Ed. Thomas Docherty. New York: Columbia UP, 1993. 1-31.

Doucey, Bruno. *La ronde de nuit*: *Patrick Modiano.* Paris: Hatier, 1992.

Drago⬜ Elena. "À propos de la stylistique structurale: Michael Riffaterre." *Revue roumaine de linguistique* 22 (1977): 99-105.

Dunn, Allen. "Forgetting to Remember Paul de Man: Theory as Mnemonic-Technique in de Man's *Resistance to Theory* and Derrida's *Mémoires*." *Southern Humanities Review* 22 (fall 1988): 355-85.

Dupuy, Josée. *Le roman policier.* Paris: Librairie Larousse, 1974.

Eagleton, Terry. *Literary Theory: An Introduction.* Minneapolis: U of Minneapolis P, 1996.

Eisenzweig, Uri. *Le récit impossible*. Mesnil-sur-l'Estrée: Christian Bourgeois Editeur, 1986.

Erkkila, Betsy. "The Poetics of Whiteness: Poe and the Racial Imaginary." *Romancing the Shadow: Poe and Race*. Ed. J. Gerald Kennedy and Liliane Weissberg. Oxford: Oxford UP, 2001. 41-74.

Ewert, Jeanne C. "Lost in the Hermeneutic Funhouse: Patrick Modiano's Postmodern Detective." *The Cunning Craft: Original Essays on Detective Fiction and Contemporary Literary Theory*. Ed. Ronald G. Walker and June M. Frazer. Macomb, Illinois: Yeast Printing, Inc., 1990. [Copyright by Western Illinois U.] 166-73.

Ezine, Jean-Louis. *Les écrivains sur la sellette*. Paris: Éditions du Seuil, 1981.

Fish, Stanley. *Is There a Text in This Class?* Cambridge: Harvard UP, 1980.

Forclaz, Roger. *Le monde d'Edgar Poe*. Berne: Herbert Lang, 1974.

Foucault, Michel. "Entretien avec Michel Foucault." *Cahiers du Cinéma* juillet 1974: 5-15.

Freadman, Anne. "Riffaterra Cognita: a Late Contribution to the Formalism Debate." *SubStance* 13.1 (1984): 31-45.

Freud, Sigmund. "Wit and Its Relation to the Unconscious." *The Basic Writings of Sigmund Freud*. Trans. A. A. Brill. New York: The Modern Library, 1938. 631-803.

Friedlander, Saul ed. *Probing the Limits of Representation: Nazism and the "Final Solution."* Cambridge: Harvard UP, 1992.

Galey, Matthieu. "*Les boulevards de ceinture* de Patrick Modiano." *Réalités* 322 (novembre 1972): 17.

Gellings, Paul. *Poésie et mythe dans l'œuvre de Patrick Modiano: le fardeau du nomade*. Paris: Minard, 2000.

Genette, Gérard. *Figures III*. Paris: Éditions du Seuil, 1972.

———. *Palimpsestes: la littérature au second degré*. Paris: Editions du Seuil, 1982.

———. *Seuils*. Paris: Éditions du Seuil, 1987.

Ginsburg, Michal Peled. Rev. of *Fictional Truth*. By Michael Riffaterre. *Comparative Literature Studies* 28.4 (1991): 450-55.

Goyet, Francis. "*Imitatio* ou intertextualité? (Riffaterre revisited)." *Poétique* 18.71 (septembre 1987): 313-20.

Guillot, Gérard. "Modiano: le jeune Vermeer du roman." *Le Figaro* 21 novembre 1978: 39.

Guyot-Bender, Martine. *Mémoire en dérive : poétique et politique de l'ambiguïté chez Patrick Modiano*. Paris: Minard, 1999.

Guyot-Bender, Martine and William VanderWolk. Editors' Introduction. *Paradigms of Memory: The Occupation and Other Hi/stories in the Novels of*

Patrick Modiano. Ed. Martine Guyot-Bender and William VanderWolk. New York: Peter Lang, 1998. 1-15.

Hammett, Dashiell. *Complete Novels*. New York: The Library of America, 1999.

Hammond, J. R. *An Edgar Allan Poe Companion: A Guide to the Short Stories, Romances and Essays*. Totowa, New Jersey: Barnes and Noble Books, 1981.

Hardy, Alain. "Théorie et méthode stylistiques de M. Riffaterre." *Langue Française* 3 (septembre 1969): 90-96.

Hartman, Geoffrey H. "Literature High and Low: The Case of the Mystery Story." *The Poetics of Murder*. Ed. Glenn W. Most and William W. Stowe. San Diego: Harcourt, Brace, Jovanovitch, 1983. 210-29.

Heine, Heinrich. *Jewish Stories and Hebrew Melodies*. Trans. Hal Draper. New York: Markus Wiener Publishing, 1987.

———. *Werke*. Vol. 1. Ed. Frankfurt a. M.: Insel Verlag, 1968.

Hutter, Albert D. "Dreams, Transformations, and Literature: The Implications of Detective Fiction." *The Poetics of Murder*. Ed. Glenn W. Most and William W. Stowe. San Diego: Harcourt, Brace, Jovanovitch, 1983. 230-51.

Jakobson, Roman. *Essais de linguistique générale*. Paris : Les Editions de Minuit, 1963.

Johnson, Barbara. "The Frame of Reference: Poe, Lacan, Derrida." *The Critical Difference*. Baltimore: Johns Hopkins UP, 1980. 110-46.

Joselin, Jean-François. "Mondo Modiano." *Le Nouvel Observateur* 8-14 janvier 1988: 59-61.

Joye, Jean-Claude. *Littérature immédiate: cinq études sur Jeanne Bourin, Julien Green, Patrick Modiano, Yves Navarre, Françoise Sagan*. Paris: Peter Lang, 1990. 89-116.

Kaminskas, Junate D. "Modiano's Female Trilogy: *Voyage de noces, Fleurs de ruine, Un cirque passe*." *Paradigms of Memory: The Occupation and Other Hi/stories in the Novels of Patrick Modiano*. Ed. Martine Guyot-Bender and William VanderWolk. New York: Peter Lang, 1998. 89-101.

———. "Les structures de l'échange dans *Fleurs de ruine* de Patrick Modiano." *Romance Notes* 33.3 (spring 1993): 239-48.

Kauffmann, Judith. "Patrick Modiano, un 'juif imaginaire'? Une relecture de *La place de l'étoile*." *Hebrew University Studies in Literature and the Arts* 12.3 (1984): 130-45.

Kawakami, Akane. *A Self-Conscious Art: Patrick Modiano's Postmodern Fictions*. Liverpool: Liverpool UP, 2000.

Kennedy, J. Gerald and Liliane Weissberg. Introduction. *Romancing the Shadow: Poe and Race*. Ed. J. Gerald Kennedy and Liliane Weissberg. Oxford: Oxford UP, 2001. xi-xvii.

Khalifa, Samuel. "The Mirror of Memory: Patrick Modiano's *La place de l'étoile* and *Dora Bruder*." *The Holocaust and the Text: Speaking the Unspeakable*. Ed. Andrew Leak and George Paizis. New York: St. Martin's Press, Inc., 2000. 159-73.

Kingston, Maxine Hong. *The Woman Warrior: Memoirs of a Girlhood among Ghosts*. New York: Vintage International, 1989.

Knight, Stephen. *Form and Ideology in Crime Fiction*. Bloomington: Indiana UP, 1980.

Koepke, Wulf. Introduction. *Peter Schlemihl*. By Adelbert von Chamisso. Trans. Sir John Bowring. Columbia: Camden House, Inc., 1993. v-xxxi.

Krieger, Murray. "An Apology for Poetics." *American Criticism in the Poststructuralist Age*. Ed. Ira Konigsberg. Ann Arbor: U of Michigan P, 1981. 87-101.

Kundera, Milan. *L'art du roman*. Paris: Gallimard, 1986.

Lacan, Jacques. *Écrits I*. Paris: Éditions du Seuil, 1966.

Laurent, Thierry. *L'œuvre de Patrick Modiano: une autofiction*. Lyon: Presses Universitaires de Lyon, 1997.

Lazarus, Joyce Block. *Strangers and Sojourners: Jewish Identity in Contemporary Francophone Fiction*. New York: Peter Lang, 1999.

Lehman, David. *Signs of the Times: Deconstruction and the Fall of Paul de Man*. New York: Poseidon Press, 1991.

Lejeune, Philippe. *Le pacte autobiographique*. Paris: Seuil, 1975.

Lemire, Elise. " 'The Murders in the Rue Morgue': Amalgamation Discourses and the Race Riots of 1838 in Poe's Philadelphia." *Romancing the Shadow: Poe and Race*. Ed. J. Gerald Kennedy and Liliane Weissberg. Oxford: Oxford UP, 2001. 177-204.

Levine, Stuart. "Introduction: The New Image of Poe." *The Short Fiction of Edgar Allan Poe*. Ed. and annotated Stuart and Susan Levine. Indianapolis: Bobbs-Merrill Educational Publishing, 1976. xv-xxx.

Lodge, David. *The Art of Fiction*. London: Penguin, 1992.

Long, Edward. *The History of Jamaica*. Vol. 2. London: T. Lownudes, 1774.

Lyle, A. W. "Practical Criticism à la Riffaterre." *Critical Survey* 4.3 (1992): 241-49.

Lyotard, Jean-François. *La condition postmoderne: rapport sur le savoir*. Paris: Les Éditions de Minuit, 1979.

MacKenzie, Ian. "Le texte, le lecteur et la référence." *La construction de la référence*. Introduction Remi Jolivet. Lausanne: Université de Lausanne, 1988. 41-58.

Man, Paul de. *Blindness and Insight: Essays in the Rhetoric of Contemporary Criticism*. Minneapolis: U of Minnesota P, 1983.

————. "Hypograms and Inscription: Michael Riffaterre's Poetics of Reading." *Diacritics* 11.4 (1981): 17-35.

Montfrans, Manet van. "Rêveries d'un riverain: la topographie parisienne de Patrick Modiano." *Patrick Modiano*. Ed. Jules Bedner. Atlanta: Rodopi 1993. 85-101.

Margolies, Edward. "The American Detective Thriller and the Idea of Society." *Dimensions of Detective Fiction*. Ed. Larry N. Landrum, Pat Browne, and Ray B. Browne. Bowling Green, Ohio: Popular Press, 1976. 83-87.

Margolin, Uri. "The Nature and Functioning of Fiction: Recent Views." *Canadian Review of Comparative Literature/Revue canadienne de littérature comparée* 19.1-2 (March-June 1992): 101-17.

Margolis, Joseph. "Reinterpreting Interpretation." *The Journal of Aesthetics and Art Criticism* 47.3 (summer 1989): 237-51.

May, Georges. *Le dilemme du roman au XVIIIe siècle: étude sur les rapports du roman et de la critique, 1715-1761*. New Haven: Yale UP, 1963.

McKeon, Richard. Introduction. *The Basic Works of Aristotle*. Ed. Richard McKeon. New York: Random House, 1941. xi-xxxiv.

Meisel, Perry. "Let a Hundred Isms Bloom." *The New York Times Book Review* 28 May 2000: 27.

Mehlman, Jeffrey. *Genealogies of the Text: Literature, Psychoanalysis, and Politics in Modern France*. Cambridge: Cambridge UP, 1995

Michaels, Walter Benn. "The Interpreter's Self: Peirce on the Cartesian 'Subject.' " *Reader Response Criticism: From Formalism to Post-Structuralism*. Ed. Jane P. Tompkins. Baltimore: Johns Hopkins P, 1980. 185-200.

Modiano, Patrick. *Accident nocturne*. Paris : Gallimard, 2003

————. *Les boulevards de ceinture*. Paris: Gallimard (Collection Folio), 1972.

————. *Catherine Certitude*. Paris: Editions Gallimard (Collection Folio Junior), 1988.

————. *Chien de printemps*. Paris: Editions du Seuil (Collection Points). 1993.

————. *Un cirque passe*. Paris: Gallimard (Collection Folio), 1992.

————. *De si braves garçons*. Paris: Gallimard (Collection Folio), 1982.

————. *Dimanches d'août*. Paris: Gallimard (Collection Folio), 1986.

————. *Dora Bruder*. Paris: Editions Gallimard, 1997.

————. *Du plus loin de l'oubli*. Paris: Gallimard, 1996.

————. *Fleurs de ruine*. Paris: Editions du Seuil (Collection Points), 1991.

————. *Des inconnues*. Paris: Gallimard, 1999.

————. *Une jeunesse*. Paris: Gallimard (Collection Folio), 1981.

————. *Lacombe Lucien*. Paris: Gallimard, 1974.

————. *Livret de famille*. Paris: Gallimard (Collection Folio), 1977.

————. *Memory Lane*. Paris: Hachette, 1981.

————. *Un pedigree*. Paris: Gallimard, 2005.

————. *La petite bijou*. Paris: Gallimard, 2001.

————. *La place de l'étoile*. Paris: Gallimard (Editions Folio), 1968.

————. *Quartier perdu*. Paris: Gallimard (Collection Folio), 1984.

————. *La ronde de nuit*. Paris: Gallimard (Collection Folio), 1969.

————. *Remise de peine*. Paris: Editions du Seuil (Collection Points), 1988.

————. *Rue des boutiques obscures*. Paris: Gallimard (Collection Folio), 1978.

————. *Vestiaire de l'enfance*. Paris: Gallimard (Collection Folio), 1989.

————. *Villa triste*. Paris: Gallimard (Collection Folio), 1975.

————. *Voyage de noces*. Paris: Gallimard (Collection Folio), 1990.

Morand, Paul. *La folle amoureuse*. Paris: Stock, 1956.

————. *Le prisonnier de Cintra*. Paris: Librairie Arthème Fayard, 1958.

Morris, Alan. *Patrick Modiano*. Oxford: Berg, 1996.

————. *Patrick Modiano*. Amsterdam: Rodopi, 2000.

Morrison, Toni. "Unspeakable Things Unspoken: The Afro-American Presence in American Literature." *Michigan Quarterly Review* 28.1 (winter 1989): 1-34.

Morson, Gary Saul and Caryl Emerson. *Mikhail Bakhtin: Creation of a Prosaics*. Stanford: Stanford UP, 1990.

Nelles, William. "Michael Riffaterre: A Checklist of Writings through 1996." *Style* 30.4 (1996): 554-65.

Nettelbeck, C. W. and P. A. Hueston. "Anthology as Art: Patrick Modiano's *Livret de famille*." *Australian Journal of French Studies* 21.2 (May-August 1984): 213-23.

————. *Patrick Modiano, pièces d'identité: écrire l'entretemps*. Paris: Lettres Modernes, 1986.

Nicolas, Michel. "*La place de l'étoile* par Patrick Modiano." *La Revue Nouvelle* 48 (1968): 343-45.

Obajtek-Kirkwood, Anne-Marie. *L'Occupation "rêvée" de l'"autre vie" de Patrick Modiano*. Copyright 1992. Ann Arbor: UMI Dissertation Services, 1994.

O'Keefe, Charles. "Hard to Swallow: A Not-So-Postmodern Reading of Patrick Modiano's Postmodern Oeuvre." *The French Review* 77.5 (April 2004): 930-41.

_____. "The *Odyssey* and Signs to the Rescue: Escaping the Labyrinth and Enjoying Gaps in Patrick Modiano's *Rue des boutiques obscures*." (To be published by *Nottingham French Studies*.)

_____. "Patrick Modiano's *La place de l'étoile:* Why Name a Narrator 'Raphaël Schlemilovitch'?" *Literary Onomastics Studies* 15 (1988): 67-74.

Pascal, Blaise. *Pensées*. Texte de l'édition de Brunschvicg. Paris: Garnier Frères, 1948.

Parrochia, Daniel. *Ontologie fantôme: essai sur l'œuvre de Patrick Modiano*. Fougères: Encre Marine, 1996.

Peirce, Charles S. *Collected Papers*. Ed. Charles Hartshorne and Paul Weiss. Vol. 5. Cambridge: Harvard UP, 1933.

Peter Pan. Walt Disney Pictures ; directors, Hamilton Luske, Clyde Geronimi, Wilfred Jackson. Burbank: Walt Disney Home Video. Distributed by Buena Vista Home Entertainment, c1998.

Pinsker, Sanford. *The* Schlemiel *as Metaphor: Studies in Yiddish and American Jewish Fiction*. Carbondale: Southern Illinois UP, 1971.

Pire, Michel. "Patrick Modiano: *Les boulevards de ceinture*." *La Revue Nouvelle* 55 (1972): 511-14.

Plato. *The Collected Dialogues*. Ed. Edith Hamilton and Huntington Cairns. New York: Pantheon Books, 1964.

Poe, Edgar Allan. *Essays and Reviews*. Ed. G. R. Thompson. New York: The Library of America, 1984.

———. *The Short Fiction of Edgar Allan Poe*. Annotated and edited by Stuart and Susan Levine. Indianapolis: Bobbs-Merrill Educational Publishing, 1976.

———. "Slavery in the United States." Rev. of *Slavery in the United States*, by J. K. Paulding, and *The South Vindicated from the Treason and Fanaticism of the Northern Abolitionists*, by H. Manly. *Complete Works of Edgar Allan Poe*. Ed. James A. Harrison. Vol. 8. New York: Fred de Fau and Co., 1902. 265-75. [The attribution of this book review to Poe is not accepted by all Poe scholars. See Whalen.]

———. *Complete Works of Edgar Allan Poe*. Ed. James A. Harrison. 17 vols. New York: Fred de Fau and Co., 1902.

Poirson, Alain. "Le malaise du passé." *France Nouvelle* 3 novembre 1978: 41-42.

Prendergast, Christopher. *The Order of Mimesis: Balzac, Stendhal, Nerval, Flaubert*. Cambridge: Cambridge UP, 1986.

Prince, Gerald. "Patrick Modiano." *Dictionary of Literary Biography. Volume 83: French Novelists since 1960*. Ed. Catherine Savage Brosman. Detroit, Michigan: Gale Research Inc., 1989. 147-53.

————. "Re-Membering Modiano, or Something Happened." *SubStance* 49 (1986): 35-43.

Rachlin, Natalie. "The Modiano Syndrome: 1968-1997." *Paradigms of Memory: The Occupation and Other Hi/stories in the Novels of Patrick Modiano.* Ed. Martine Guyot-Bender and William VanderWolk. New York: Peter Lang, 1998. 121-36.

Rey, Alain et al. *Dictionnnaire historique de la langue française.* Vol. 1. Paris: Dictionnaires Le Robert, 1998.

Ricardou, Jean. *Nouveaux problèmes du roman.* Paris: Editions du Seuil, 1978.

————. *Problèmes du nouveau roman.* Paris: Editions du Seuil, 1967.

Richard, Claude. "Destin, Design, Dasein: Lacan, Derrida and 'The Purloined Letter.' " *The Iowa Review* 12.4 (fall 1981): 1-11.

Ricoeur, Paul. "Guilt, Ethics and Religion." *Experience of the Sacred: Readings in the Phenomenology of Religion.* Ed. Sumner B. Twiss and Walter H. Conser Jr. Hanover: N.H.: University Press of New England, 1992. 223-37.

————. *A Ricoeur Reader.* Ed. Mario J. Valdés. Toronto: U of Toronto P, 1991.

Riffaterre, Michael. *Essais de stylistique structurale.* Paris: Flammarion, 1971.

————. *Fictional Truth.* Baltimore: Johns Hopkins UP, 1990.

————. "L'illusion référentielle." *Littérature et réalité.* R. Barthes, L. Bersani, Ph. Hamon, M. Riffaterre, I. Watt. Paris: Editions du Seuil, 1982. 91-118.

————. "The Interpretant in Literary Semiotics." *American Journal of Semiotics* 3.4 (1985): 41-55.

————. "The Intertextual Unconscious." *Critical Inquiry* 13 (winter 1987): 371-85.

————. Interview. *Diacritics* 11.4 (1981): 12-16.

————. "The Making of the Text." *Identity of the Literary Text.* Ed. Mario J. Valdés and Owen Miller. Toronto: U of Toronto P, 1985. 54-70.

————. "The Mind's Eye: Memory and Textuality." *The New Medievalism.* Ed. Marina S. Brownlee, Kevin Brownlee, and Stephen G. Nichols. Baltimore: Johns Hopkins UP, 1991. 29-45.

————. "On Narrative Subtexts: Proust's Magic Lantern." *Style* 22.3 (fall 1988): 450-66.

————. *La production du texte.* Paris: Editions du Seuil, 1979.

————. *Semiotics of Poetry.* Bloomington: Indiana UP, 1978.

————. "Text, Textuality and Interpretation." Interview with Vijay Mishra. *Southern Review* 18 (March 1985): 109-19.

————. "La trace de l'intertexte." *La Pensée* 215 (octobre 1980): 4-18.

————. "Undecidability as Hermeneutic Constraint." *Literary Theory Today.* Ed. Peter Collier and Helga Geyer-Ryan. Ithaca, New York: Cornell UP, 1990. 109-24.

Robert, Marthe. *Roman des origines et origines du roman*. Paris: Gallimard, 1976.

Robert, Paul. *Le petit robert 1: dictionnaire alphabétique et analogique de la langue française*. Rédaction par A. Rey et J. Rey-Debove. Paris: Le Robert 1990.

Rosenthal, Bernard. "Poe, Slavery, and *The Southern Literary Messenger:* A Reexamination." *Poe Studies* 7.2 (December 1974): 29-38.

Roth, Marty. *Foul and Fair Play: Reading Genre in Classic Detective Fiction*. Athens: U of Georgia P, 1995.

Roudiez, Leon S. *French Fiction Revisited*. Elmwood Park, Illinois: Dalkey Archive P, 1991.

Rousso, Henry. *Le syndrome de Vichy de 1944 à nos jours*. 2e édition. Paris: Editions du Seuil, 1990.

Rowe, John Carlos. "Poe, Antebellum Slavery, and Modern Criticism." *Poe's Pym: Critical Explorations*. Ed. Richard Kopley. Durham: Duke UP, 1992. 117-38.

Roux, Baptiste. *Figures de l'Occupation dans l'œuvre de Patrick Modiano*. Paris: L'Harmattan, 1999.

Ruszniewski-Dahan, Myriam. *Romanciers de la Shoah: si l'écho de leur voix faiblit....* Paris: L'Harmattan, 1999.

Rycroft, Charles. "The Analysis of a Detective Story." *Imagination and Reality: Psycho-Analytical Essays*. London: The Hogarth Press and the Institute of Psycho-Analysis, 1968. 114-35.

Salaün, Franck. "La Suisse du Cœur." *Patrick Modiano*. Ed. Jules Bedner. Atlanta, GA: Rodopi 1993. 15-42.

Saltz, Laura. " '(Horrible to Relate!)': Recovering the Body of Marie Rogêt." *The American Face of Edgar Allan Poe*. Ed. Shawn Rosenheim and Stephen Rachman. Baltimore: John Hopkins UP, 1955. 237-67.

Scherman, Timothy H. "Translating from Memory: Patrick Modiano in Postmodern Context." *Studies in Twentieth Century Literature* 16.2 (summer 1992). 289-303.

Smadja, Robert. "La solitude dans *Livret de famille* de Modiano, et *L'invention de la solitude* d'Auster." *Solitudes, écritures et représentation*. Ed. André Siganos. Grenoble: ELLUG, 1995.

Spanos, William V. *Repetitions: The Postmodern Occasion in Literature and Culture*. Baton Rouge: Lousiana State UP, 1987.

Steele, Stephen. "Modiano*bis*." *French Studies Bulletin* 54 (spring 1995): 12-14.

Steiner, George. Foreword. *The Damned and The Elect: Guilt in Western Culture*. Friedrich Ohly. Trans. Linda Archibald. Cambridge: Cambridge UP, 1992. xi-xiv.

Streight, Irwin Howard. "A Good Hypogram Is Not Hard to Find." *Flannery O'Connor and the Christian Mystery*. Ed. John J. Murphy et al. Provo: Brigham Young U, 1997.

Still, Judith and Michael Worton. Introduction. *Intertextuality: Theories and Practices*. Ed. Judith Still and Michael Worton. New York: St. Martin's Press, 1990. 1-44.

Swales, Martin. "Chamisso: *Peter Schlemihl*." *The German* Novelle. Princeton: Princeton UP, 1977. 77-98.

Tadié, Jean-Yves. *Le récit poétique*. Paris: PUF, 1978.

Tani, Stefano. *The Doomed Detective: The Contribution of the Detective Novel to Postmodern American and Italian Fiction*. Carbondale: Southern Illinois UP, 1984.

Taylor, John. "France." *The Oxford Guide to Contemporary Writing*. New York: Oxford UP, 1996. 142-64.

Terdiman, Richard. *Discourse/Counter-Discourse: The Theory and Practice of Symbolic Resistance in Nineteenth-Century France*. Ithaca: Cornell UP, 1985.

———. *Present Past: Modernity and the Memory Crisis*. Ithaca: Cornell UP, 1993.

Thompson, Jon. *Fiction, Crime, and Empire: Clues to Modernity and Postmodernism*. Urbana: Illinois UP, 1993.

Thompson, William. Introduction. *The Contemporary Novel In France*. Ed. William Thompson. Gainesville: U of Florida P, 1995. 1-31.

Tillich, Paul. *The Courage to Be*. Introduction Peter J. Gomes. 2nd ed. New Haven: Yale UP, 2000.

Todorov, Tzvetan. *Poétique de la prose*. Paris: Editions du Seuil, 1971.

Trilling, Lionel. *The Liberal Imagination: Essays on Literature and Society*. New York: Harcourt, Brace, Jovanovitch, 1950.

Trioreau, Odile. "La représentation de la seconde guerre mondiale dans les manuels d'école primaire de 1945 à nos jours." *Paris sous l'Occupation*. Ed. Wolfgang Drost. Heidelberg: Universitätsverlag C. Winter, 1995. 187-203.

Tritsmans, Bruno. "Les secrets de la bibliothèque dans *Villa triste* de Patrick Modiano." *The Documentary Impulse in French Literature*. Ed. Buford Norman. Atlanta: Rodopi, 2001. 113-24.

Van Leer, David. "Detecting Truth: The World of the Dupin Tales." *New Essays on Poe's Major Tales*. Ed. Kenneth Silverman. Cambridge: Cambridge UP, 1993. 65-91.

Van Meter, Jan R. "Sophocles and The Rest of the Boys in the Pulps: Myth and The Detective Novel." *Dimensions of Detective Fiction*. Ed. Larry N. Landrum, Pat Browne, and Ray B. Browne. Bowling Green, Ohio: Poppular Press, 1976. 12-21.

VanderWolk, William. *Rewriting the Past: Memory, History and Narration in the Novels of Patrick Modiano*. Atlanta: Editions Rodopi B.V., 1997.

Vanoncini, André. "Analyser 'Poisson soluble': ombres et lumières du structuralisme éclairé de Michael Riffaterre." *Archiv für das Studium der neueren Sprachen und Literaturen* 224.2 (1987): 329-45.

Walker, Jeffrey S. "Aristotelian Poetics: Reading Ezra Pound with Michael Riffaterre." *Style* 18.1 (winter 1984): 43-63.

Wardi, Charlotte. "Mémoire et écriture dans l'œuvre de Patrick Modiano. "*Les Nouveaux Cahiers* 1985: 40-48.

———. "Mémoire et identité dans *La place de l'étoile* et *Rue des boutiques obscures* de Patrick Modiano." *Revue d'Histoire Littéraire de la France*: 14.1 (1981): 87-96.

———. "Mémoires romanesques de la Shoah." *The Conscience of Mankind*. Eds. Elrud Ibsch, Douwe Fokkema, and Joachim von der Thusen. Amsterdam: Rodopi, 2000. 117-31.

Warehime, Marja. "Returning to the Scene of the Crime: *Rue des boutiques obscures*, *Quartier perdu*, *Dimanches d'août* and *Fleurs de ruine*." *Paradigms of Memory: The Occupation and Other Hi/stories in the Novels of Patrick Modiano*. Ed. Martine Guyot-Bender and William VanderWolk. 37-53.

Weigand, Herman J. *Surveys and Soundings in European Literature*. Princeton: Princeton UP, 1966.

Wellek, André and Austin Warren. *Theory of Literature*. New York: Harcourt Brace, 1949.

Whalen, Terence. "Average Racism: Poe, Slavery, and the Wages of Literary Nationalism." *Romancing the Shadow: Poe and Race*. Ed. J. Gerald Kennedy and Liliane Weissberg. Oxford: Oxford UP, 2001. 3-40.

Whitehead, Alfred North. *Process and Reality: An Essay in Cosmology*. Ed. David Ray Griffin et al. New York: Free Press, 1978 (c1929).

Wright, Katheryn. "Patrick Modiano." *The Contemporary Novel in France*. Ed. William Thompson. Gainesville: U of Florida P, 1995. 264-78.

◆ ◆ ◆

Index